$16.95

P9-CRO-434

The Devil's Casino

The Devil's Casino

Friendship, Betrayal, and the High-Stakes Games Played Inside Lehman Brothers

Vicky Ward

WILEY

John Wiley & Sons, Inc.

Copyright © 2010 by Vicky Ward. All rights reserved.

Published by John Wiley & Sons, Inc., Hoboken, New Jersey.
Published simultaneously in Canada.

No part of this publication may be reproduced, stored in a retrieval system, or transmitted
in any form or by any means, electronic, mechanical, photocopying, recording, scanning,
or otherwise, except as permitted under Section 107 or 108 of the 1976 United
States Copyright Act, without either the prior written permission of the Publisher,
or authorization through payment of the appropriate per-copy fee to the Copyright
Clearance Center, Inc., 222 Rosewood Drive, Danvers, MA 01923, (978) 750-8400, fax
(978) 646-8600, or on the Web at www.copyright.com. Requests to the Publisher for
permission should be addressed to the Permissions Department, John Wiley & Sons, Inc.,
111 River Street, Hoboken, NJ 07030, (201) 748-6011, fax (201) 748-6008, or online at
http://www.wiley.com/go/permissions.

Limit of Liability/Disclaimer of Warranty: While the publisher and author have used
their best efforts in preparing this book, they make no representations or warranties
with respect to the accuracy or completeness of the contents of this book and specifically
disclaim any implied warranties of merchantability or fitness for a particular purpose. No
warranty may be created or extended by sales representatives or written sales materials.
The advice and strategies contained herein may not be suitable for your situation. You
should consult with a professional where appropriate. Neither the publisher nor author
shall be liable for any loss of profit or any other commercial damages, including but not
limited to special, incidental, consequential, or other damages.

For general information on our other products and services or for technical support, please
contact our Customer Care Department within the United States at (800) 762-2974,
outside the United States at (317) 572-3993 or fax (317) 572-4002.

Wiley also publishes its books in a variety of electronic formats. Some content that appears
in print may not be available in electronic books. For more information about Wiley
products, visit our web site at www.wiley.com.

Library of Congress Cataloging-in-Publication Data:

Ward, Vicky.
    The devil's casino : friendship, betrayal, and the high-stakes games played inside
Lehman Brothers / Vicky Ward.
        p. cm.
    Includes bibliographical references and index.
    ISBN 9781118011492
        1. Lehman Brothers.   2. Investment banking—New York (State)—New York—
History.   3. Investment advisors—New York (State)—New York—History.
    4. Finance—New York (State)—New York—History.   I. Title.
    HG5129.N5W37 2010
    332.660973—dc22

                                                                    2010000762

For my sons, Orlando and Lorcan Doull.
Without your laughter,
your hugs and your very good-natured patience,
"Mummy's annoying book" would not exist.

The mind is its own place, and in itself
Can make a heav'n of hell, a hell of heav'n.

Paradise Lost by John Milton, 1:254–255

Contents

Part Two: The Echo Chamber

Cast of Characters

Key Players

Richard S. "Dick" Fuld Jr., Lehman's chief executive officer. An underachiever in youth, Fuld got a job trading commercial paper at Lehman in 1969.

Joseph M. "Joe" Gregory, president and chief operating officer. Gregory started at Lehman in 1968 as a summer intern when he was 16 years old. He used to cut the lawn of Lehman's top trader, Lew Glucksman.

T. Christopher "Chris" Pettit, Lehman president and chief operating officer. A West Point graduate, decorated Vietnam veteran. He joined the firm in 1977 and rose through its ranks—until, that is, 1997.

Lehman 1984–1994, the Slamex Years

Board Members of Either Amex or Shearson Noted in the Book
David Culver
John Byrne

President Gerald Ford
Richard Furlaud
Henry Kissinger
Dina Merrill (actress)

CEOs

Howard L. "H" Clark
Peter A. Cohen
Lewis L. "Lew" Glucksman
Harvey S. Golub
J. Tomlinson "Tom" Hill
James D. Robinson
Sanford I. "Sandy" Weill

Managing Directors

James S. Boshart III
Herbert Freiman
Ronald A. Gallatin
Jeffrey Lane
Robert "Bob" Millard
The Hon. Peregrine Moncreiffe
Theodore "Teddy" Roosevelt V
Peter J. Solomon

Executives

Jim Carbone, senior deputy to Chris Pettit
Steve Carlson, head of emerging markets
John F. Cecil, chief financial officer (later also chief administrative officer)
Steven "Steve" Carlson, global emerging markets
John Coghlan, managing director of fixed income
Leo Corbett, deputy head of equities
Martha Dillman, sales
Robert A. "Bob" Genirs, Shapiro's successor as CAO
Nancy Hament, human resources
Allan Kaplan, banking
Bruce Lakefield

Stephen "Stevie" Lessing, senior deputy to Tom Tucker

Robert Matza, Stewart's successor as CFO

Paul Newmark, senior vice president and treasurer, Lehman Commercial Paper Inc. (LCPI)

Michael Odrich, chief of staff to Dick Fuld

Marianne Rasmussen, head of human resources

Thomas Russo, chief legal officer until 2008

Mel Shaftel, chief of investment banking

Robert A. "Bob" Shapiro, chief administrative officer

Richard B. Stewart, chief financial officer

Kim Sullivan, sales

Thomas H. "Tom" Tucker, sales

Jeff Vanderbeek, rose to run all of fixed income, then capital markets

James "Jim" Vinci, Pettit's chief of staff

Paul Williams, equities chief

Lehman 1994–2008: From Independence to Meltdown

Executives

Madeleine Antoncic, head of risk

Steve Berger, briefly co-head of banking

Steven Berkenfeld, global head of legal, compliance, audit

Jasjit "Jesse" Bhattal, replaced Tyree as head of Asia in 2000

Tracy Binkley, head of human resources

Erin Callan, chief financial officer

Steve Carlson, head of emerging markets

Jerry Donnini, head of equities

Eric Felder, replaced Reider

Scott J. Freidheim, office of chairman, later chief administrative officer

Mike Gelband, McDade's successor at fixed income

David Goldfarb, chief financial officer turned chief administrative officer turned global head of strategic partnerships

Hope Greenfield, chief talent officer

Jeremy Isaacs, head CEO of Lehman Europe from 2000 onward

Bradley Jack, banking, then co-COO

Ted Janulis, head of mortgages

Todd Jorn, hedge funds

Alex Kirk, high-yield business

Fran Kittredge, philanthropy

Bruce Lakefield, Europe until 1999

Ian Lowitt, treasurer, later co-chief administrative officer, then chief financial officer

Herbert "Bart" McDade, fixed income and later equities

Hugh "Skip" McGee, investment banking

Michael McKeever, briefly co-head of banking

Christian Meissner, Europe

Maureen Miskovic, risk

Andrew Morton, Nagioff's successor in fixed income

Roger Nagioff, European equity derivatives, then Gelband's successor in fixed income

Chris O'Meara, CFO, then head of risk

Rick Rieder, head of credit

Thomas A. Russo, chief legal counsel

Benoit Savoret, Europe

Robert "Rob" Shafir, global equities

David Steinmetz, Chris Pettit's chief of staff

Paolo Tonucci, treasurer

C. Daniel Tyree, Asia until 2000

Jeffrey Vanderbeek, head of fixed income turned vice president

George Herbert Walker IV, investment management

Mark Walsh, real estate

Ming Xu, analyst

Lehman Staff of Note

Holly Becker, equities

Marianne Burke, Dick Fuld's secretary

Barbara Byrne, investment banking

Kerrie Cohen, press officer

Andrew Gowers, press officer

Ros L'Esperance, investment banking

Lara Pettit, sales

Marna Ringel, Scott Friedheim's assistant
Craig Schiffer, bond salesman
Peter Sherratt, Europe

Key Lehman Spouses

Celia Felcher Cecil
Isabelle Freidheim
Kathleen Fuld
Teresa Gregory
Niki Golod Gregory
Karin Jack
Sandra Lessing
Martha McDade
Mary Anne Pettit
Michael Thompson, ex-husband of Erin Callan
Heather Tucker
Nancy Dorn Walker

The Original Lehman Brothers

Henry, Emmanuel, and Mayer Lehman, founders
Philip Lehman, managing partner, 1901–1925
Robert "Bobbie" Lehman, took over as head of Lehman from father
  Philip in 1925

Industry Players

Gary Barancik, partner, Perella Weinberg Partners
James L. "Jamie" Dimon, chairman and CEO, JPMorgan Chase
David Einhorn, chairman, Greenlight Capital
Kenneth D. "Ken" Lewis, president, chairman, and CEO, Bank of
  America
John Mack, chairman of the board and CEO, Morgan Stanley
Joseph R. "Joe" Perella, chairman, Perella Weinberg Partners

Daniel Pollack, lawyer for Chris Pettit

Robert K. "Bob" Steel, president and chief executive, Wachovia, also domestic undersecretary at the U.S. Treasury

Min Euoo Sung, CEO, Korea Development Bank

Mark Shafir, partner and senior investment banker, Thomas Weisel Partners

Bruce Wasserstein, the late chairman and chief executive, Lazard

Andrew Zimmerman, analyst, SAC Capital

Barclays

Archibald Cox Jr., chairman, Barclays Americas

Jerry del Missier, president, Barclays Capital

Robert E. "Bob" Diamond Jr., president and CEO, Barclays Capital

Michael Klein, independent adviser, Barclays

Rich Ricci, chief operating officer, Barclays

John S. Varley, CEO

The Law

H. Rodgin Cohen, chairman, Sullivan & Cromwell

Steve Dannhauser, chairman, Weil, Gotshal & Manges

Victor Lewkow, attorney, Cleary Gottlieb Steen & Hamilton

Harvey R. Miller, partner, business finance and restructuring guru, Weil, Gotshal & Manges

James M. Peck, judge, United States Bankruptcy Court for the Southern District of New York

Daniel Pollack, lawyer for Chris Pettit

Simpson Thacher & Bartlett, Lehman's primary law firm, Erin Callan's former employer

Anton R. Valukas, official examiner probing the Lehman bankruptcy

Bankruptcy Administrators

Tony Lomas, PricewaterhouseCoopers partner and administrator of Lehman's London estate

Bryan Marsal, chief restructuring officer and co-CEO of turnaround firm Alvarez & Marsal LLC

Government Players

United States

Ben S. Bernanke, chairman, Federal Reserve

C. Christopher Cox, chairman, Securities and Exchange Commission (SEC)

Michele Davis, assistant secretary

Timothy F. Geithner, president, Federal Reserve Bank of New York, later secretary of the Treasury

Dan Jester, Paulson's adviser

David G. Nason, assistant secretary

Henry M. Paulson Jr., secretary of the Treasury

Steven Shafran, Paulson's adviser

Kendrick R. Wilson, adviser to the secretary of the Treasury

United Kingdom

Alastair M. Darling, chancellor of the Exchequer

Sir Callum McCarthy, chairman, Financial Services Authority (FSA)

Hector Sants, chief executive, FSA

Prologue

The most crucial talent required in business is an ability to understand people. You have to know what motivates them, what their strengths and weaknesses are. . . . If you're a good judge of character, you will go very far. If not, it's over.

— *Stephen A. Schwarzman (2009), former Lehman Brothers partner and current CEO of the Blackstone Group*

What do I think when I look back on that period when I interviewed all those Lehman bankers in the 1980s? Honestly, I was relieved that I'd never have to see many of them ever again. They were, with some exceptions, a greedy, selfish, deeply unpleasant bunch of people.

— *Ken Auletta (2009), author of* Greed and Glory on Wall Street: The Fall of the House of Lehman (1986)

When I started researching this book, I thought I'd be telling the lurid story of the final few months of America's fourth-largest investment house, Lehman Brothers, which was almost 160 years old when it gasped its last breath on September 15, 2008.

When it filed for bankruptcy, credit markets around the world trembled, and U.S. Treasury Secretary Henry Paulson Jr. and Federal

Reserve Chairman Ben S. Bernanke realized with terror that they were facing the worst economic catastrophe since the Great Depression of the 1930s.

I thought I would simply be telling the dramatic story behind that harrowing moment, viewing Lehman's history through the lens of Paulson, Bernanke, and Lehman's chairman and CEO, Richard S. "Dick" Fuld, who held his position for nearly 15 years, and once joked—during better times, when Lehman stock rose to its all-time high—that "they'll be carrying me out of here feet first." And they almost did.

What I had failed to realize until I dug far deeper into the annals of Lehman's history was that the drama of the ending was no match for the saga of its life. The story of the 160-year-old firm up until 1984 had been well-chronicled (in particular, by Ken Auletta in *Greed and Glory on Wall Street: The Fall of the House of Lehman*). But what happened to it in those crucial intervening years—from 1984 until 2008—had not.

Ironically, Lehman had tried to tell this story itself, and failed. In 2003, Joseph M. "Joe" Gregory, the firm's president, asked the chief players of the preceding 20 years (among them himself, Steve Lessing, Jeff Vanderbeek, John Cecil, and Paul Cohen) to each give their accounts in the hope of compiling "The Modern History" of Lehman. He gave up after fifty pages. But in one of those rare, extraordinary gifts that biographers pray for, those fifty pages—and, more important, the many pages written by each individual—were handed to me by a source to whom I am forever deeply indebted.

"The Modern History" opened in 1994 as Lehman gets spun out of American Express and Dick Fuld, the new CEO, stood in front of a cascade of balloons in the Winter Garden, the party space in the World Financial Center, across the street from the World Trade Center towers in the heart of Wall Street. Fuld proudly proclaimed: "It's a new day. We have the opportunity to create our own destiny, and I need you to do it."

There is talk among the senior executives about the "remarkable will of Lehman Brothers," and the "nonnegotiable values of the Lehman culture," which include "integrity, strength of character, open communication, loyalty, and teamwork." The unfinished manuscript discusses rating these values above the more superficial inclinations of Wall Street: Valuing spirit over education, for example, makes Lehman a "special place to work." The firm was small but the employees were united. They were, they proudly proclaimed again and again, "one firm." The Lehman mantra was "Do the right thing." They were the good guys of Wall Street.

But were they?

There's a reason "The Modern History" was never finished; the individual contributions—like journal entries—make it clear what happened to the project. And former CFO John Cecil confirmed my suspicions.

As Joe Gregory poured through the "diaries," he realized that there were two major problems. One was that the portrait being painted of Dick Fuld, the leader of the firm, was negative—he was not the great general that Gregory wanted him to be, but a man who either was invisible or needed to be told what to do by a stronger subordinate. The second was that the accounts were so different from one another that they could scarcely be said to represent a united front, the "one firm" ethos.

So the project was abandoned, waiting until someone wanted to write a history of the way things had actually been at Lehman, without concern for the egos, or the agendas.

The irony was that had Gregory really thought about why his project had failed, he might have understood the firm's inherent problems, and realized that a cacophony of opinions at the top was something not to be ignored, but embraced. Had he interpreted the material differently, Lehman might still be alive.

■ ■ ■

Despite appearances and the endlessly self-perpetuated myth of being a mighty gorilla, Dick Fuld was never truly synonymous with Lehman (never mind that it was a public securities house, and therefore owned by its shareholders and not by him).

No, the hopes—and heart and spirit—of modern Lehman lived and died with two men with huge presences, both of whom served as Dick Fuld's number twos, his confidants, his presidents, his victims.

Lehman was made great and almost brought down twice in the past thirty years, thanks to these two men. Dick Fuld was pretty much a lieutenant to each, which is why in some ways the second half of this book reads like an echo of the first. Some men refuse to learn from the past.

The first Lehman president is buried in Farmingdale, Long Island. He was 51 when he died in 1997. T. Christopher "Chris" Pettit stood six feet two inches and had dark hair and piercing brown eyes; when he spoke both male and female hearts melted. Prior to joining Lehman, he graduated from West Point and was an Army Ranger in Vietnam.

On a tip from a friend, in 1977 Pettit applied for and got a job with Lehman Commercial Paper Inc. (LCPI), the commercial paper trading unit of the investment house Lehman Brothers. With his extraordinary leadership skills, Pettit rose with almost unprecedented speed to be head of sales, effectively Fuld's number two within LCPI.

LCPI at the time was run by Lewis "Lew" Glucksman, an obese giant of a bond trader who ran Lehman's capital markets division; Glucksman had ousted Peter G. Peterson, the urbane former secretary of commerce, as the chairman of Lehman Brothers in 1983. Glucksman had argued that since he made the most money, he should run the business. He won that argument.

Fuld was one of Glucksman's protégés. He operated the way Glucksman had: tyrannically. The men were similar, though they looked nothing alike. Fuld, who is five feet eleven inches and has dark eyes, was a fit squash player, in contrast to his slovenly mentor. Both men said little in the office, but were notorious for shouting insults and expletives.

In 1984 when Shearson American Express acquired Lehman and Glucksman was bought out of the business, Fuld rose to run Lehman's fixed income division. Pettit was his complementary number two. Pettit was the man on the ground, in the trenches with his soldiers. He could be tough, but he was respected. Pettit was the man the traders really worked for, the leader they revered. Pettit would go to Lehman parties and give speeches that left everyone ready to put down their cocktails and head straight back to the office.

For 10 or so years, while Lehman was merged with Shearson and American Express, Fuld reigned largely unseen. He was "neither a leader nor a dazzling intellect," one former trader says.

After Lehman was spun out of American Express and became a public company in 1994, the only person who could threaten Fuld's place as head of the new investment bank, Lehman Brothers, was Pettit. And as long as Pettit had the loyalty of the troops, there was nothing Fuld could do about his rival.

Until, that is, his rival, for the first time in his life, made himself vulnerable. Pettit was struggling to manage his private life at that time; he had a dying sibling and a dying marriage. He was also having an affair. None of this ought to have mattered in the workplace, but his three best friends ensured that it did. Their names were Joseph "Joe" Gregory, Stephen "Steve" Lessing, and Thomas "Tom" Tucker. All worked for Lehman. In fact, together, they ruled Lehman, at least the fixed income division that was essentially the new independent Lehman. All had carpooled together since the 1970s from Huntington, Long Island, until fights over compensation drove them apart.

Joe Gregory persuaded Tucker and Lessing to go to Fuld and essentially ask for Pettit's resignation in March 1996. Fuld knew that with Tucker, Lessing, and Gregory behind him, he finally controlled the firm; he demoted Pettit to head of client relations. The episode is still called the Ides of March by senior Lehman executives because the demotion occurred on March 15, the day Julius Caesar was killed by his former friends in 44 B.C.

Six months later, Pettit resigned. Three months after that, he was dead.

With Pettit gone, Fuld was able to tighten his grip on the firm. He took elocution lessons, and evolved into the leader he had never before been. Lehman's stock soared over the next ten years as it evolved into an investment bank. The stock price rose to $86, and Fuld was the hottest CEO in town, featured in a 2006 issue of *Fortune* magazine as the man who had transformed the "notoriously fractious" firm into a "super-hot machine." The chief banger of the drums, the man urging the firm to take more risk, was the man who had orchestrated the ousting of Pettit—and had replaced him: Joe Gregory, the second Lehman President.

But inside Lehman's headquarters at 745 Seventh Avenue, people worried that dangerous corners were being cut in Fuld's haste to beat what he perceived as the enemy: Goldman Sachs. On June 9, 2008,

Lehman reported its second-quarter loss of $2.8 billion, the company's first quarterly loss since going public in 1994. The stock fell 9 percent that day. Yet for months, Erin Callan, the new CFO and a Gregory "pet," had been telling the market that Lehman had plenty of capital— that the company was in good shape.

On June 12, Lehman announced that Joe Gregory was out. When he left, he took Callan down with him, but the damage they had done was irreversible. Disaster loomed.

For a while Dick Fuld could not see where he had gone wrong. As he later testified before Congress about the fall of Lehman, "I wake up every single night thinking, 'What could I have done differently? What could I have said? What should I have done?' And I have searched myself every single night. And I come back to this: At the time I made those decisions, I made those decisions with the information that I had. I can look right at you and say, this is a pain that will stay with me for the rest of my life. . . ."

This was before he learned that Gregory, who had cashed several hundred million out of Lehman, asked for a further $233 million from the Lehman estate after the company had been declared bankrupt plus, according to filings, another employee benefit plan for $700,000 per year for 25 years at the firm and a further $2.4 million per year for 15 years.

Fuld, who had asked for nothing when the end came, was reportedly horrified. He, like a handful of others, had deluded himself into thinking that Gregory was a good guy; Gregory was the guy who told young Lehman managing directors he didn't want to hire people "who regularly checked their bank balances." Yet Gregory was, in the words of his former friend and carpooler, Steve Lessing, "a phony."

So, no, this is not yet one more book about the crash of 2008. Rather it is a parable about the foibles of men, the corrosive influence of money, and the dangers of hubris.

■ ■ ■

"One firm" was the Lehman Brothers mantra, and most people thought Fuld had dreamed up the slogan. But he hadn't.

That was the handiwork of Lew Glucksman, who used to stand in his office by the trading floor and snap a single pencil in front of his employees. He would then hold a group of pencils together and say, "Watch: When they are together, I can't break them."

The man who embodied that slogan best was not Fuld. It was Chris Pettit, who once, in a sly tribute to Glucksman and the camaraderie Pettit had instilled at Lehman Brothers, handed out pencils with all the senior executives' names on them as party favors. He was the man who once staked his career and his lifesavings to protect the jobs of the traders, back-office workers, and secretaries in his unit. He was Lehman Brothers at its best. Yet now he is all but forgotten, nearly erased from the public record by a culture of ruthless avarice.

Part One

THE PONDEROSA BOYS

Character is destiny.
—*Heraclitus*

Chapter 1

A Long, Hot Summer

I just remember the nights. George would come in from the office at what seemed like 4 A.M. every single night. I don't know how he got through those months. I don't know how any of them did. It was crazy.

—*Nancy Dorn Walker*

By nightfall on Saturday, June 7, 2008, the Manhattan streets were still radiating heat, an unwelcome harbinger of a long, stifling summer. At the Skylight Studio, a sprawling private event space in SoHo, George Herbert Walker, a 39-year-old second cousin of then President George Walker Bush, and at the time head of Lehman's Investment Management division, was celebrating his marriage to Nancy Dorn, 31, a pretty blonde hedge fund analyst from Texas. The couple—who had exchanged their vows at New York's City Hall a few weeks earlier and had already celebrated with family down in Texas—ate Southern food, danced to the overwrought musical stylings of a suitably ironic wedding singer, and drank margaritas with 400 of their friends. It was, however, a celebration tempered by the first signs that Lehman Brothers was about to come crashing down.

The newlyweds had planned for their party to be casual and low-key—cushions on the floor and a buffet. Dorn wore a strapless Missoni dress that was asymmetrical and calf length. Walker—tall, bespectacled, a "cuddly bear," some friends said—rather typically and charmingly cannot recall what he wore that night.

The last thing the couple wanted was to be perceived as grandiose. In fact, Walker had instructed their friend, party planner Bronson van Wyck, "Just make sure we don't make it into Page Six," the gossip page of the *New York Post*. The public outrage over the $3 million extravaganza hosted by Blackstone Group CEO Stephen A. Schwarzman for his 60th birthday on February 13, 2007, was still echoing throughout New York City. The star-studded, 500-guest event held at the Park Avenue Armory, featuring performances by Rod Stewart (who was paid $1 million) and Patti LaBelle (who sang "Happy Birthday"), had been an ill-timed disaster of self-congratulation: Blackstone's stock had fallen steadily ever after and was then teetering at $18 per share, nearly half of its value a year earlier. And now, *all* of Wall Street was suddenly standing on the edge of a precipice, and everyone—especially those in attendance at the Walkers' party—were acutely aware of it. "We wanted people to come and go when they wanted to, and not force them to sit down for a formal dinner," Dorn said. The band—a Neil Diamond cover band, Super Diamond—was chosen by Walker in order to keep the mood light.

Just months earlier, on March 17, Bear Stearns had imploded, and was scooped up by JPMorgan Chase, which paid $2 per share (that was eventually elevated to $10 per share with the aid of a $29 billion government nonrecourse loan); the rescue operation had stunned the financial market. Worried eyes were now staring at the next domino in Wall Street's Big Five: Lehman Brothers. Walker had moved to the bank only two years before from the larger, more capitalized (and therefore safer) Goldman Sachs.

Since March, most of Lehman's senior management had been working nights and weekends, furiously trying to shore up their balance sheets. That weekend, many of the guests at the Walkers' "second wedding" had come directly from the Lehman offices on 745 Seventh Avenue at 50th Street. Most, like David Goldfarb, Lehman's global head of Strategic Partnerships, Principal Investing, and Risk, had met their wives at the office and had simply grabbed their jackets from the backs of their chairs before heading hurriedly, their minds elsewhere, out the door. Even Walker hadn't been home much recently; on the day of the wedding party, Nancy Dorn had gone to a movie by herself. The June earnings were due in two days. As the new 41-year-old CFO, Erin Callan, worked on them (she did not attend the party), her colleagues knew they'd be announcing Lehman's first losses since spinning off from American Express—$2.8 billion. They were deeply concerned.

"Everyone was stressed that night—we felt badly for George," Goldfarb said. "We were more tired than downbeat. No one at that time had any inkling that we would go down. We just knew we had a lot of work to do." Despite the tumult, nearly all the core senior management team of Lehman came to the party. Longtime chairman and CEO Dick Fuld was there with his wife of nearly thirty years, Kathy, 56, then the vice chair of the Museum of Modern Art. Sticking close to them were Joe Gregory, Lehman's president, and his second wife, Niki, a beautiful Greek-born brunette. Then there was the urbane, silver-haired Tom Russo, Lehman's chief legal officer. Famous for his charm and eloquence, he was nicknamed "the Mayor of Davos" because, as one colleague put it, "he arrives first and leaves last" at the annual financial powerhouse conference in Switzerland. Beneath his twinkling eyes is a steel core—after Lehman Brothers collapsed, in late September, Russo would offer his consolation to Lehman Europe by way of a terse telephone call, in which he told them: "You're on your own."

"Never be fooled by Tom's charm," a colleague said. "He's as tough as anyone when he wants to be."

The last member of Fuld's inner circle in attendance that night was Scott Freidheim, whom Fuld looked upon almost as a son. Freidheim, then 41, is the son of former Booz Allen & Hamilton vice chairman and former CEO of Chiquita Brands International, Cyrus Freidheim. Scott was yanked out of Lehman's investment banking unit in 1996 and appointed managing director, office of the chairman. He quickly rose to the top echelons of the organization, which earned him as many enemies as friends.

Most of the executive committee was there: Hugh "Skip" McGee (the head of investment banking), Herbert "Bart" McDade III (head of equities), and Ted Janulis (mortgages). Also present were Steven Berkenfeld (chairman of the investment banking committee) and John Cecil, the small, earnest former McKinsey director who had risen to become the CFO of Lehman in the late 1990s and who, though he had left Lehman in 2000, was still being paid as a consultant. Also gathered were a large number of senior executives of NeubergerBerman, Lehman's asset management division, commonly referred to as its "crown jewel."

Months earlier Joe Gregory had taken Walker aside. "You know, you didn't have to invite all these people," he said. "Remember: These are just the people you work with. They are not your friends."

Gregory was the only person at Lehman who had been at the firm longer than Fuld. Their careers began in the early 1970s when Lehman was one of the leading advisory mergers and acquisitions (M&A) houses on Wall Street, before it became a bond and mortgage shop.

Fuld and Gregory had fought in what became known as "the Great War" of 1983 and 1984, an epic battle for control of Lehman between their professional mentor, the bond trader Lewis "Lew" Glucksman, and Peter G. "Pete" Peterson, the former commerce secretary. A preening sophisticate who dominated luncheons with his prattle, Peterson was widely disliked by the relatively blue-collar traders for his patrician demeanor. Glucksman and his traders won the Great War and ousted Peterson, chiefly because by the mid-1980s the traders were making more money than the advisory bankers aligned with Peterson. But the fight cost the firm dearly. Top banking talent fled and revenues plummeted, making it vulnerable for a takeover by the newly merged entity of American Express Shearson in April 1984. Peterson hadn't left without implanting a lethal sting. It was greatly in his financial interests to get Lehman sold. In fact, it was greatly in the interests of pretty much *all* the senior investment bankers to get it sold. This was precisely what happened, as detailed in a 1986 saga chronicled by Ken Auletta in *Greed and Glory on Wall Street*. Glucksman was offered a $15.6 million noncompete buyout fee (on 4,500 shares). He and most of the other partners took the money and ran.

And Gregory and Fuld began their ascents into the ruling elite of the new Lehman Brothers.

■ ■ ■

The firm was founded in 1850 by three cotton trader brothers—Henry, Emmanuel, and Mayer Lehman. The cotton business had evolved from trading and general merchandising into an exchange in lower Manhattan. With the post–Civil War expansion of trading in stocks and bonds, the firm prospered and expanded. The next great leap for Lehman Brothers occurred after World War II, under the reign of Bobbie Lehman, who had a Rolodex bursting with names like Whitney, Harriman, and most of the rest of New York's ruling class. He decorated the walls of Lehman's offices downtown at One William Street with works from his private art collection—paintings by Picasso and Cezanne, Botticelli and Rembrandt, El Greco and Matisse. He was a gentleman, and his great strength was that he knew how to unite the people who worked for him.

Andrew G.C. Sage II, a former employee, told Ken Auletta, "Bobbie was not much of an investment banker. He wouldn't know a preferred stock from livestock, but he was a hell of a psychologist." Under him, Lehman became the *gentleman's* banking house.

"The partners at Lehman were all men of stature," Felix Rohatyn, the banker who kept New York City from the throes of bankruptcy in the 1970s, told Auletta. "They were principals. You dealt with them as owners of a great house. You felt that if there was any such thing as a business aristocracy, and at the same time a highly profitable venture, that was it."

The firm's stellar reputation survived Bobbie's death in 1969. Many of its M&A bankers in the 1970s and early 1980s are still famous, still the icons of their profession. Their ranks included Eric Gleacher, Stephen A. Schwarzman, Peter Solomon, J. Tomlinson "Tom" Hill, Robert Rubin, Roger Altman, and a young Steve Rattner; they all achieved great success—and wealth—after leaving Lehman Brothers. It was infighting—typical in the firm's last half-century—that brought Lehman low enough to be bought by Shearson American Express in 1983. And through that strange marriage ("Shearson taking over Lehman is like McDonald's taking over '21,'" a Lehmanite told Bryan Burrough and John Helyar for their 1990 book, *Barbarians at the Gate*), Lehman stewed. And schemed. Its Lehman Commercial Paper Inc. (LCPI) unit grew to eclipse Shearson's own department, and provided enough momentum for Lehman Brothers to finally spin out once again, its egos intact.

As for Fuld and Gregory? It had taken immense grit, courage, and a warlike mentality to restore the burnish to the once golden brand. They had defied the naysayers who believed that a tiny bond shop would never survive the Mexican peso crisis of 1994; and they did the same again through the Russian crisis of 1998. They had weathered rumor, had survived scandal, and had even ousted their longtime colleague, T. Christopher Pettit, to preside over a fully fledged global investment bank.

Since Lehman, in their hands, had gone public and had grown from 8,500 employees to 28,000, the stock price had risen by a factor of 16. The partners were all rich. In 2007, Fuld was named CEO of the Year by *Institutional Investor* magazine in the Brokers and Asset Managers category. The bank was once again competitive, once again a respected force on Wall Street. They weren't now going to let it go down just because of an asset and housing crisis. They had survived 9/11, when their three floors of offices in the World Trade Center had been destroyed and their headquarters in the nearby World Financial Center badly damaged. They'd been through far worse.

■ ■ ■

And so, on this evening, for the sake of the well-liked George Walker, Lehman's top management tried to have a good time, tried to forget about their troubles. They chatted, they danced, they drank.

Gregory and Fuld slipped away early. This was not unusual—Fuld had never been much of a party guy. He was famous for showing up at in-house cocktail parties for ten minutes and then leaving to be with his family. "We're going to be fine," Fuld told a stranger who approached him just before he left the party. And if worse came to worst, he believed, the U.S. government wouldn't let Lehman fail.

We're going to be fine.

Chapter 2

The Beginning

> You had this senior group of guys; there was Dick, obviously,
> but also the four guys in the carpool who started to run the
> businesses: Joe, Tommy, Stevie and Chris. They ran Lehman.
> They *were* Lehman.
>
> — *Craig Schiffer, founding partner at Sevara Partners,*
> *LLC, and former Global Head of Equity*
> *Derivatives at Lehman Brothers*

The five men who would forge the culture of the new Lehman Brothers, the *post-Shearson* Lehman, could not have been more different from the polished Lehman partners of the 1970s. They were street fighters, traders who had no time for the condescension of snobbish bankers who wore fancy suits but made less money than they did.

Lehman's resurgence was led by Dick Fuld—and four men known as "the Ponderosa Boys." This was a now badly outdated reference to *Bonanza*, the popular TV series in the early 1960s about an intrepid rancher and his sons, each of them born to a different wife. Lehman's Ponderosa Boys were T. Christopher "Chris" Pettit, Joseph M. "Joe"

Gregory, Thomas "Tommy" Tucker, and Stephen "Stevie" Lessing. Each morning at 5 A.M. they'd meet at Lessing's house in Laurel Hollow, on Long Island's north shore, for the 45-minute drive in to Wall Street.

They took turns driving. Chris was the tallest and oldest of the group, the clear leader. Tommy was his sidekick and confidant—his blond, good-looking best friend since kindergarten. Stevie was the youngest—and the chubbiest—but he exuded charm. He'd married well and it showed. Joe was the wild card. A man as nervous as he was voluble, lithe, with long hair, huge glasses, and rope bracelets, Joe looked completely out of place on Wall Street, and in that carpool. He looked like he ought to have been in a rock band, not a bank. He looked like Barry Gibb.

■ ■ ■

Dick Fuld was the son of upper-middle-class parents from Harrison, New York, a posh bedroom community north of Manhattan. His father, Richard, ran a company that wrote short-term loans for textile companies. Growing up, Richie, as he was known then, wanted to go into the Air Force.

Betsy Schaper, a media publicist who grew up across the street from him, remembers that he was doted on by his parents and was a local heartthrob. "Everyone wanted to date Richie," she recalled. He was good-looking, straightforward, masculine.

Dick excelled in athletics at Wilbraham & Monson Academy, a boarding school in Massachusetts—but otherwise left little impression on the faculty there. "If you'd asked me back then, 'Is this a man with burning ambition?' I would have said absolutely not," said Schaper.

Fuld next studied at the University of Colorado, and his legacy there had nothing to do with his efforts in the classroom. He stood out mostly for the reckless passion he brought to parties, and for the fierce loyalty he showed his friends, and demanded in return.

Even then, he had grit, and didn't back down. There is an oft-repeated story of the time he was expelled from his college Reserve Officers' Training Corps (ROTC). One officer delighted in tormenting Fuld during weekly inspections about the shine on his shoes. This officer would step on Fuld's shoes and then send him back to his dorm to shine them again. During one such inspection, Fuld returned from a second round of shoe polishing to find the officer tormenting a fellow cadet in a similar fashion, even stomping on the young man's foot until he dropped to the floor in pain.

"Hey, asshole," Fuld said. "Why don't you pick on someone your own size?"

"Are you talking to me?" the officer asked, astonished.

"Yes," Fuld said, and the two men started fighting.

After they were separated, Fuld was summoned by his commanding officer. "Do you want to know my side of the story?" Fuld asked.

"No," came the answer. "There's only one side to the story."

With that, Fuld was kicked out of the program for insubordination, thus ending what he had hoped would be a career in the Air Force.

He graduated in 1969, with a degree in international business.

Later that year, Lehman partner Herman Kahn told Paul Newmark, then a senior vice president and treasurer of Lehman Commercial Paper Inc. (LCPI), that the grandson of one of his clients was coming to work at the firm. Newmark was not surprised—such friendly inbreeding had been common practice at Lehman Brothers for a long time.

"*My son, my cousin, my* . . . you know. Anyone who was a relative could get a job at Lehman Brothers," Newmark says. "People at Lehman said Dick Fuld's grandfather was an important man. No one was going to turn down his grandson. And anyway, Dick's father had accounts at Lehman. That's how he got the interview."

Fuld got the job, and was sent to LCPI, which was run by the infamously intimidating head trader Lew Glucksman.

Glucksman would hurl objects across his office when he was in a bad mood, which was quite often. Newmark once saw him rip the shirt off his back in anger—and, on another occasion, throw a 20-pound adding machine. An ex–Naval officer and the son of a lamp manufacturer, Glucksman was increasingly riled by the fact that his unit was generating more than half the firm's profits, but his traders were openly derided by the investment bankers—a well-born, well-educated, and well-groomed elite comprising most of the firm's 77 partners, and led by CEO Peter G. Peterson. The bankers looked down on the traders and never paid them as well as they paid their fellow bankers. But as the capital markets grew, so did trading instruments and the opportunity for

Glucksman's division to make even more money, which only increased the tension within the firm.

Glucksman quickly took a liking to Fuld. "Dick was a very bright guy," recalls Newmark. "If you were a good trader working for Lew Glucksman, you had it made.

"Lew loved people who would sit with him from 6:30 in the morning till 10:00 at night," Newmark says. Glucksman's home life had almost entirely evaporated following a divorce, so "people who were willing to spend 14, 15 hours" with him "were the ones who . . . went to the top." Fuld rose quickly under his mentor.

Fuld and Glucksman were in many ways alike. Both were taciturn, ruthlessly competitive men who swore loudly, and often, in and out of the office. Both thought the most effective tool for managing a trading floor was fear. Both were swift, instinctive traders—never hampered by details.

According to a Lehman partner, in those early days when Fuld participated in the morning traders' meeting, "everyone would say what they wanted to say, and Dick would say, 'I like it. Buy it.' So everyone would go back to their desks and buy *everything*, you know? Basically, everybody did what Dick said—they made money because Dick was right often enough." Almost no one dared cross Fuld and take an alternative view, because if they lost money on a trade he hadn't sanctioned, there was "hell to pay," according to this trader.

Glucksman had an us-versus-them mentality, and "them" included Lehman's investment bankers. In those days, the traders would put their positions on five-by-seven-inch cards on a wall so that everyone could see what had been bought and sold. The color of the ink indicated which type of security it was. According to a senior person at LCPI, if ever the traders heard that Arthur Schulte, Lehman's partner responsible for trading, was on his way over from One William Street (Lehman Brothers' headquarters) to 9 Mill Lane (then the headquarters of LCPI), the cards were quickly pulled off the board. There were limits to the total value of their positions, and at midday those positions might be higher; essentially, they were hiding their volatility, how much risk they were taking on a daily basis.

When Arthur left, the cards went back up. "It was a game," says Newmark, "that was ingrained in people. That's how Glucksman ran his business." It was a game that taught these traders they "had to hide the facts." It was also a very profitable game. And Dick Fuld was good at it.

One anecdote starring him quickly turned into legend.

It was the 1970s. Fuld was an associate trader and needed a trade signed by Allan Kaplan, then a partner and banker in charge of the commitments committee, to move forward. He went to see Kaplan, who was on the phone and motioned for Fuld to wait outside.

Fuld came in anyway, and said, "I need you to sign something." Kaplan again signaled for Fuld to wait for him outside.

Fuld did not budge. "I know, but I need you to sign this."

Kaplan continued with his phone conversation and Fuld barked at him again. An irritated Kaplan got off the phone. Who was this annoying young guy? Didn't he know you couldn't just barge into an office on the banking floor, much less interrupt a phone call? Fuld explained he had a trade that needed Kaplan's signature before he could make it.

Kaplan decided to teach the impudent trader a lesson in protocol.

He motioned toward his desk, strewn with paper. "You see all these piles on my desk? When they are gone, I will sign your paper."

Fuld leaned across the desk and cleared it in one sweep. Papers flew across the office as Fuld said, "Now may I have your signature?"

Kaplan was astonished, but he signed. The legend of Dick Fuld— the gorilla—had begun.

■ ■ ■

By 1984 Fuld had just a few close friends on the trading floor. One was Glucksman. Another was James S. "Jim" Boshart III, a managing director, who had been hired in 1970 by Glucksman mostly because of his jump shot. Boshart was six feet five inches tall and a former Wake Forest University basketball star, and Glucksman badly wanted the LCPI team to win the Lehman basketball championship. (The team had lost its first four games before Boshart joined them, but then ran off 12 straight wins to win the Wall Street basketball league.) That Boshart, who would rise to be a partner and chief administrative officer (CAO) by 1983, had a superb gift for crunching numbers was a happy coincidence. When he'd joined, Glucksman had rushed across the trading floor to greet him. "I know who you are. I've read your resume. You're not qualified to work here." He paused. "But I'll give you a contract for three months so you can play on the basketball team. It's up to you if you make it work on the trading front."

And Boshart had.

A joke went around Lehman after Boshart was hired that "if you could jump up and touch the ceiling you'd be hired."

It was not surprising that Glucksman liked Chris Pettit, either. Pettit had joined the firm in 1977. As a former military man, Glucksman liked recruiting from the military. Pettit, with his commanding demeanor and distinguished military resume, was a natural fit.

Tucker, Gregory, and Lessing—all seen as "Pettit's men"—benefited from Pettit's rise even though Pettit had joined the firm long after Gregory. The son of a lithograph printer, Gregory had never imagined he would end up on Wall Street. He'd been recruited by a family friend way back in 1968, and he'd spent his summers there as an intern in his teens.

Steve Lessing was the youngest of the group. He joined in 1980.

They all watched in awe as Pettit, with zero financial background, shot up through LCPI's ranks. Pettit was made head of LCPI sales in 1980 and partner in 1982. He was now essentially the deputy to Fuld, with whom he got on very well.

Newmark recalled that the partnership of Fuld and Pettit worked well in the early 1980s, particularly while Glucksman watched over both of them.

"It was the type of firm in the eighties that you thought couldn't be any better. It was Glucksman, it was Fuld, it was Pettit, it was a team," Newmark said. "Lehman Brothers in those days was a team. And the team worked together, and we were all successful. We all got paid."

Tucker became Pettit's deputy in sales while Lessing, a salesman, rose to be Tucker's deputy; Gregory worked in mortgage securities in the 1970s and rose to become head of high-yield bonds and, in the 1990s, of fixed income.

Gregory was always considered to be bright, although also unusually impetuous and emotional for a banker. He was sometimes seen openly crying in the office, which he tried to hide, and sometimes seen losing his temper, which he didn't attempt to hide. He was, in those days, very much a Pettit man, constantly mocking the more taciturn Fuld. "Joe used to be considered a loose cannon," recalls Robert "Bob" Genirs, a partner during this period. He remembers Fuld in particular shaking his head at some of the things Gregory either said or did. "Dick confided in me at times that he was skeptical of Joe," says Genirs.

■ ■ ■

Before work each weekday morning, the Ponderosa Boys would stop off at a gym in lower Manhattan, just a short walk from their office, and, alongside business competitors from Goldman Sachs (including its future CEO, Jon Corzine, and Robert Giordano, its co-chief economist), run on treadmills and lift weights. They took pride in being the first through the doors of that gym, and were often greeted with the *Bonanza* theme music as they walked in. Liz Neporent, who was a trainer at the gym, had coined the nickname for the bunch, and assigned each of them a character from the show. "Tommy was the good-looking one—*Adam*; Steve was *Hoss*, and Joe, for obvious reasons was *Little Joe*." She said Chris, "the leader . . . always the first in, was *Pa*."

Neporent came up with the idea because Lessing, the chubbiest of the group, was always the most reluctant to "do what he was told" when it came to personal fitness. While the others ran and lifted competitively, pushing each other, Lessing was often strolling on the treadmill. Occasionally, though, he'd crank it up to full speed for about a minute and yell, "Come on!" as he ran and "Yee-haw! Yee-haw!"

Those screams were what gave Neporent her *Bonanza* theme: It sounded as if he was rounding up cattle.

Neporent remembers that the four men were, by far, the most generous members of the gym. "Other bankers would give us a card with $20 in it for a holiday tip. These guys gave us thousands of dollars. They never knew it, but we really relied on their Christmas bonus to live. And sometimes if they called us out to their homes for a personal training session, they'd send a limo to pick us up. I remember stepping into this limo while my neighbors were gawping. No one else did anything like that for us."

The Ponderosa Boys were driven, competitive risk takers, unafraid of peers with better resumes and sharper suits—and they were completely united. Between 1984 and 1995 they were the architects of what would become the new Lehman Brothers. Their tiny division fought for its life and grew into an investment bank whose values would reflect, for a short while, what those men dreamed of creating: a firm that encouraged a militaristic loyalty and a hardscrabble resourcefulness exemplified by the credo "The Trader Knows Best" and a selfless embrace of the "one firm" mantra.

In 1980, as they looked around Wall Street and saw the excesses of the era, Tucker and Pettit made a pledge to one another—they swore they would never turn into assholes if they made money.

They would be unique. They would be the good guys of Wall Street.

Chapter 3

The Captain

"Team," "team," "team" . . . I'm not sure Chris Pettit uttered
a sentence that didn't mention the word.

—*Ronald A. Gallatin, former Lehman partner*

A pickup basketball game delivered Chris Pettit from the
Vietnam War. He had served nearly three of his required
eight years of military service after graduating from West
Point and hoped to eventually study medicine. He had received two
bronze stars for valor while in Vietnam. He piloted a small motorboat
for the Mobile Assistance Training Team, and his wife, Mary Anne
Pettit, remembers his letters describing the fear he felt as he trolled up
and down the river with the Vietcong watching from both banks. He
believed he would die at any moment.

After six months in Vietnam, Pettit was ready to go home. His
good friend and high school lacrosse rival, Lieutenant Ray Enners, had
been killed in an ambush, and the futility of teaching military maneu-
vers to the South Vietnamese was wearing on him. He wanted to go
back to Long Island, back to his wife.

In tenth grade, he'd started dating Mary Anne Mollico, a pretty, auburn-haired cheerleader and gymnast at Huntington High School, where Pettit had been a top athlete and scholar. They married six years later, in 1967. Though they were poor, Mary Anne regarded their marriage as a "fairy tale." Chris was, it seemed to those who knew him then, a prince of a man. There was something about him, they recall, that held your attention—when he looked at you, it was as if he saw straight into your soul. He was a man other men and women instinctively followed.

Pettit had chosen West Point over Harvard because it offered a salary, and he knew his family needed the income. Additionally, Pettit wanted to play for the West Point lacrosse coach, James F. Adams, who was a legend in the sport. At West Point, Pettit was the academy's leading scorer and team captain, and was twice named to the All-American team. He graduated with honors in 1967, the year General Westmoreland declared U.S. victory in Vietnam. After two and a half years of training at the Nike Hercules Missile Battery Site in Zweibrucken, Germany, Pettit was shipped off to Vietnam.

When Mary Anne received a telegram at their home in Huntington, New York, in May 1970, she assumed the worst. She and Chris had planned to spend his upcoming R&R together in Hawaii, and Mary Anne now feared that that wasn't going to happen. Her hands shook as she opened the envelope, and read: "Captain Pettit has suffered a severe hematoma to his right thigh, and it's traveling toward his heart. We have to Medevac him to Japan."

It was only a bruise—a nasty bruise that felt as if he'd broken his femur, but still only a bruise. He'd caught a knee from another player while fighting for a loose basketball at district headquarters in Vietnam, and a week later was in Japan being diagnosed by Captain Marvel, a marvelously named Army doctor who assured him, "We'll fix you."

But Pettit didn't want to be fixed—at least, not in order to return to combat in a war he no longer believed in. He wanted out. According to Mary Anne, her husband—like so many other soldiers—had been traumatized by the war. A devout Roman Catholic (in the 1980s he would become a eucharistic minister in his local church, Lady Queen of Martyrs), he'd had serious philosophical issues with what he and the U.S. military were doing in Vietnam. He'd had especial difficulty with carrying out his assigned task of teaching the Vietnamese how to fight once he realized that they didn't want to learn. They'd rather die.

Captain Marvel was surprised when Pettit told him that he didn't want to go back. "This is not going to be my career," he said. Pettit was shipped to St. Albans Hospital, in Queens, New York, and he was there for six weeks, until the hematoma dissipated. He resigned his commission in June 1971.

Major Peter Bouton, his commanding office, wrote:

> It is extremely unfortunate that this outstanding young officer will not continue to pursue an Army career, as he has the potential of surpassing the vast majority of his contemporaries in individual professional development.

Pettit still wanted to become a doctor. He had hoped that his outstanding high school record, his schooling at West Point, and his service in Vietnam would be enough to get him into a top medical school, but he was now 27, and couldn't afford to pay his own way. He received rejection letter after rejection letter. According to Mary Anne, it crushed him.

"This was a man who was always the captain of every sports team," she said later. "President of every class. He had never lost, never failed. It was a reality check."

By now, Chris and Mary Anne had two daughters, Lara and Kari, and Chris needed to do whatever he could to pay the bills. The young family lived in his late grandmother's house, which was owned by his father, a window salesman. Chris got hired to teach science and math to seventh and eighth graders at his old high school and coach the football team.

"When he came back [from the war] he was very troubled, and I found him crying so many nights, just sobbing, trying to understand the ludicrous business of war," Mary Anne says.

He planned to write a book about his troubles, but didn't get very far. He read Aristotle and Plato, and tried to make sense of his experience.

Pettit's childhood best friend, Tom Tucker, had heard from his mother that Pettit was home, and having trouble. Tucker hadn't seen Pettit for years, and was eager to reconnect with his old buddy. He invited

Chris to join him in Chicago, where he was working with Greg Marotz, a Colgate University fraternity brother, in sales for the Northern Screw Company, a small importer and distributor of industrial fasteners used by farm implement manufacturers in the Midwest.

"When I called him in January 1973, he told me no—that Mary Anne was pregnant with their third child, Suzanne, and moving from Huntington was out of the question," recalls Tucker.

But Tucker didn't give up, and after a week Chris relented enough to go to Chicago for an interview. He was hired, and six months later so was his brother, Rusty. The trio spent two years there, and more than tripled the productivity of the company; but they had a falling out with the owner, who they claimed cheated them on their compensation. They swore that they "would never work for a jerk again," says Mary Anne.

They came home to Huntington in 1975. With help from Chris's father, they purchased Finnegan's Restaurant and Tap Room, the oldest bar-restaurant in town. On the wall they hung a picture of Fiver, the runt rabbit in Richard Adams's epic allegory, *Watership Down*. They incorporated a company under the same name.

But the revenue from Finnegan's was not enough to support three families. The Pettits were so hard up that Mary Anne was denied a Woolworth's credit card that she needed to buy blinds for her bedroom. By 1977, the Pettits and their three children often ate whatever food Chris could bring home from the bar. Mary Anne was pregnant with her fourth child (Chris Jr.), but she was so worried about their finances that she didn't tell her husband for the first few months, not wanting to burden him. "Chris, in high school, had been the most likely to succeed and now he couldn't even afford to support his own children," she recalls.

Then in January 1977, Jim Boshart, who had known Pettit since they were on rival high school basketball teams and had heard that he and Tucker were struggling, invited them to interview at Lehman Commercial Paper Inc. (LCPI). Pettit happily accepted the invitation, Tucker says. Both men had realized that Finnegan's was not a growth business, and "We learned that there was a lot of money to be made on Wall Street."

For their big interviews, both men bought new suits from a local department store, Abraham and Strauss—Tucker says the suits cost $49.99.

Later that month, they met with Paul Cohen, then a partner and the chief administrative officer for LCPI, and Morton Kurzrok, the chief administrative officer for equities, before having a brief meeting with Lew Glucksman.

At the start of Tucker's interview, Cohen said, "New suit?"

Tucker blushed. Quietly, he said, "Yep."

Cohen smiled. "You realize the price tag is still on it?"

Neither man impressed their interviewers hugely—mainly because of their lack of financial experience. For Boshart this was hugely embarrassing, but he insisted they'd be good hires.

"Okay, so pick one," he was told. Boshart picked Pettit.

Pettit refused the job out of loyalty to his friend, but Tucker insisted that he accept it, so he did. Six months later Pettit had shown he was an invaluable hire, and Tucker got another interview. He showed up for this grilling wearing the same suit he'd bought for the first session. This time the tag was cut off. This time, he was hired.

What was it that Boshart had seen in the tall, earnest, brown-eyed Pettit and in the good-looking, fair-haired Tucker? "I just felt that they were extraordinarily high-quality people who had an element that Wall Street clearly lacked, which was a sense of how to build a team."

■ ■ ■

Given his military background, the demands of a grueling Wall Street day weren't much of a challenge for Pettit. Of all the Ponderosa Boys, he was the quickest to ascend Lehman's ranks. In 1979 he was made head of sales in the San Francisco office. He moved his family to the West Coast without hesitation. But they weren't there for long. By 1980 he was head of all sales in LCPI, and he made partner of Lehman Brothers Kuhn Loeb (LBKL) in 1981.

"I think because he was quite old when he started, he was in more of a hurry than the rest to succeed," says Lara Pettit, 40, his eldest daughter. "So he got in earliest and he worked through lunch."

Unlike Fuld, Pettit had a charisma that people still recall with awe. He was an excellent—and often inspirational—impromptu speaker. Unlike Pete Peterson, Lehman's CEO, Pettit offered humble, practical advice. He often liked to remind colleagues of how John F. Kennedy had once bumped into a janitor cleaning the floors of

NASA's vast corridors. "What are you doing?" JFK had asked the janitor. "Mr. President, I am helping put a man on the moon," the janitor had replied. Pettit said he wanted every person at Lehman to have that janitor's spirit. Every man and woman had his or her part in the firm's business.

Bond salesman Craig Schiffer recalls that "Chris had an ability that I have never seen"—people often walked away inspired even after he had ripped into them. "He was particularly hard on me, kind of like a tough dad. He would beat the living crap out of you. Scream at you. But he's the only person I've ever met who could do that to you, and you didn't walk out of the room going, 'What an asshole!' You'd walk out of the room and think, 'I've gotta do a better job for that guy!'"

Pettit was blunt and honest with people, and revered for it. He also had a knack for spotting talent. Jim Vinci was an accountant for what was then Coopers & Lybrand and had been hired to update Lehman's antiquated operational systems. He had a reputation for being mean, pig-headed, and tough—and knew it. He had never met Pettit when he was summoned to his office in the mid-1980s, when Pettit was Fuld's number two.

"I was six months into my tenure there," Vinci recalls. "He calls me into his office, and he says, 'Jim? I've heard you're the biggest asshole we've ever hired.'

"I was thinking, 'Okay, this is going to be a good meeting. . . . I think I can probably go back to my old job . . .' And then Pettit says, 'But I've also heard that you're one of the brightest people we've ever hired.' He added, 'I came across your sort in the military. And so what I'm going to do is save you. You're going to come work for me.'" Vinci quickly morphed into Pettit's chief of staff.

■ ■ ■

Pettit remained untainted—or so it seemed for many years—by his swelling paycheck. His four children all attended the same public school he had attended in Huntington. The moment he got home he'd rush to help them with their homework.

"We would have all the kids coming over—their parents would drive them over—because he was the only one who could figure out our chemistry homework," says Lara. "And he'd be doing this at eight o'clock at night, right after he got back from work, trying to sit with a text book, figuring it out." He rarely missed a game played by any of his children. "I remember him running to catch the last quarter, his tie flying behind him—he was late because he'd been caught in traffic on the way home from the office," says Mary Anne. Once he arrived, everyone knew he was there because he shouted and cheered louder than any other parent.

On weekends he hung out with his family and with the Tuckers, the Lessings, and sometimes the Gregorys. Occasionally the Fulds, Dick and his beautiful blonde wife Kathy, came out from their apartment in the city. "Be on your best behavior, because my boss is coming," he'd say to the children, who remembered liking Dick and Kathy Fuld. "She was so pretty," says Lara.

Dick took photographs of them all sitting in the Pettits' backyard with the children and their pets: two golden retrievers and two cats.

The romance of Dick and Kathy Fuld was by now part of Lehman lore. Kathleen Bailey, a statuesque blonde, the youngest of eight Catholic siblings, had been hired in the 1970s to work on the sales desk. Fuld had not wanted to hire her. "She's too pretty—she'll distract someone and marry them and will be no use to the firm," he had said.

He was partly right. "We all pretended not to notice that when Dick traveled for work Kathy would be going, too, but no one was fooled," recalls Paul Newmark. They got married on September 24, 1978, the day after Fuld was made partner. Kathy converted to Judaism for her husband, and the couple had three children, Jacqueline and Chrissie, twins, and Richie. To the amusement of the Lehman staff, once they were married Dick called his wife "Fuld."

Pettit's simple lifestyle was a dramatic contrast to that of most of his Lehman peers, the majority of whom in the early 1980s were on LBKL's banking side. They were men with last names like Gleacher, Altman, Rubin, Solomon, and Schwarzman. They were famous for their brains, their smooth talk, and their tough negotiating skills; but most of all they were guys who'd made money—lots of it (although *they* believed there was much more to be made, and in many cases, they were right). They had multiple houses, large domestic staffs, and as they got richer, many of them traded in the first wife for a younger one.

Pettit took all this in and told Mary Anne, "I only want to do this for 10 years. I'm worried it will change me if I do it for longer than that."

The Lehman partners in the early 1980s regularly ate lavish lunches, washed down with expensive wine and dirty martinis. There was a barber in-house, free cigars (for which the annual bill ran as high as $30,000), and fresh raspberries at the ready. "Lehman's dining room, and its chef, was as fine as any restaurant in the world," recalls Newmark. "It was hard to get a reservation. You had to come with a client. But if you were a partner, you could go up and eat every day. But this wasn't just 'Come up and grab a sandwich.' This was a three-course, four-course [meal], the finest food, no expense spared, with cigars, with alcohol, with wine, and then you had Robert Lehman's art collection up there, with Picassos and Rembrandts, and all that other good stuff. It was a fascinating place."

Back then the traders in LCPI never really partook of that lifestyle. They wore belts; the bankers wore suspenders. When Pettit first arrived, he found the traders reading *Playboy* magazine at their desks during lunch, and as soon as he was in a position to impose his will and taste, he put an end to that. In this way, he was like Fuld, who had strict moral principles and believed in the sanctity of family values.

What Pettit also loved about LCPI in those early years was that his little unit always fought above its weight. Its profits were disproportionally high, and this was in large part due to the camaraderie of the people who worked there. This was what all of the Ponderosa Boys were proudest of.

Mary Anne says, "What they loved about Lehman was its insistence on *team, team, team.*"

She recalls that during one LCPI Christmas dinner in the late 1980s, "Chris was recapping the year's growth and success, and he looked around the room and said, 'Now look at this! Every single person here is with their original spouse. That is why we are successful: because our word is our honor. We succeed in business because people can trust us.'"

He was seen as messianic, says Kim Sullivan, a secretary on the sales side. "I can remember when I first started working on the trading floor, and he brought me out one day—it was like my second day—and said, 'You're going to see a lot of things go on here. You're going to see a lot of people make lots and lots of money. Just remember one thing. One day you'll be there, too. But remember how you started in your career. And don't ever lose sight of who you are and where you came from. Because that is easy to do when we all make lots of money.'"

Sullivan recalls the day she found a trader in hysterical tears. "His daughter had been brought to the emergency room in Long Island, and the hospital used the wrong aspirator for her, and the poor thing went into a convulsion, and went into a coma. He had just been notified that he had used up all his health insurance. He was new to Wall Street; he had not made any money yet."

"I told him, 'You've got to go talk to Chris.' And he said, 'I don't know Chris.' I said, 'Well, you're going to know him in about five minutes.'"

Sullivan quickly briefed Pettit on the situation and recalls that he said, "Sure, I know him." "Chris knew everybody's name on the trading floor. He was amazing! And he brought this guy into his office. They talked for about a half an hour, and when the guy came out, he was all smiles. Chris had given him a bridge loan so he could get a house in New Jersey, so the child could be moved to a better hospital facility. The house was like a block away from the hospital, and Pettit made sure that Lehman took care of everything. There was no limit on our health coverage, because we were a self-insured company.

"The guy said to me, 'Wow, this is really an incredible place! They actually care about you!'"

Pettit's ethos so infused and inspired LCPI that a corporate video about the firm's history referred to the period before his arrival as a chaotic, unenlightened time: "B.C.—Before Chris."

Chapter 4

The "Take-Under"

The biggest and most fundamental change on Wall Street in my career has been the migration of private and public ownership to a place where private partnerships and publicly owned firms determine their own capital, and where, to quote Vikram Pandit, "the traders play with the house's money."

—Joseph R. Perella, chairman and CEO,
Perella Weinberg Partners

Peregrine "Perry" Moncreiffe, the younger son of Sir Rupert Iain Kay Moncreiffe of that Ilk, 11th Baronet, joined Lehman's fixed income division in 1982. A tall, Scottish aristocrat (and Oxford rower), Moncreiffe was an affable, affluent anomaly on the New York trading floor. But he was also smart, extremely low-key, and charming.

He had been attracted to Lehman because of Lew Glucksman's lack of pretension, which he considered a blast of fresh air in the stuffy confines of Wall Street. "I thought, 'This is the first guy I like because he's a no-nonsense trader,'" says Moncreiffe. "There were no airs and graces with Lew, but he was so intelligent—like an old Russian general. He was always there working in his shirtsleeves, his tie loosened and collar open. When I first had lunch with him, we talked about Marx, and I thought, '*This* gentleman I can work for.'"

When Moncreiffe met with Pettit and Fuld for his interview, he told them, "Lew is fantastic!" and, imitating Glucksman's slovenly manner, took a piece of Brie from the welcoming spread and put it on his tie. "I really like him, because he's not smooth," he said. "But he's able to lead a large trading organization, so he has got to be good at what he does."

Like Pettit, Moncreiffe rose swiftly—though he clashed with Fuld. "When you are a trader, and working for someone else who's a trader, you are always going to come up against a different point of view," says Moncreiffe. "Dick had good instincts and usually knew when to run for the hills when things were going wrong. He also had the requisite toughness to run a trading operation. We didn't always see eye to eye. I used to tell him that in trading there's many ways to skin the cat. I'm not sure that he agreed with me."

But Fuld and the other partners recognized Moncreiffe's talent, and before long he was put in charge of trading the money markets side in London. One morning, he sold the entire London certificates of deposit position because he saw the market trading badly. "I remember the shock of colleagues," he says. "They asked: 'Why didn't you get Dick's permission?' I replied, 'What's the point? By the time he wakes up it will be too late.' I was right. But their reaction showed the fear he inspired."

In fact Fuld was impressed by that move and Moncreiffe was brought to New York to manage money markets and U.S. Treasury trading. That's when the Scotsman's relationship with Pettit was cemented.

"When it came to management decisions, Dick listened to Chris, who was never afraid to speak his mind. Dick respected Chris. It made them a good team," Moncreiffe says. The Scot became great friends with Pettit, whom he regarded as "such an inspiring person. Chris and I got along really well together. And I think Chris was all ready to dislike me. I think he thought, 'Oh no! Perry's going to be another one of these single-smartest-guy types.' Chris had a thing against a 'single smartest guy,' because I think there was a tendency on the part of Lehman—maybe Dick and some other senior colleagues—to sort of say about new hires, 'Ah, this is the single smartest guy,' and then you'd find out they had feet of clay."

The two men found a lot to talk about, including Vietnam and Scottish and military history. One of Pettit's historical heroes was the Scottish independence warrior King Robert the Bruce, and Moncreiffe was descended from that line.

■ ■ ■

Moncreiffe had arrived back in New York just in time to watch Lew Glucksman plot his coup while Pete Peterson went on being "Mr. Outside," the public face of the firm. Glucksman was fed up of being talked down to and treated like a second-class citizen who had to be tolerated. Peterson thought he was doing Glucksman a great favor by making him co-CEO in May 1983. Of course, Glucksman didn't see it that way. Glucksman thought he deserved more.

On July 13, 1983, Glucksman got to the office before Peterson, who was at a breakfast meeting, and, according to Ken Auletta, who chronicled the ouster of Peterson in *Greed and Glory on Wall Street*, began leaving "urgent" messages with Peterson's executive assistant. When Peterson came in, he walked to Glucksman's office, not expecting anything out of the ordinary. "I just thought it was one of our weekly meetings," Peterson told Auletta.

But Glucksman was tense, and Peterson asked him what was on his mind.

"I've been giving a lot of thought to my life," Glucksman said. "You know how important boats and cruising and ships are to me. Kind of in the same way I have satisfaction when I'm in charge of a boat, I'm beginning to get the same feeling about Lehman."

He was unhappy in his role and thought his abilities were under-utilized, that he, unlike Peterson (a cultured New York intellectual and gadabout, who published essays in the *New York Review of Books* and counted Henry Kissinger as a friend), didn't have any "alternatives."

"This is my whole life," he said.

"Lew, let me see if I understand what you're saying," said Peterson. "Are you saying you want to run the business alone?"

Glucksman didn't just agree with that summation; he told Peterson he wanted him gone by September 30. Everyone knew that Glucksman ran day-to-day operations of the firm, and Glucksman knew that he could count on the support of the board, if it came to a vote.

On July 26, 1983, a special meeting of the board was called, and the directors arrived at 2 P.M. not having a clue what was going on. By the end of the afternoon, Peterson had ceded completely.

Bob Genirs, a partner, recalls being summoned into the Lehman executive committee meeting where Glucksman made the announcement.

"Lew and Pete stood together while Lew said that Pete was stepping down, and then, to our astonishment, he asked Pete to leave so that 'I can talk to my partners,'" remembers Genirs. "I thought, as I watched Peterson's face, 'We haven't heard the last of this.'"

■ ■ ■

After Glucksman ousted Peterson, the market nose-dived for a brief period. Unfortunately this happened at precisely the same moment Glucksman got long in the bond market—and the firm lost a ton of money Quite suddenly, Lehman was vulnerable. Unfortunately for Glucksman, this played into Peterson's hands.

Moncreiffe explains: "Peterson's severance package contained a clause that stated that if Lehman was sold within a specified number of years, he would get an uplift on his equity—as would all the partners, most of whom were bankers, not traders. Most of the bankers had a vested interest in Lehman getting sold at any price. They thought if it doesn't get sold, they're not going to get a premium on the equity that they've got in the business. He [Lew] will redistribute their shares to his constituency and they'll get taken out at asset value. It is an example, in a sense, of absolute power being perhaps a negative thing."

On May 11, 1984, Lehman Brothers Kuhn Loeb was absorbed into Shearson, a retail brokerage firm acquired in 1981 by American Express, for $360 million. American Express was then run by James D. Robinson III. It had luminaries like Kissinger, President Gerald Ford, and Vernon Jordan on its board. Shearson was the second-largest retail sales force in the country, run by Sanford I. "Sandy" Weill, who left almost immediately after the deal was done and was supplanted by his deputy, Peter A. Cohen, a brash-talking, dark-haired cigar smoker.

Peterson made $6 million from the transaction ($12 million today); Glucksman, $15.6 million ($32 million today); Peter Solomon,

$7.8 million ($16 million today); Jim Boshart, $6.2 million ($13 million today); Ron Gallatin, $6 million ($12 million today).

But before the merger could be completed, each Lehman partner who owned over 800 shares was asked to sign a noncompete clause. (According to Cohen, there was a secret list with the 53 names Shearson American Express thought they needed. "We didn't really care if the others didn't sign," he says.) Fuld held out until his mentor, Glucksman, capitulated. Then he agreed, with a handful of other senior Lehman bankers, to join the newly merged firm. Fuld then got a signing fee of $7.6 million.

Robinson's reason for buying an investment bank was to create the first financial supermarket. He had a credit card business with American Express, and he had a brokerage to sell it (Shearman); and—the third essential ingredient—he now had an investment bank to stake his ground on Wall Street. But most of Lehman's most famous bankers left as soon as the merger was completed. Most of them went on to richer pastures. Peterson and Steve Schwarzman (who left six months into the merger, meaning he never signed a noncompete clause) founded the private equity firm Blackstone Group.

The most senior Lehman partners left in the new firm (nicknamed Slamex) included Shel Gordon, Peter Solomon, Bob Rubin (who left soon after Schwarzman), and Dick Fuld. One by one, except for Fuld, they left. Peter Solomon was the last to go, in 1989. "I saw how the new business was shaking out, how capital markets were rising and supplanting the advisory business, and I realized it just wasn't my area of expertise," Solomon later said. "I didn't want my reputation dependent on people I really didn't know, trading securities I didn't fully understand, in time zones I rarely visited." He started his own firm, Peter J. Solomon Company, the first independent investment bank on Wall Street.

By 1990, Fuld, who had been a low-key partner in the old Lehman, was the most senior person left in the newly merged entity. He was made a senior vice chairman and a board member, and was placed on the planning group of the new firm. He was nominally in charge of commercial paper, government, mortgage, and money market securities. According to Robert "Bob" Shapiro, the senior trader on the LCPI desk, some of the surviving Lehmanites sympathized with Fuld over his capitulation to the takeover.

"He was boxed in, and I think we all knew it. He had a lot of money at stake," says Shapiro.

One person who did not agree with what Fuld had done, however, was his best friend, Jim Boshart. Boshart was leaving out of loyalty to Lew, and he thought the firm had just been murdered.

He thought Fuld should have made a similar stand, so they had some angry exchanges. Their friendship never fully recovered.

Others agreed with Boshart. "They thought, quite frankly, that Dick had sold out," says Moncreiffe. "No one thought much of what he'd done."

■ ■ ■

At first it did not occur to Moncreiffe that the merger would directly involve him. He had expanded the government securities trading operation and then run the mortgage-backed securities trading desk. But because he wasn't that close to Fuld, he thought he was "no longer a key player" on the trading side by the time the Shearson American Express takeover happened in 1984.

But suddenly, just before the deal was done, Moncreiffe and Pettit, the two most junior Lehman partners (who were barely on any of the senior partners' radars) were asked to sign noncompetes. To the dismay of the other partners, they refused. Why? They believed that they needed to protect LCPI, the little unit that employed 454 people and might be broken up unless they kept it together. LCPI drew its success from its loyalty and team spirit. Pettit and Moncreiffe were not going to allow it to be dismembered in the takeover. "We believed in truth, justice, and the American way," says Moncreiffe with a smile.

Initially Robinson had felt he didn't need noncompetes from Pettit and Moncreiffe, since together they had only a thousand LBKL shares. Neither was on his list of 53 essential partners. But then the American Express board noticed just how profitable LCPI had been before the meltdown of the past six months, and there was a sudden panic.

Moncreiffe says, "Chris and I agreed that we would refuse to sign unless we could protect every single person in LCPI—secretaries and back-office people included. We had to be kept together; we had to be paid as a unit. It's no good paying us extra to sign a noncompete.

What we need is a viable business going forward. We insisted that we get a bonus pool based on profits. We also secured a guarantees pool for the first year because of the business disruption because of the takeover."

Moncreiffe says Cohen summoned him and Pettit to a meeting with his deputy, Jeff Lane, and Herb Freiman (the executive in charge of all capital markets for Shearson), and asked for their signatures. Moncreiffe says the meeting became "quite heated" as they "outlined the incompatibilities that needed to be bridged."

After the meeting, Pettit called a conference at 6.30 P.M. Moncreiffe says Fuld was there, but said very little.

"It was vintage Chris to do this. . . . [It] didn't matter that Dick was his boss, nor that Lew was his boss . . . he was going to call this meeting."

Pettit later described the scene in a dramatic video that was taped for Bob Genirs's farewell on April 1, 1993:

The leadership of that group [LCPI] had gathered—a small group of us—one afternoon in great consternation in my office at 55 Water Street. And we were trying to figure out what to do, and as we talked about our options, we realized, well, we didn't have a lot of options. But the one we did have was possibly to draw a line in the sand, so to speak, with Shearson. And just simply go in to them and say, "Look—we have 454 people. We're united as a group. And we're either going to come as a group, or we'll not come as a group." It was a very high-risk strategy because by making demands upon Shearson, they might look at us and say, "We're not taking your demands, fellas—you're fired," or they might just say, "We're not taking your demands," and then we would have to quit. Because we'd make that the option—"You either take our demands or we're gone."

So as that idea was being formed that afternoon, we sort of stopped the meeting and looked at Bob [Genirs], and Bob was sitting—there was a long couch in the office, a very long couch—he was sitting there with the other fellas. And I said, "Bob, you're the longest-term partner, one of the longest-term partners at Lehman, certainly the longest-term partner in this room. You have your whole financial security at risk, what you promised your family you would get out of this business. And if they fire us, or we have to quit, you're going to lose all that. So, why don't you leave [the room] now before we make a decision—which we're probably going to make—and if it works, you're with us, and if it doesn't, you can go on." So the room got quiet, and we fully expected Bob to get up and say, "Okay, guys, I'll step out now." But we looked over and . . . he was shaking his head back and forth, sort of looking at the floor. And all of a sudden, he looks up, and he goes, "I'm with you guys. I want to be part of this. Put my name on the list." And we spent about two seconds trying to say, "Bob you don't wanna do that," but it was pretty clear that Bob wanted to do that. And those of us who were there will never forget that.

Pettit also privately told Steve Lessing that he should feel free to leave with no ill will. Lessing was by the far the youngest of the Ponderosa Boys. His father-in-law was Andrew J. Melton Jr., the former chairman of Dean Witter Reynolds. He could start over. But Lessing did not leave. In fact, he set up a meeting between Pettit and Melton. The two met and Melton made it clear that Dean Witter might be prepared to take all of LCPI, which gave Pettit some leverage.

"When we held that meeting we really did feel we could lose everything," remembers Moncreiffe.

Yet everyone was prepared to follow Pettit. "The Captain" had put his livelihood on the line for them.

When Glucksman heard about the insurrection his protégés were cooking up, he was livid. He had made his own peace with the deal. After all, he was taking $15.6 million for standing down. Someone close to Pettit remembers Glucksman screaming at him: "You're going to fail! You're scum!"

"Chris was so disheartened," says this person. "He was always respectful of rank, and Lew Glucksman was older. I mean, Chris still called people like that 'sir.' But Chris thought he was doing the right thing, sticking with the people of Lehman. And that is why he didn't leave."

Pettit told that video camera that Moncreiffe called him at 10 the night before they were due to deliver their ultimatum to Robinson and asked him, "What do you think's going to happen?"

"I said, 'I think what's going to happen is this: I think Lew's going to fire us as soon as we get in in the morning so that we're not partners anymore, so we don't have to sign a noncompete and the issue goes away. That's what I think is going to happen.'"

He was wrong. A short time later, American Express agreed to all the demands of the rebels. "I don't remember Chris calling a meeting to announce what had happened, but I do recall word getting out that we were all safe, and we were jubilant," says Bob Shapiro.

Moncreiffe and Pettit got their terms and finally signed. LCPI, and all the people in it, were kept together. What the press reports never recorded was that some, including Moncreiffe, feared that the name Lehman might have been eradicated from the new merged entity of Shearson and Lehman had Pettit not held out. Peter Cohen emphatically denies this: "We wanted Lehman; we wanted the name." But the reality was that Lehman was a dying brand and at the time of the merger (May 1984) the only former Lehman Brothers entity that kept the Lehman moniker *was* LCPI. Had it not been for Chris Pettit, the name Lehman *could* have ended up on the cutting-room floor. The new company *could* have evolved into American Express Shearson.

No more Lehman Brothers.

■ ■ ■

Pettit's victory signaled the rebirth of the "one firm" spirit that Glucksman had wanted to instill in his people, and tried—but failed—to spread throughout the firm.

Bob Shapiro says, "In that meeting, Chris and Perry were essentially anointed as the leaders for LCPI. It's a meeting that, for many people, has taken on mythic, almost religious, proportions. It was the beginning of the esprit de corps that LCPI took on then."

"From that moment on, Chris Pettit was the hero and the real leader of what came to be Lehman Brothers," says J. Tomlinson "Tom" Hill, at the time a top Lehman investment banker and now the vice chairman of the private equity giant Blackstone Group.

There were some casualties in this war. Joe Gregory did not speak to Lew Glucksman for 12 years—which was remarkable given that Glucksman not only had given Gregory that internship when he was 16, but had also paid some of his tuition at Hofstra University when Gregory had flunked a course and was broke.

Boshart, loyal to Glucksman to the end, took several years off and eventually went to work for James L. "Jamie" Dimon at Bank One in Chicago. He did not speak to Fuld for many years, though eventually he got over his bitterness and regretted it

■ ■ ■

Unsurprisingly, Dick Fuld's life at Lehman was thereafter complicated; he was now responsible for negotiating for a firm that didn't really see him as its leader.

"Pettit was our leader," says Moncreiffe. "Fuld—well, Fuld was the front man who was tough enough to negotiate with the almost-as-tough guys at Shearson who tried to wiggle out of some of the assurances we had elicited. They were not all nice people. Their culture was about the individual. Dick did a good job of facing off with them."

Others were less diplomatic: "Dick sucked up to Peter Cohen, which no one else wanted to do," says one employee. Fuld's role at this point was a lonely one; he didn't receive much recognition from the troops below him.

Initially both Fuld and Pettit kept glass offices on the ninth floor (the trading floor), but Pettit was the manager who knew your name if you worked on the floor. Fuld did not.

If you had a problem, you went to Pettit. If you'd messed up, you went to Pettit.

Pettit understood why Fuld did what he did—and, according to Moncreiffe, was grateful that Fuld was the one who had to negotiate with the tough guys upstairs.

Contrary to some people's beliefs, the two men actually worked quite well together at this point. "Chris was far more interested in running the business than in battling upstairs," says Bob Shapiro.

On the corporate videos that got made in the late 1980s and early 1990s, Pettit's preeminence at LCPI is easily deduced from the simple fact that Fuld scarcely appears on them at all.

In "Citizen Genirs," the video tribute to Bob Genirs, the chief administrative officer, the entire firm comically searches for Genirs's Rosebud (which turns out to be a calculator called Victor). It's Pettit who appears as the boss.

"Dick was on the sidelines at this time," says Moncreiffe. "He wasn't the main guy urging people to do the right thing and stick together. Chris did."

Jim Vinci, Pettit's chief of staff, says Pettit convinced everyone that "they were part of something really special. And people believed him."

They were right to. According to Moncreiffe and others, they made way more money than their Shearson counterparts.

And Jim Robinson noticed.

As a result, by 1990 LCPI was running all of fixed income for Shearson Lehman. The Lehman traders had taken over the house. And the man pulling the strings was Chris Pettit.

"He took such pride in LCPI," says Mary Anne. "To him they were family; it felt like he was coaching a team; everyone had a part. They were going to be different, stand apart from the other Wall Street players."

"He was a Marine; they were all a bunch of Marines," says Peter Cohen, the CEO of Shearson, now the chairman and CEO of the securities firm, Cowen Group. Cohen admits he loathed Pettit. "I can guarantee you that if you asked anyone in investment banking if they liked Chris Pettit the answer would have been no. . . . He always wanted more money, more independence for LCPI. They may have worshipped him—but it was like a cult thing. They were soldiers and he was their captain."

Moncreiffe says, "Of course Cohen and Pettit didn't get on. Cohen understood Fuld's motivation but couldn't deal with Chris's altruism."

Shearson had bought Lehman, and yet it was Lehman that seemed to be incubating its power.

"The truth is, Chris understood that unless we retained independence we would lose control of our business, our revenues, our accounting. We'd disappear," says Vinci. "By hanging on to those, we eventually submerged Shearson into *our* culture."

Steve Carlson, then in the mortgage business, said that within LCPI the troops took to snickering that the Shearson takeover ought better to be known as the "take-under," for it was clear almost from the start that there was no quit in Lehman Brothers.

Chapter 5

Slamex

On our corporate videos we had music from *Les Miserables*. In Chris's mind we were fighting tyranny—just like the French Revolution."

—*Ronald Gallatin, Lehman's "minister without portfolio" and chief bonus negotiator*

The fight led by Chris Pettit and Perry Moncreiffe might have been over, but the war in the offices of the newly fashioned Shearson Lehman Brothers was just beginning. It was inevitable, really—here was the shotgun marriage of two of Wall Street's most culturally diverse houses, a combined firm that, as Helyar and Burroughs note in *Barbarians at the Gate*, "came to be marked by a peculiar blend of elegance and streetwise chutzpah: brass knuckles in a velvet glove."

Shearson was a vast brokerage of 8,000 salespeople who made money purely on commission. They neither cared about nor understood investment banking, whereas Lehman had its deep roots in providing initial capital to firms like the Woolworth Company, Sears, Roebuck & Company, the Studebaker Corporation, and RCA.

The Lehman executives thought that the Shearson brokers were self-centered idiots; the Shearson brokers had little comprehension of what the Lehman guys were doing. As for Lehman Commercial Paper Inc. (LCPI)? They thought they were the modern-day equivalent of the Three Musketeers—"all for one, one for all."

"They were the only unit in the entire organization which had salaries and systems entirely for themselves," says Peter Cohen. More than 20 years later he still sounded irritated by that.

They proudly identified themselves as the working class of Wall Street, and in their rarefied circles—and bank accounts—they were. They smirked at the extravagances of Cohen, who at 38 was the CEO of Shearson Lehman. He was an easy target. At a year-end party hosted at the Greenbrier resort in White Sulfur Springs, West Virginia, Cohen arrived atop an elephant.

"A circus had been provided as part of the entertainment, and someone said 'Why don't you ride an elephant?' so I did," he explains.

But the moment became a running joke among the Lehman traders.

Cohen had worked his way up the operational side of Shearson, but had little experience in investment banking and none in capital markets; he was resented.

Joe Gregory told people that Cohen's first meeting with the Lehman team was a disaster—Cohen had come to placate his new employees, but he only enraged them. He came across as high-handed and was met not with obedience, but with derision.

"Basically he came in and told us that each January his brokers knew they would make a million dollars that year," says Bob Shapiro. "It was meant to be inspirational but what it showed was that he had no idea who his audience was. We were people who could lose a million in the final two weeks of the year. That was our business. It showed us he had no clue about what we actually did."

"Of course they didn't like me," Cohen retorts. "I was younger than a lot of them, I was their boss, and they were a bunch of difficult guys."

■ ■ ■

The Lehman veterans continued to isolate themselves from the rest of the company. In a small sign of rebellion, Pettit's troops answered their phones with "Lehman," snipping off the prefix "Shearson."

"They were tough people, and they made money," recalls John Cecil, a McKinsey consultant who was brought in by Pettit and who would later become the firm's chief financial officer. "No one wanted to mess with them, because they were known as people who'd push back if you'd try to tell them what to do. They took over other businesses in the company, and they hired most of the other people who went on to be senior management."

Cohen tried to exert control over LCPI, but this was a revolution that wouldn't be put down. The Lehmanites took pride in running circles around him.

■ ■ ■

Cohen had to negotiate between LCPI and Shearson/American Express mainly over two subjects: LCPI's compensation and the amount of leverage (or, as the American Express board saw it, risk) that was kept on its books. The latter was always a subject that greatly alarmed the American Express board, mostly made up of industrialists, like David Culver and Richard Furlaud, who had a collective heart attack when they saw a balance sheet of $90 billion. "To them this meant huge risk must be being taken," says Cohen.

In fact this was not necessarily the case. The balance sheet was often inflated by low-risk hedged U.S. Treasury trades and repurchase agreements (repos)—a common practice on Wall Street, but not in the more conservative credit card business. "They [Amex] didn't quite get the mechanics of the whole thing," said one source.

Cohen told Fuld to make sure that at the end of each quarter the leverage got taken down, to placate both the board and the rating agencies. (In fairness to Lehman, it was not the only bank that made money by raising leverage between quarters—all banks did it.)

Cohen suspected that LCPI had a secret cushion, but according to several senior LCPI executives, he was never told the precise size of what was known on the LCPI floor as "Dick's reserve."

The Lehman traders did their best to make sure Cohen and Robinson couldn't tell what gambles they were making, and what enormous stakes were on the table. "Dick's reserve" might as well been called "the daily fiction"—which, in fact, it was. A former managing director says it worked like this:

> Every day we would report up to Shearson and American Express our P&L [profits and losses] for the day. We knew that the management upstairs, if they saw the P&L going up and down dramatically—one day we made a lot of money, and the next day we lost a lot of money—they'd know that we were betting a lot of money, and taking a lot of risk. But if our P&L looked like a nice steady EKG kind of thing, then everything was okay. So on the days we made a lot of money, Dick didn't report all of it, and when we lost a lot of money, he took a little out of that kitty to make that day's P&L not as bad. We called that kitty [kept on a piece of paper] "Dick's reserve."

A nice story, but neither Peter Cohen nor the rating agencies were fooled for long. Toward the end of each quarter, it was standard practice for rating agencies like Moody's Investors Service and Standard & Poor's to ask banks to write down their risk. Cohen told Fuld to get it done. Fuld went to Pettit, who managed the deleveraging. But on one memorable occasion the chain was broken and chaos ensued.

In 1987 Cohen told Fuld to take his leverage down. Dick passed on the news to Jim Vinci, Pettit's staff officer.

Fuld said, "I made another deal with Peter Cohen, but I haven't told anybody yet. We have to get the balance sheet (as in risk) lower than expected." Fuld hadn't told Pettit yet about the new agreement with Cohen, and yet Vinci went over to Jeff Vanderbeek, a friend at the trading desk, and said to the man who ran the repo book, a book of short-term loans, "Jeff, look—Dick's just told me that you're going to have to be a lot lower."

Vanderbeek (now the owner of the New Jersey Devils), according to Vinci, was tired of getting picked on in the quarterly deleveraging issue. ("The repo book was always the place with the most elasticity," says Vinci.) His bonuses were taking a hit because they no longer reflected his true performance.

Vanderbeek was furious. Fuld was negotiating with Cohen, seemingly to the detriment of his business and LCPI's loans. He bolted from his desk and went to Pettit's office. Vinci recalls, "I'm watching from across the trading room. And there's a lot of arms being waved, and a lot of screaming and yelling. Next thing I know, Pettit gets out of his chair, leaves his office, slams the door, and goes into Dick's office. And now Pettit and Fuld are yelling and screaming at each other.

"Pettit leaves Fuld's office, slams *that* door, walks back to his office, and goes back to work. I see Fuld coming for me across the trading floor, making a beeline. I have never been so belittled and berated in my entire life. He backs me into a corner and starts screaming expletives—'You little bleep! This is my fucking trading floor! I don't know what the fuck you were thinking when you betrayed me!'"

Fuld felt that Vinci had broken the chain of command and had usurped Pettit's role by telling Vanderbeek, albeit with the best of intentions.

"I was just doing the right thing, but Dick didn't like getting yelled at by Pettit, who was just trying to protect the business. That's why we were all loyal to Pettit. That's why Vanderbeek didn't go in to talk to Fuld. He went to talk to Pettit, because he knew Pettit always wanted to do the right thing for the business. Fuld just wanted to do what was politically correct for Peter Cohen and Shearson.

"Now the stupid thing about it then was that when we delevered, it was all window dressing. We just took off the least risky assets, which were the easiest to sell. We would make the books look like they were delevered."

Once the quarter was over, the loans would go back onto the repo book. It was just like the cards coming on and off the wall at 9 Mill Lane a few years earlier.

■ ■ ■

LCPI must have really grated on the management of Amex and Shearson. Despite the open arrogance of Pettit's people, it was impossible to deny their talents.

By 1990, Tucker had risen to the top of all of Shearson Lehman fixed income sales; Lessing was Tucker's deputy, and Joe Gregory was made head of mortgage-backed securities sales. The Ponderosa Boys and Dick Fuld were the face—and brains—of Shearson Lehman fixed income.

"A group of us had grown up together and worked together a long time," Lessing said later. "We were strong. We had a certain culture. We kept pushing."

Lessing's version of "pushing," according to someone who worked for him, meant that he spent a lot of his day climbing onto his desk and shouting "Sell!" to whip up enthusiasm. He wasn't considered the brightest at the firm. "They only put him on the operating committee—a committee formed of around 20 people in senior positions—so that they could talk business in the car," someone senior to Lessing said. said. But he did have a knack for charming clients.

Fuld was increasingly isolated from the trading floor, even though his office was right next to Pettit's.

One person remembered watching Fuld's secretary, Marianne Burke, work through a stack of L.L. Bean receipts. Fuld would have an assortment of L.L. Bean polo shirts spread across his desk—two of almost every shade, and whatever he didn't like he'd have Marianne return. "He orders them in two different sizes and then makes up his mind," she explained. The story wound its way across the trading floor and through the halls: This was how Fuld frittered away his workday, ordering from the L.L. Bean catalog.

One of the people who made most of the rude jokes about Fuld in those years was Gregory, who was known to be both a hothead and a chatterbox. "When I first met Joe back in 1980," Lessing would later say, "he was a young ball of energy—clean-shaven, constantly in motion, the fastest man who had ever been on a calculator in the history of mankind. But he had one problem: He looked very young."

Gregory went to the Virgin Islands in the mid-1980s and came back with a beard. He grew it in hopes of looking older, more commanding, and thereby more appropriate for running the trading desk. Though it didn't have the desired effect—his colleagues still remembered his baby face—it became a kind of signature. In a world of clean-shaven, immaculately groomed men, Gregory's beard was a power play, a defiant sign of his confidence.

He was also known for fits of road rage. "There was one time when a cabbie cut us off in Manhattan, just by the South Street Seaport,"

Tom Tucker says, "and Joe railed at him from the car. The cabbie pulls over. Joe gets out of the car. The cabbie pulls out a tire iron, and Joe starts to go after him. And we're like, 'Joe, get in the car! You idiot!'"

Colleagues wondered if it was tremendous insecurity that made Gregory so susceptible to emotional fits. "We wondered if he could never get over where he had come from and where he got to," says one. "It was as though he'd moved up so far beyond his dreams, he really had no idea who he actually was."

One of the many people lashed by Gregory's temper was bond salesman Craig Schiffer. Schiffer was bright and bold; he had a habit of skipping his boss's morning meetings, and eventually this irked Gregory so much that in the early 1990s he went to Pettit and demanded that Schiffer be fired. Pettit talked to Schiffer, and then told Gregory they couldn't let him go. Gregory, according to someone in Schiffer's department, went berserk. "He screamed at Craig like I've never seen. Joe appeared to be furious that he had lost, that he wasn't able to get rid of Craig. It was unbelievably threatening."

■ ■ ■

Fear was very much the management style of that era, and it began with Fuld.

In 1989 Pettit sent Dick Dorfman—who covered the government-sponsored enterprises (GSEs) Fannie Mae and Freddie Mac—and Steven Carlson, a managing director, to Fuld's ninth-floor office. They had to explain why Lehman needed to buy mortgage assets from government-owned asset management company Resolution Trust Corporation (RTC) stock, which was responsible for liquidating the assets of insolvent savings and loans (S&Ls) in the 1980s crisis. According to someone in the room, Carlson said to Fuld: "We've got to get staff on this. We've got to get full-time coverage on this. You've got to spend some money to make money that is going to become available, in terms of cheap assets to buy." He felt it would be the buying opportunity of the decade because these assets were going to be dumped on the market and be cheap.

Fuld's response was typically curt: "How much money do I need to spend?"

"We think it's three or four million dollars for these kinds of things," Carlson said.

Fuld rushed to the point: "How much money are we going to get?"

Carlson and Dorfman just looked at each other. "A lot. You know, *lots*," which wasn't specific enough for Fuld, who said again, "How much money are you going to make?"

"Dick, it's an opportunity—lots."

Fuld just growled, "Get the fuck out of my office." And before they could say anything else, he shouted: "Get the fuck out!"

The next day they came back, and Fuld didn't even look up from his desk. "How much money are we going to make?"

"Fifteen million."

"Okay," Fuld said. "Spend the money."

Fuld was a classic capital markets thinker in that he valued a simple figure over detailed explanations. He wanted things easy. He didn't want to be bogged down with the minutiae of data reasoning; that was a job for other people, Pettit for instance. Pettit was there to corral the staff, to keep it in line, to do whatever he could to inspire them to do whatever they had to do to get Fuld the number he wanted. Fuld was there for the big decisions. In his mind, this didn't make him a tyrant; rather, it made him efficient. And while Pettit was his deputy, he didn't need to evolve because Pettit had his back on the small stuff.

But Fuld also knew that if the grand plans for LCPI were to become real, then he'd have to change. He'd have to be a better manager. He'd have to learn to delegate; to be a people person. He couldn't really be "the gorilla."

He'd been given the nickname because of his habit of grunting, his prominent forehead, and his fondness for expletives. To further the myth, he kept a stuffed toy gorilla in his office on top of a basketball hoop, but it was all theater to mask his social anxieties.

He secretly started working on his weaknesses.

He was inarticulate and introverted. He was a solid trader, but knew next to nothing about investment banking, despite having put himself through New York University's prestigious Stern School of Business at night during his early years at Lehman.

So he began to carefully study the men around him, as he had with Glucksman, who had qualities he admired but had also lacked qualities Fuld lacked.

For example, Fuld was nowhere near as good a negotiator as 64-year-old Ronald L. Gallatin, an intellectually nimble partner who created many of Lehman's financial products during the years of Slamex. Gallatin was once described as a "man who could juggle so many balls that only he could keep track of them all." Fuld paid close attention to what made him effective. "Dick listened carefully to everything Gallatin said. In fact, he listened carefully to everything everyone said. He absorbed far more than people realized," said someone familiar with the situation.

Fuld got a brutally blunt reminder of how much he still had to learn when he was joined at the helm by the man appointed in 1990 to run Shearson Lehman's investment banking division while Fuld ran fixed income. That man was J. Tomlinson Hill—otherwise known as Tom Hill.

■ ■ ■

The appointments had come about almost organically. Fuld was the head of the toughest traders in Shearson Lehman while his counterpart in banking, Hill, had shone among all the bankers. Hill was in the mold of the famous Lehman bankers of yore. He was known to be one of the toughest fighters on the Street. Immaculately dressed, his hair slicked back, Hill was the ultimate smooth-talking barracuda as banker.

One former Shearson Lehman executive says: "If Tom Hill were not actually as good a banker as he was, he still would have been hired by Central Casting. He absolutely looked the part. He went to the right schools, had the right physical build—in every way, shape, or form, this was your classic investment banker. He knew everybody from business school, knew everybody from the country club."

Hill's sublime arrogance left many people cold, if not mortally wounded. Many sources say he has since matured into one of the most effective and liked investment bankers on Wall Street (an impression confirmed by this author who met with Hill twice). But back then he was young and hard-edged. A mutual friend once sent a young Harvard MBA to be interviewed by Hill, who reportedly told the young man he clearly did not have the "drive and energy" required to be a success in investment banking since he was making only $200,000 a year at his current job.

Hill came by his arrogance honestly. A senior Lehman executive says, "Tom went from being a very, very good cutthroat—because that's what you're supposed to be as a mergers and acquisitions banker—to actually running the investment banking area." It was Hill who drafted the blueprint with both the Shearson Lehman board and the Amex board that branded the Lehman divisions as "one firm."

■ ■ ■

In an effort to show that this realignment was not mere lip service, once Hill and Fuld were appointed co-heads of Lehman in 1990 (Hill was responsible for banking; Fuld for fixed income with Chris Pettit as COO), Hill built one office next to Fuld's on both the trading floor and another on the banking floor. The goal was to cement the idea of Shearson Lehman as one firm, with no more feuds between the bankers and the traders.

And for a while it worked, in part because Dick Fuld needed it to work. He knew he had to learn what Tom Hill knew, how to *be* him, if he was ever to make it to the top echelons of Wall Street.

Over the next two years, according to one insider, Fuld studied Hill so intensely "he should have been given a postgraduate degree in learning how to become Tom Hill. He had studied and studied and studied Tom Hill. If you walked into a meeting in Dick's office between 8:30 and 10:00 in the morning, Tom would always be sitting there, they would both have their nail clippers out, and they would both be filing and clipping their nails at almost exactly the same time.

"I really believe that if Tom had regular bowel movements at 9:15 in the morning, and that's what an investment banker's supposed to have, [Fuld] would have followed him to the men's room.

"And as bright as Tom is, I don't really think he believed—understood—that he was really like an animal in the zoo that was being studied. Dick was able to take mannerisms that he saw in Tom; he was able to take the essential personality."

These were lessons Fuld knew were essential for him to learn if he was one day going to lead an investment bank of his own. And to do that, he'd have to get rid of Shearson and American Express—and Tom Hill and Chris Pettit.

Chapter 6

The Phoenix Rises

Do you honestly think, given what you know about Dick
Fuld, that he tried to save my job? Of course he didn't. He
needed me gone.
  —*J. Tomlinson Hill, Vice Chairman of the Blackstone Group*

One of the biggest challenges Dick Fuld, Chris Pettit, and the
other senior people at Lehman embraced during their years
under Shearson and American Express was not just to protect
their bonuses. They were protecting the brand of Lehman so that one
day it might stand alone. They didn't do this just out of idealism—it
was the only way they'd get *really* rich.

In an attempt to reshape the merged company and expand his little
unit into all of fixed income, Pettit hired John Cecil and a team from
McKinsey & Company, the consulting firm. Until 1990, the Lehman
retail brokers knew they would always be involved in equity (stock)
underwritings, of which they took a percentage for themselves, while
the Shearson brokers depended on over-the-counter stocks, municipal
bonds, and tax shelters (which paid less commission). There was much

less upside in this, so the Shearson brokers never gelled with their Lehman counterparts.

Meanwhile, irking the American Express and Shearson leadership was the fact that the Lehman banking had been weakened when so many of its top bankers left with, or soon after, the merger. This meant that while Goldman Sachs had the topflight clients, Lehman was left with middling seconds.

And although, on the equity side, Lehman was in many deals controlled by Goldman Sachs, Merrill Lynch, or any of the other titans of Wall Street, it was rarely the lead banker in a quality deal. In other words, IBM, or any other huge conglomerate with mountains of money to throw around, would not make Lehman the banker of choice if it wanted to do an offering or an acquisition.

■ ■ ■

Further muddling things was the fact that on May 14, 1987, Shearson Lehman went public; it sold 27 percent of its stock—13 percent had been bought by Japan's largest insurance company, Nippon Life, and the rest was owned by American Express.

By 1990, Jim Robinson had decided it was time for a change.

Shearson Lehman had started to lose money as the market turned sour at the end of 1989. The high-yield bond market started to crash and, in its wake, down came the equities and mergers and acquisitions deals.

Peter Cohen had also made what now looked like two bad missteps. A year earlier, in the fall of 1988, he and Robinson had stepped on their own feet when they bid unsuccessfully for the snack and tobacco conglomerate RJR Nabisco. In a battle that exemplified the excesses of the 1980s, they were beaten to the prize by buyout king Henry R. Kravis—events chronicled by Bryan Burrough and John Helyar in *Barbarians at the Gate*.

In the fall of 1988, F. Ross Johnson, a Canadian originally from Winnipeg, who was the president and CEO of RJR Nabisco, was looking to pull off a company buyout of RJR Nabisco and take the company private. Johnson first approached buyout specialist firm Kohlberg Kravis Roberts & Co. (KKR) about doing the deal, but he ultimately went with Shearson Lehman Hutton (SLH). They offered Nabisco shareholders $75 per share, or $17 billion. But a fierce bidding war between KKR and Shearson ensued, and in April 1989, KKR emerged victorious, taking control of RJR Nabisco with its bid of $109 per share, or $25 billion. It was a humiliating defeat for Cohen and Robinson. Johnson retired and all of a sudden both Cohen and Robinson looked vulnerable.

Then came another fiasco.

In 1988, Cohen had bought the upscale brokerage E.F. Hutton & Company—at a vast premium—for almost $1 billion, because he believed that Dean Witter's CEO, Philip J. Purcell, was bidding low. (According to multiple sources, it was widely believed within Lehman at the time that Purcell was bidding merely to drive up the price.)

When Cohen called Ron Gallatin into his office and told him what he wanted to do, and how he wanted to do it, Gallatin said straight off that he wouldn't get involved in something like that. Cohen asked him why, and Gallatin said: "Because it's going to take us down."

"What are you talking about?" Cohen responded, clearly annoyed. Gallatin privately thought Cohen was empire building, that he wanted E.F. Hutton for its size. He thought Cohen wanted to be bigger than Merrill Lynch, which had approximately 13,000 brokers.

"Your timetable does not allow for enough due diligence," Gallatin said, "particularly given their [Hutton's] tax shelter liability." Gallatin was reminding Cohen that Hutton was being sued by almost every customer who had bought a tax shelter from the firm. Hutton had also recently (May 1985) pled guilty to 2,000 counts of mail and wire fraud, and agreed to pay a $2 million fine plus $750,000 for costs and $8 million in restitution to the victims of a so-called check-kiting scheme. Gallatin thought buying the brokerage was idiotic. "Hutton is falling on its ass, the markets aren't in good shape, and you're out of your fucking mind," he told Cohen.

Jim Vinci also came to the same conclusion. In late November he and Robert Druskin, the CFO at Shearson Lehman, met to try to get a handle on Hutton's value. Vinci says they began with the book value and started subtracting liabilities. It took all day.

At the end, the number they were left staring at was a big, fat *zero*.

"After all the adjustments, there was no book value," Vinci said. "I went home to my wife and told her I'd just wasted Thanksgiving."

But Cohen went ahead with the acquisition. (He now says that Robinson had promised him a cash balance of $1 billion the following year to pay for it, but that Robinson failed to deliver—hence the implosion.)

Whatever the reason, Gallatin and Vinci were proven right. The deal went through, and again there was a clash of cultures. Hutton brokers left Shearson Lehman Hutton in droves. Hutton regarded itself as the superior brand, and thought of Lehman, in an unusual twist, as retrograde. By the early 1990s what had been a brokerage of over 13,000 employees was down to 9,000 and SLH was shutting down branches throughout the United States.

Hutton was the second nail in Cohen's coffin.

■ ■ ■

In 1990, Robinson decided he wanted to streamline his American Express credit card business and separate it from the Shearson Lehman business, so he took a write-down of $1 billion on Amex.

Meanwhile, Shearson Lehman, which was worth $400 million, was bleeding $60 million a month and Robinson had to recapitalize it with $1 billion. Given those cash flow problems, he didn't see why he needed to pay Lehman people their bonanza bonuses.

The job of schooling him fell to Gallatin, who patiently explained the situation at Robinson's lavish penthouse apartment in the Museum Towers (near the Metropolitan Museum) one night in late fall (bonus conversation time).

"It was my job to help Jim explain to his board that even if Shearson Lehman had lost $650 million, they had no choice but to pay Lehman bonuses on what they'd made," says Gallatin.

The two men sat in Robinson's spacious living room, tired but eager to find a resolution. Robinson, who was from Atlanta, looked at Gallatin and said, in a charming Southern drawl that belied his exasperation, "What are you talking about, paying a bonus? You lost money."

"I said to him, 'No, Jim, Lehman *made* money.' *They*, Shearson, had lost money. We went back and forth—and he's one of the nicest gentlemen you'll meet in your life—but eventually I said, 'Fine, you don't want to pay the bonuses. But I'm going to go down in the elevator now.'

"And he looks at me and he says, '*What* are you doing?' It was one o'clock in the morning. He says, 'Of course you're going to go down the elevator. You're not going to walk down the stairs.' I said, 'Jim, you don't get it. I'm going down in the elevator.' He may think the capital of the firm was the balance sheet, but the real capital of the firm is the people. And if he wasn't going to make the bonuses, tomorrow the key Lehman people are going to [go] down the elevator."

Meaning that Robinson would be encouraging his best people to leave if he didn't pay up.

Lehman employees got their bonuses paid that year.

■ ■ ■

On January 30, 1990, Robinson forced Peter Cohen to resign and replaced him with Howard L. Clark Jr., or "H," whose father, Howard Sr., had been Robinson's predecessor at American Express. Cohen had lost his power in part because of the RJR Nabisco and E.F. Hutton deals, and was undermined further by impressions that followed the gratuitous purchase of a $25 million ski lodge and conference center in Colorado. "There were just excesses," Lessing later wrote of Cohen and his cronies: "They took their eye off the ball. We kept working and taking on more power. Eventually we ended up running both firms."

The Lehmanites did not hide their joy at Cohen's firing. They made a satirical short film, which was shown at the 1991 holiday party at the Museum of Natural History. Entitled "The History of Lehman Brothers, Part One," the film mocked Cohen using the tune from "If I Only Had a Brain" from *The Wizard of Oz*. The lyrics went like this:

I could while away the hours
Conversing in the towers
Consulting with the lame.

And my head I'd be scratching
While my schemes they'd be hatching
If I only had a brain.

I smoke a big cigar
My deals are quite bizarre.

So what if KKR took RJR
We got first cap
So it was crap.

Oh some day I'll find a way, sir
To make this business pay, sir
And though it sounds insane

With the stuff I'll be struttin'
I could give back E.F. Hutton
If I only had a brain.

At the end of the video LCPI traders dance and sing Billy Joel's "We Didn't Start the Fire."

"H" Clark immediately saw the extraordinary energy and spirit that bonded LCPI and tried to utilize the passion so that it had a more constructive purpose. He had reorganized Shearson Lehman's management, starting with the elevation of Fuld, who became co-CEO of Lehman with Tom Hill. Chris Pettit was their COO. Lehman Brothers was also allowed to officially be called "Lehman" again, since "H" recognized that it now had superior brand recognition to Shearson.

The three Lehman leaders immediately got to work on their plans to dominate Shearson and then consume it. One of their first tasks was to reduce overhead. But they weren't going to have Lehman's bonus pool reduced in the process. One senior employee recalls a meeting convened to restructure the overall bonus pool, already tilted heavily toward Lehman's side.

The man representing Amex was in charge of the retail business, Jonathan S. Linen. Opposing him were Hill, Fuld, and Pettit.

Fuld remained quiet for most of the negotiation, allowing Pettit and Hill to divide and conquer. "They sort of sliced [Linen] up," says someone in the room. John Cecil, the McKinsey consultant hired in 1990, recalled that Pettit and Hill "came out of the meeting with the bonuses skewed [in their favor] even more than before."

The trio was always looking for ways to subvert their putative masters. Their job was made easier, says one senior Lehman executive from that era, because "H" Clark was seen as easy to manipulate. "There was a joke that he was called 'H,' unlike his father, who was called 'Howard,' because he had one-sixth of his father's brains," said one former senior Lehman leader.

"H" conducted the search for Lehman's CFO on his own. It took several months, and when he finally sent down a potential candidate, Richard B. Stewart Jr., Cecil thought he was weak and told Clark so. Clark seemed surprised. "But Dick and Tom love him," he said.

Cecil says he went to see the Lehman co-heads and told them he thought Stewart was weak.

"Of course he is," Cecil says that Hill responded. "We want to control him." (Hill says this never happened.)

■ ■ ■

Hill and Pettit were clearly the leaders of the transformation of Lehman from 1990 to 1994. "Dick didn't have that much of a role," says a former colleague. "That was Chris. Except for banking—Tom, even when he was co-head, really was the head of banking. And so, as long as they were there, there wasn't much for Fuld to do.

"And he was certainly not very visible to the organization. The bankers wouldn't see him going out to see banking clients. Nobody in the organization would see Dick running things."

When they did see Fuld working, he didn't exactly dazzle.

One person recalls a meeting at the Plaza Hotel in Manhattan, in which Clark had asked Fuld and the other senior managers to stand up for a few minutes and describe their respective parts of the business.

"Dick stood up there, and it was the most awkward meeting I've ever seen in my life. He'd say a sentence—[long pause]—and then he'd say—[long pause]—a sentence and then he'd say—[long pause]—a word. It was unbelievable."

Around that time, Jim Vinci was asked to help Fuld with his speech for the year-end meeting at New York's American Museum of Natural History. Vinci gave him a draft of the speech, and Fuld went through it and began inserting the word *clearly* every chance he could get. According to a source who was present for the conversation between the two men, Vinci said, "Dick, you can't say 'clearly' that often. As a matter of fact, you can't say it at all." Vinci finally closed the door to Fuld's office and said, "Look, you need a coach. You need someone to help you."

Fuld took Vinci's advice. He attended courses at Dale Carnegie Training, a training center founded by the author of *How to Win Friends and Influence People* to assist in "bringing out the best" in business leaders.

He never forgot Vinci's help. Many years later, in October 2007, Lehman Brothers had an alumni cocktails event at the Four Seasons restaurant in midtown Manhattan. Fuld began by giving a speech, and later, in front of four or five former managing directors, put his arm around Vinci and said, "Gentlemen, I want to introduce you to the first person who told me no, that I can't do something."

Vinci says he smiled, and thought to himself, "Yeah, and probably the last."

■ ■ ■

While Fuld worked on his public speaking skills, it was becoming clearer and clearer to many that Jim Robinson wanted out of the banking business. Word went around the Lehman offices that Gallatin, who negotiated all of Lehman's compensation, had been described to the American Express board by Robinson as a "man who enters revolving doors after me and somehow reaches the other side first." The board was not exactly thrilled to hear this from their CEO. Befuddlement doesn't wear as well as bespoke suits.

On January 25, 1993, American Express fired Robinson and replaced him with Harvey Golub, a man one senior Lehman person described as "a crazy guy, with a bizarre sense of humor and difficult to deal with." Golub, nicknamed "Ego Harv," was known to have installed a car wash at his house in Minnesota.

When he moved to New York, Golub quickly established a reputation for micromanaging, which did not go down well with the Lehmanites. Golub and Hill immediately tangled over Lehman's compensation agreement, which Golub wanted torn up.

"I'm not asking—I am telling you what to do," Golub told Fuld, Hill, and Pettit. Hill threatened to take the matter to the Amex board, where he knew he had a supporter in John "Jack" Byrne, the insurance industry executive. Hill pointed out to Golub that he and Fuld would lose all credibility with their staff if they reneged on the compensation program.

Golub backed down—but it seemed that Hill was a marked man from then on. According to someone close to Fuld, Golub had intended to rid himself of Hill (whom he viewed as a Robinson loyalist) from the start, and after the disagreement over compensation he was looking for any excuse.

For a while, however, he concentrated his energies elsewhere.

Fuld and Hill soon learned what Golub was up to. Through the trading floor rumor mill they heard that he was planning to shed Shearson, and that Sandy Weill, who had sold Shearson to American Express in 1981 and was an old friend of Golub's, was prepared to buy it for $1 billion. The catch: He didn't want Lehman. He knew about its rowdy culture and prickly senior management.

Not being told of these discussions greatly irked Hill and Fuld, and Hill confronted Golub. He asked him, "What's the price tag for Shearson?"

Hill says, "He threw out a number. And I said, 'Well, who's the buyer? What was the process?' He said, 'I've decided this is the best offer.' And I said, 'Well, were there other bidders? Was there competition? How do we know this is the best price out there?' He said, 'I've made a strategic decision to sell it. I want you to do one thing, and that's to make sure this deal closes. If I hear anything that you are getting in the way of this deal closing, I'm going to fire you.'"

Worried that Lehman was going to get hammered in the deal because it would lose distribution, Hill went behind Golub's back and talked to an acquaintance, Sandy Weill's then-deputy, a rising financier named Jamie Dimon.

Hill says he told Dimon: "'I know what's going on. Sandy knows Harvey has told us to roll over. But we're not going to do that. We're not going to get in the way of this deal, but you can't screw us. We're going to defend the value here, just as you would be defending the value if you were in our shoes.' And Jamie agreed to work with us."

The only leverage Hill had was his friendship with Dimon. Their daughters went to the same school in New York. Perhaps both sensed that Wall Street is a small place and that they were destined to cross paths again (they did), or Dimon knew that in the long run there was no upside in upsetting Hill. "Jamie knew that he was already getting one hell of a deal on a plate and that he didn't need to make it worse for us," says Hill. "There was zero upside for him in doing that."

Fuld and Hill knew they had only forestalled the inevitable—that Golub would dump Lehman. He just wanted Amex. After meeting with Golub in order to discuss his concerns going forward, Hill told Fuld: "He [Golub] doesn't like the securities business. He wants to be in the credit card business. And he's going to get rid of us just as soon as he can, too."

Hill was right. But he had not foreseen one important detail in Golub's grand plan. On March 29, 1993, Golub fired *Hill*.

"Where's Dick on this?" was Hill's first question to Golub. "In the office next door," replied Golub. In other words, Fuld already knew.

Gallatin, who had by now earned the official title "minister without portfolio," says that Hill's exit was inevitable. "Golub knew he had to spin off Lehman, and between the two of them [Hill and Fuld], the one he least wanted to deal with was Hill, because Hill was this mature, brilliant M&A banker he didn't want to have to negotiate with. It didn't cross his mind that maybe by now Dick Fuld had every attribute that made Tom who he was."

Gallatin thinks that Fuld was now finally ready to apply all that he'd learned in his so-called postgraduate studies of Tom Hill. "He realized that there was only going to be one leader—but who? In Dick's mind, that was a silly question: it was going to be him."

Chapter 7

Independence Day

I knew I would be retiring soon. I thought: "What the heck."
I will take it upon myself to fight one last battle for Lehman
Brothers.

—Ronald Gallatin

I n early winter of 1994, Harvey Golub hosted a meeting in a
conference room in lower Manhattan to negotiate the spin-off of
Lehman with his hand-picked opponent, Dick Fuld. With Hill
gone, Fuld knew he needed help getting favorable terms from Golub,
who knew Fuld wanted desperately to be the next CEO of Lehman
Brothers. If Fuld was too disagreeable in these negotiations, Golub had
the power to fire him, thus ending Fuld's campaign to get the top job.
To help him, Fuld had brought John Cecil and Ron Gallatin.

After announcing that he planned to spin American Express out,
Golub blithely told Fuld, Cecil, and Gallatin that he'd leave Lehman
with $2.8 billion in equity—enough, he said, for them to get a single
A rating.

Gallatin smiled at Golub and said, "Three point six."

Gallatin's counter-proposal was understandable. He believed Golub was trying to shortchange Lehman. With only $2.8 billion on their books, with a strong fixed income department but weak banking and equities arms, Lehman needed a cushion. But Golub thought Lehman could get by on $2.3 and was furious that his half-billion of padding wasn't enough for Gallatin. He screamed, "Two point eight!"

Gallatin, still calm, his voice low, repeated, "Three point six."

Perhaps thinking he hadn't much to lose—he was nearing retirement—Gallatin decided he would be the one to fight for Lehman's future, and maybe establish his legacy as well.

Golub screamed at Gallatin, "You can convince them to give you an A rating with $2.8 billion!" Gallatin smiled again and said, "Maybe I could, but I'm not going to."

Golub told everyone at the table that it was $2.8 billion or "I will crush you like a fly!" Some executives were startled at his display of temper.

Gallatin calmly threatened to take the story to the press—and reminded Golub that he had already announced he would be doing the spin-off at a single A rating. Gallatin's implication was obvious: Did Golub want to look like he wasn't keeping his word? Would people start to wonder about the sincerity of the management of American Express?

In the end, Gallatin won out; but when Lehman was finally spun off, it had a few onerous terms foisted on it by Amex.

Golub forced Lehman to buy from Amex several floors in the World Financial Center at top-of-the-market prices, so they were now "co-tenants." Together, Lehman and Amex had issued $700 million to $800 million of long-term notes to finance the property. Lehman's share of this debt was about 50 percent, but the debt was guaranteed by Amex, to whom Lehman had to pay a "guarantee" fee of 928 shares, and Nippon Life Insurance Company acquired 72 shares of Lehman redeemable voting preferred stock. There was also a noncompete clause with regard to bankers; Lehman could not hire any American Express bankers for eight years (fortunately the Lehmanites didn't want to). Amex would be entitled to 50 percent of Lehman Brothers' net income over $400 million for each of the next eight years, with a maximum of $50 million in any one year. The Lehman senior management saw it as a "Get Out of Jail Free" card. The terms weren't that bad—and finally they were in charge of their destiny.

To fund the spin-off, Amex agreed to inject over $1 billion into Lehman—$904 million to buy Lehman common shares that would then be distributed to Amex shareholders as a special dividend, plus another $200 million to buy Lehman preferred shares. American Express would not hold a single common share of Lehman, nor have a single seat on its board.

The deal still had to be approved by American Express's board— most of whom were skeptical that a spin-off was a good thing. Lehman, after all, made money. Golub placated them by saying that the spin-off would be tax-free.

Golub asked John Cecil and Lehman investment banker Michael Odrich, a good-looking, personable banker who was then Fuld's chief of staff, to make a presentation to the board, explaining how Lehman could be successful as a public company. It was set for January 20, the day of the AT&T Pro-Am golf tournament at the legendary Pebble Beach golf course, and Odrich says he appealed to Fuld for a dispensation so that he could play in that event. He reminded his boss that if one played even once in the Pro-Am, one was "in" for life, but if one declined an invitation, one wasn't invited back. Golf was an obsession for both Fuld and Odrich (and was the hobby of choice at Lehman), but Fuld told him no, and said he'd make it up to him. (He never did.)

The presentation—a basic run-down of the businesses within Lehman, and what the economics looked like going forward—went over well, and the board signed off on the deal. Two memorable moments occurred, first, when former Secretary of State Henry Kissinger, then on the American Express board, opened a sweetener packet, emptied it into his iced tea, then stirred the beverage with his pencil—eraser end first.

The second was when another board member, former U.S. President Gerald Ford, asked Golub if he could please explain the difference between "equity" and "revenue." There was an awkward moment of silence as everyone digested this.

One person in the room recalls that Golub "did a very skillful job. I was very impressed. It's a very basic concept, and he explained it to the former president without making it sound like he was talking down to him."

■ ■ ■

On May 2, 1994, Lehman went public. By the end of the month, the spin-off complete, Golub reportedly exclaimed, "Let this puppy fly!" Cecil had been persuaded to come onboard—theoretically as chief administrative officer (CAO). Cecil understood implicitly that he was number three in the food chain, with Pettit immediately above him.

It was an arrangement that sat well with all three. Neither Pettit nor Fuld felt threatened by Cecil, who was aided in this regard by his unimposing physique and academic manner. Traders regularly joked about his analytical brain being woefully out of place in a bank made up of rough-and-tumble brawlers.

At one meeting Fuld said, "John, what do you think?"

"I'm still thinking," came the reply.

"Well, get yourself warmed up," said Fuld. "We're waiting."

But Cecil was a valuable member of the team. He was able to analyze the new bank objectively, identify its strengths and weaknesses, and give Fuld and Pettit guidelines for what they needed to do.

The short answer: There was a lot that needed fixing.

Despite the valiant predictions to the American Express board and the garish celebration held in the Winter Garden Atrium, a party venue in downtown New York where balloons cascaded down from the ceiling and where Lara Pettit recalls her father standing "very proud, upright, his fist in the air" reminiscent of a triumphant French revolutionary, the new Lehman Brothers was very fragile.

By September, Lehman began buying back stock from investors who owned fewer than 100 shares. Earnings in the second quarter of 1994 dropped 79 percent from the prior year, and profits fell by over half. In July, the employees who could afford to do so bought Lehman stock; Fuld sensed that at $14 the purchase would be a steal. He bought a lot.

By the end of October, Fuld owned more than 179,000 Lehman shares, the majority purchased at $25.54 per share; Pettit owned more than 132,000 shares. It wasn't a tactic they could use forever, but it worked in the short term; and over the long term, it made them all very rich, at least on paper. "We had the last laugh," says Ronald Gallatin.

"The stock did trade poorly initially," says Cecil, "in part because there hadn't been a market created for the stock, really, as a new company, but also because these shares were given to American Express shareholders, who really wanted to own American Express." Those folks quickly dumped their Lehman stock, devaluing it.

Adding to the new company's problems: In 1994 the Federal Reserve tightened interest rates, which, as a general rule, impacts the price of bonds negatively, and thereby weakened Lehman's fixed income division. Its share price fell 30 percent in just five months, from $20 per share when it first went public in May to $14 per share in October. (In a final kick to the 14 or 15 executives on Lehman's operating committee, Golub had made them buy the stock at book value. They had to pay $20 per share when it was trading for $14.)

Less than a year after Lehman went public, Moody's would downgrade its rating.

It was time for Fuld, Pettit, Gregory, Tucker, Lessing, and their band of merry men to do what they did best—roll up their sleeves and go to war.

■ ■ ■

According to the methodical John Cecil, Lehman had to do four things if it hoped to survive.

Above all, it had to cut costs—there was still a vast amount of fat, including luxuries such as the barbershop and shoe-shine stand on the executive floor, and Lehman was paying out over half of its revenues in compensation and another 41 percent in "nonpersonnel expenses."

Not only was cutting costs "the right thing to do," Cecil argued, but it would also buy them time and capital to grow their other businesses. Still, there was the inevitable push-back. One person joked, "When the milk came out of the refrigerator and they replaced it with dairy creamer, we knew it was a bad market."

Cecil also decreed that the nepotism had to stop. Family members and friends could no longer be hired unless they actually merited a spot. (Steve Lessing, in particular, was infamous for placing an inordinately large number of alumni from Fairfield University, his alma mater.)

The new recruiting strategy was largely led by Joe Gregory and Pettit, and only the best would be hired. According to Tom Tucker, "the best" did not mean "the elite." In other words, Harvard MBAs were welcome in areas such as investment banking, where Harvard MBAs were likely to do well. In other areas, like bond sales, Lehman was looking for people who were hungry and could work in a team.

The third goal was to be competitive in all capital market areas, globally, beginning with Europe and Asia.

The fourth and most important part of Cecil's survival strategy was to fix the culture of the firm. "Doing the right thing for the firm" and "One firm" had to be more than platitudes. Everybody had to buy into that ethos if Lehman was to become the place Dick Fuld, Chris Pettit, Joe Gregory, Steve Lessing, and Tom Tucker wanted it to be.

Cecil thought this was crucial for many reasons, but chiefly because he knew that a securities house could be ruined at the whim of a single trader. The only way to stop "selfish" or "foolish" acts of trading, as he called them, was to get people to always consider the firm's return on equity (ROE)—and not just their bonuses—before acting. In pursuit of this Cecil introduced the restricted stock unit (RSU)—as a form of payment to every "firm member."

The higher up you were, the higher the percentage of your bonus paid in company stock. Top-tier executives received 50 percent of their bonuses in stock that was restricted for five years while it vested. The amount of stock each employee got was scaled according to pay, but even the janitors participated in this compensation plan.

While there was much about Pettit's "one firm" culture that Cecil lauded, there was one aspect that nagged at him—and this issue never went away. He saw a dark side to the mantra of sticking together—it encouraged people to place a value on loyalty over ability.

Even so, Cecil was optimistic. He reflected years later: "I don't think I would have joined Lehman if it hadn't gone public and if I hadn't seen that the culture could change. Until then, it hadn't been run for profitability. It had been run for the bonus pool."

■ ■ ■

But Cecil was dismayed by the firm's first earnings report in the fall of 1994.

It was $22 million.

When Cecil first heard that, he shook his head and thought, "The world's going to hate that number." He was surprised and annoyed that Fuld and Pettit didn't seem disturbed by that posting. He says Pettit told him, "Twenty-two million dollars is a good number." Tom Tucker, however, hotly disputes this. "Chris Pettit would never have thought $22 million is a good number." What Pettit may have meant, his friends believe, was that there was no point dwelling on it. Certainly everyone must have agreed with Cecil that the next quarter's results needed to be over double that—especially once the firm was put on review for a ratings downgrade.

Cecil asked Bob Matza, the new CFO, if Fuld and Pettit understood what would happen if Moody's downgraded the firm—Lehman would not be able to issue commercial paper, which meant, as Matza put it, "We're toast." Matza told Cecil that neither Fuld nor Pettit understood this, so Cecil called a meeting with both men to enlighten them. He says, "They did not take this very well, particularly Chris."

Cecil says both Fuld and Pettit had grown up in a subsidiary of a subsidiary; they had no experience running a public company and didn't know they had to look out for rating agencies. They had to learn on the job.

Still, by the fourth quarter, Cecil had almost met his objective. The firm announced a $46 million after-tax profit and Moody's affirmed them.

A relieved Cecil said to Matza, "I think we should ban the phrase 'We're toast.' I don't want to have to hear it ever again."

■ ■ ■

Cecil believed that Fuld, not Pettit, was his best ally in the cost-cutting battle. He remembers patiently explaining to Fuld that by cutting costs and not plowing the savings back into remuneration, the share price would go up. Cecil says this was Fuld's "lightbulb moment."

"Dick is very pragmatic," he says, "and he is, more than almost anybody I know, a lifelong learner. Most people get to a point in their career, and they kind of are who they are. Dick, however, at a fairly late stage in his life, went through this transition of being on a trading desk to running Lehman as a public company. That's a huge change in just five years. Also, he went from being a trader, heavily influenced by all the bad habits of the old-fashioned trading floors, to head of the firm, trying to do the right thing, trying to keep the firm together, recognizing the value of all the different parts of the firm, recognizing the importance of a good culture.

"He also changed personally, becoming a good public speaker and all those things. Becoming good with clients. He went through a remarkable transition in a short period of time."

Fuld began spending more and more time not just with capital market clients, but with investment banking clients; he already knew men like Henry Kravis (head of KKR) and Leon Black (now at Apollo), but now he had to treat them not just as acquaintances, but clients; he had to pitch them. They needed to see him differently, not just as an introverted trader, but as the visionary head of a major securities firm.

One meeting that did not go so well was with the late Bruce Wasserstein, then the co-chief executive of the boutique mergers and acquisitions (M&A) outfit Wasserstein Perella. Fred Segal, a former Lehman partner who was working for Wasserstein at the time, brought his boss down to Lehman's offices and introduced him to Fuld. Wasserstein told Fuld a harsh truth. "You'll never get a premium valuation, because you don't have a decent advisory banking business," he said. "So you should buy us." The meeting ended swiftly.

Later Fuld called up Segal. "Fred," he said, "never bring that fat fuck here again."

■ ■ ■

Pettit, however, stayed Pettit, rallying the troops and diving into staff problems. The only trouble with this approach was that Lehman was growing too big for one man to micromanage.

But it was also around this time that Pettit first realized just how far he had come. Mary Anne Pettit recalls Chris saying to her one

Sunday evening as he was paying his bills in his study in Huntington. "You know, I think we are rich."

Yet this never really changed his lifestyle, despite certain luxuries. There was an annual holiday in the Caribbean with the Tuckers. The Pettits owned a boat with the Gregorys—*Miss T* after Joe's wife, Teresa—and they started plans for a new, big house down the street in Huntington. But otherwise, their lives stayed the same.

Mary Anne recalls: "Chris sort of had a little prejudice against wealth. He would not consider putting our kids in private school. We lived pretty simply. The Tuckers, Lessings, and Gregorys—the four guys in the car—that was our social circle. We rarely went out. We never did anything with anybody other than them."

When Pettit came home, he rarely talked about work. Mary Anne was petrified her children would get spoiled, and refused to dole out the sort of generous allowances that were so common among the firm's families. At the age of 15, Lara Pettit got a job at an animal clinic because she didn't have enough spending money to buy lunches at school.

Her father was horrified when he discovered that she had a job. "What are you doing?" he said. "You should be focusing on schoolwork." He put an end to that distraction by giving her an allowance.

Years later, as Lehman was going public, Lara, who by then had worked at Lehman for three years, still had no idea what her father made. According to the proxy released that year, it was close to $7 million. Despite that impressive number, he still seemed determined to never live large—although he seemed to have forgotten the promise he'd once made to himself: *Only spend 10 years on Wall Street and then get out. Otherwise you will change.*

■ ■ ■

Inside the firm, Cecil was increasingly viewed as power-hungry. It's a claim he disputes as revisionist, but Pettit's acolytes began to see him as their nemesis, someone who wasn't falling into line.

The two men could not have been less alike. One managed by instinct (Pettit), the other by intellect (Cecil). Cecil's cerebral style was viewed as somewhat antithetical to the Lehman way. "All head, no heart" is how one senior executive put it. Another says: "We all bristled at John Cecil." He was a typical perfectionist, too sharp for his own good. He had this "tiny handwriting, perfectly formed lines. People weren't employees, they were 'firm members'"—which was the punch line to an infinite number of sophomoric jokes, according to Bob Shapiro, who briefly served as CAO of Lehman Brothers before it was spun off from American Express.

Some brokers were wary of Cecil, convinced that he would have been happy if Lehman had become a profitable "boutique bank," while Pettit had much grander ambitions. "He [Pettit] had one goal in sight and it was to beat Goldman Sachs. His—and Fuld's—dream was for Lehman to be the best investment bank on the Street."

In 1994, Cecil hired a few of his former colleagues from McKinsey and put together a group charged with cutting nonpersonnel expenses at Lehman. The team discovered extremely wasteful habits and did their best to curb them.

For instance, they worked out that in 1993, Lehman had spent $11 million moving people around inside 3 World Financial Center. If a new trader joined a desk, the entire desk had to be rewired and altered. This created a domino effect, which required paying union workers massive overtime since the reconfiguring had to be done at night. The bankers demanded the same perk.

Cecil immediately prohibited anyone from moving their desk without getting his permission. He told a new hire, "Why don't you just ride the elevator or walk from one side of the building to the other?"

None of this made him popular, but he did cut costs. In 1995, he got Lehman's total expenses down to about $950 million from $1.3 billion, and he held it there for four years. Meanwhile, net profits went up to $71 million, compared to the disappointing $22 million a year earlier.

While all this was happening, Fuld and Pettit still had neighboring offices on the trading floor, as well as offices on the executive floor—but their relationship started, very gradually, to sour.

"I think [initially] they had a relationship of convenience," says one trader who was closer to Pettit. "They knew they needed each other and both brought something to the table, but as they became more senior, I feel they became less tolerant of each other and gave less credit to the other. I think what friction they had was below the surface and I feel Chris resented Dick."

"Chris knew that Dick might want to fire him and have all the glory for himself," said Perry Moncreiffe. "He said to him, 'That's fine, but you'll have to pay me out.'" Pettit drew up an agreement that stipulated that if Fuld fired him, Pettit would be paid $10 million.

Moncreiffe says Fuld signed without thinking twice about it.

■ ■ ■

One of the reasons Fuld was aloof to the foot soldiers was his devotion to family, a quality he tried to instill throughout the company—although on occasion he got mocked for it. Fuld had two priorities: Lehman and his family.

"With Fuld, it didn't matter who was in the room; it didn't matter if it was clients in the room. It just didn't matter," says Bob Genirs. "If his secretary came to the door and said, 'Your wife's on the phone,' Dick always took the call! I'd never met anybody in business who'd do that."

The Fulds lived first in Bayshore, Long Island, and then New York's Upper East Side before moving to Greenwich, Connecticut, with their three children. (They also bought homes over the years in Florida and Sun Valley.)

On trips to Asia, while his colleagues and clients would visit geisha houses after dinner, Dick always went back to his hotel. When he was still fairly new to the firm, Glucksman once told him: "Take our most important client out to dinner. Don't fuck this up." Fuld took the man to dinner. As soon as Fuld had paid the check, he wanted to leave (he was taking night courses at New York University's Stern School of Business at the time), but the client was adamant that their evening was not over.

"Let me be plain," Mr. Very Important Client said. "You are going to take me downtown and get me laid. And you are going to pay for it."

Fuld said, "Fuck you," and left.

The next morning, Glucksman was livid when he heard that his client had not had a good time. He summoned Fuld to his office and screamed at him. In an echo of Fuld's ROTC fallout in Colorado, Fuld said to his boss, "Do you want to hear my side?"

"No!" roared Glucksman.

Later that day, though, Gucksman came into Fuld's office and said, "So what is your side?"

When he told Glucksman what had happened, Glucksman cut off business with that client.

And now, Fuld was the one sending young brokers out to butter up important clients. And he expected to them to behave the way he had. He expected them "to do the right thing."

■ ■ ■

In early January 1995 Joe Gregory, then the head of fixed income, walked down the corridor of the glass doughnut-shaped space that comprised the trading floor into Chris Pettit's office with some bad news. He had just discovered the firm had $5 billion of gross exposure to Mexican bonds and related counterparties and it looked like Mexico could default soon. At the time, Lehman was worth only $3.5 billion.

Steve Carlson, the head of emerging markets, which had put $1 billion of Lehman money into Mexican *tesobonos* (dollar-indexed, peso-denominated short-term government bonds), was exposed firsthand to Pettit's fury, which was aimed more at Gregory than at Carlson. Pettit had known about Carlson's $1 billion exposure; he had not known about the other $4 billion that cropped up in other parts of the business—fixed income, derivatives, financing desk, and foreign exchange. "He was really pissed off with Joe," says Carlson. "Pettit told Carlson to consolidate and manage all of the risk underneath the emerging markets umbrella. This earned Carlson the sobriquet "Five-Billion Guy."

Carlson and his team aggressively halved the positions and moved the remaining exposures into a special purpose vehicle (SPV), which got them off the balance sheet and shielded the firm from mark-to-market losses on those assets.

Still, as long as Mexico was vulnerable, so was Lehman. Moody's downgraded the firm. Mexico was saved only when Robert Rubin, Clinton's Treasury secretary, stepped in on February 21, 1995, and underwrote the country's debt.

While Lehman waited to see if the peso was going to bring them down, Pettit called Gregory and Carlson into his office every Friday for a risk-management meeting and update. "Take me through what you got—how is the risk reduced?" he'd ask sarcastically. "Nice work, buddy," he'd add to Joe. Carlson winced. He liked Gregory and felt bad for him.

The real purpose of these meetings with Pettit, it seemed to him, was to chew Gregory out. "He was really pissed at Joe," says Carlson. "He would say really nasty things to Joe," "and I could see that the blood between them was toxic." In fairness to Pettit, it's true that Gregory had not been watching the store. Pettit also demanded that most of the emerging markets employees be fired.

Tensions got so high that during an emerging markets executive committee meeting headed by a senior confidant of Pettit's, Jim Carbone, Carlson started to thump the table in anger. Somebody had made a comment about "crazy poor risk management." Carlson felt that it had been forgotten that his business was not responsible for the $5 billion mess and banged the desk because he felt the emerging markets team was doing a good job under the circumstances.

Gregory called Carlson into his office. He said, "Don't lose your temper." Carlson replied, "Just like Chris does with you?" He added that he was tired of watching Pettit berate Gregory each week. "It makes me sick," he said.

At this, according to Carlson, Gregory turned around and kicked his trash can, shattering it. "He got in my face," says Carlson. "I said, 'Looks like I touched a nerve, didn't I?'"

A week later, Carlson was demoted.

Gregory told Carlson he had decided that Carlson had become the symbol of the "Mexico" problem. Gregory cried when he told him the news. Carlson believed that Gregory was doing this only because he thought this would help repair Gregory's relationship with Pettit. He told Carlson that he had to move him off the floor in order to protect him to get him out of Pettit's line of fire.

But the rift between Gregory and Pettit was by now irreparable.

Even the Pettit family noticed they no longer saw as much of Joe. Now—according to Lara Pettit—her father was tight-lipped and never discussed Gregory.

She also says she never heard her father say anything remotely derogatory about Fuld. "He was always completely respectful of him," she says.

In a telling sign, the carpool was breaking up. Tucker and Lessing still drove in together, but Pettit and Gregory gradually found their own ways in. Pettit drove; Gregory got himself a driver.

Chapter 8

The Stiletto

The thing about Martha Dillman is she definitely wasn't a femme fatale or some sort of Mata Hari who tried to reel Chris in; I always thought she was just very nice. I think that's important to remember.

—Peregrine Moncreiffe

By 1995, Chris Pettit's temper seemed to be on a constant simmer. Even though his troops were still loyal, it was becoming clear that he could no longer manage the firm day-to-day in the intimate way he used to run things. The business was growing too fast. To make matters worse, he'd been busy contacting oncologists around the country for his brother, Rusty, who was dying of brain cancer. He was on a short fuse.

"We had to evolve more toward a model of decentralization," says John Cecil. "As we pushed harder for the performance levels we wanted, it was more difficult for Chris or any individual to exercise the kind of control he had in mind."

Pettit appeared to be unmoored by this change. He became unusually short with people like Ron Gallatin, who had an impish quality about him—once, according to Cecil, Pettit told Gallatin to "fuck off" when he popped his head in Pettit's office door. This was out of character. "Usually Chris only yelled when someone deserved to be yelled at," says one of Pettit's colleagues.

On another occasion he got so animated in a meeting over hiring choices with Fuld and Cecil that Cecil recalls that Pettit's voice rose to a shout. He came around to the back of his chair, and while he continued a long diatribe, his hands grasped either side of the back the leather chair. He gradually, ever so slowly, lifted it off the ground. He kept talking, apparently completely oblivious, until Fuld said to him quietly, "Chris, put the chair down."

"Ordinarily Chris was unemotional, thoughtful, listened as much as he talked—but he became someone who had a temper, didn't listen, was adamant and not objective," says Tucker.

■ ■ ■

Most damaging to Pettit's sainthood status among the traders were the stories about his office romance with a married, redheaded mother of three named Martha Dillman. Joe Gregory later wrote in the ill-fated "Modern History" of Lehman that when Pettit was caught in this relationship, "he would turn negative on the firm. The guy went crackers and it was the beginning of a very rough period."

Martha Dillman was hired in 1981 from JPMorgan by Tom Tucker, to run commercial paper research in Lehman Commercial Paper Inc. (LCPI). By 1995 she headed up research for all of fixed income and was the highest-paid woman in the company. She was soft-spoken, which sometimes masked her sharp wit. She was nicknamed "The Stiletto" for her ability to puncture holes in people's arguments. Her husband worked in asset management for the Bank of New York. Unlike Mary Anne, who was thrifty, Martha had a driver, designer clothes, and lavish homes. She was 11 years younger than Mary Anne Pettit.

Dillman and Chris Pettit had gotten to know one another through a shared affection for Johnnie Walker Black, which they knocked back after work. At first no one had believed the rumors about them, which began to circulate in early 1993. Dillman was attractive, but everyone knew that Pettit, like Fuld, was an ardent family man.

Though no one knew it, Pettit had moved out of his Huntington home in the fall of 1993, and into an apartment Lehman kept for him and Tucker in New York City.

When he moved out he never mentioned Dillman; he told Mary Anne that he was confused and needed space. But he still came home for weekends with his children. He still spent Thanksgiving and Christmas with his family. The Pettit children had no idea he was gone.

But Tucker had noticed his friend behaving oddly since the Christmas party held at the Puck Building in New York in 1992. He, Pettit, and Dillman all got into a limo; they were planning to drop Dillman off before heading out to Huntington. They were all drunk. "We always got hammered at things like that," says Tucker, who sat in the front seat.

Tucker was stunned when he saw Pettit lunge for Dillman in the backseat, kissing her.

Later, after Dillman got out, he said to Pettit, "Are you crazy?" He thought his friend had simply had too much to drink. (Pettit in his cups was a legend. He once gave a much-quoted speech on the various ways you could use the word *fuck*—as a noun, as a verb, as an adjective, and so on.) But over the next six months, it became obvious to Tucker that Dillman and Pettit were growing more and more intimate. Complicating things further, Dillman was pregnant that year and gave birth to a son, Tom Dillman.

Pettit let an inkling of his feelings for her slip out after the 1993 Christmas party in the Museum of Natural History. Shearson had just been spun off, and once again Pettit soaked his sorrows in Scotch.

At the end of the evening, Pettit and Dillman and others were walking to the Stork Club on the Upper West Side when one person recalls that Pettit started mumbling, over and over: "Martha, I love you."

The rumors slowly crystallized into fact. During a Eurobond conference held in Brocket Hall, a stately home in Hertfordshire, England, one Lehman attendee, David Bullock, told people he had seen Dillman coming down the stairs near Pettit's hotel room at 6 A.M. A few hours later, the New York headquarters was abuzz with the news.

Dillman was viewed as highly ambitious. Some people thought she was fantastic at her job and enormously likable. Craig Schiffer (who didn't work for her) was godfather to one of her children. She was not afraid to air her views and succeeded in alienating some people—particularly Gregory, whom she told people she considered "dumb as rocks" and "untrustworthy." Gregory in turn once told Tucker he thought she was "evil." Others said she was a prima donna. She had risen swiftly to the head of research position, yet according to Tucker she also had a reputation for taking breaks during the day to run personal errands, which was not considered a Lehman-like work ethic. Now she began showing up to meetings with Pettit that Mary Anne felt she had no business attending. Some people wondered: Had she slept her way to the top?

For many months Pettit kept the affair from his family. Lara Pettit recalls that one evening a week her parents would go off together, supposedly to see the architect supervising the construction of their grand new house down the road. What she didn't know was that they were seeing a marriage counselor.

But since Lara now worked for Lehman (in structured credit sales), it was inevitable that she would hear the office gossip about her father. In 1993 Lara marched into her father's office and confronted him.

"If I find out you're lying to me, I am gone," she said. "I will not be lied to like this."

She says he looked at her a moment, then said, "Lara, I am not having an affair."

In February 1994, Mary Anne found two plane tickets to Washington in Chris's coat; the passengers were listed as Martha Dillman and Christopher Pettit. She phoned Tucker late that night and asked what they were for and he had to pretend he had no idea. He liked Mary Anne very much, and the guilt ate at him. Why, he thought, won't Chris just end the affair and go home?

Pettit still phoned Mary Anne every day from the office. He rented a house in Oyster Bay to be near his son, Chris Jr., who was in high school in the area. Dillman often stayed over.

Still, Mary Anne waited for him to come home. She continued to believe Dillman was just a drinking buddy of Chris's. "We were the Cinderella couple," she says years later. "I felt that he really loved me."

When Chris asked Mary Anne for a divorce, she refused to cooperate. Years after Chris had moved out, Steve Lessing told people she kept Chris's slippers under the bed and his clothes in the closet.

Chris Pettit and Martha Dillman officially "came out" when he brought her as his date to the wedding of Bob Genirs's daughter in October 1994. Martha had divorced her husband in November 1993; Martha had told people her husband first learned about her affair when he saw a diaphragm in her briefcase.

■ ■ ■

The affair was enormously divisive in the Lehman offices, and destabilizing for Pettit. Even so, he never contemplated leaving the firm, even when John Mack of Morgan Stanley offered him the job of running fixed income there.

But he began to drink more. A colleague saw him sit at the table in the Lehman dining room and knock back a drink in one gulp before turning to greet people. "I was shocked," says this person. "Ordinarily Chris was the most perfect host; he'd always wait for everyone else to have their glasses filled and make a toast before taking a sip; I realized what a strain he must be under. Clearly he was drinking for medicinal purposes."

He had reason to be stressed. The lines dividing work and family had been blurred for so long that the consequences of his infidelity were manifold. The Pettits and the Lessings built homes in Hobe Sound's Loblolly Bay neighborhood near Jupiter, Florida, and Steve Lessing's father-in-law, Andrew J. Melton Jr., got Chris, Joe, and Tom into his country clubs. Tucker's wife, Heather, and Lessing's wife, Sandra, in particular, felt horrible for Mary Anne. And Tom Tucker, reeling, blamed himself, says a colleague, because he'd hired Dillman.

Colleagues say Pettit became increasingly isolated in the office. He wouldn't listen to anyone; he became hot-tempered, apparently changing into someone that even Tucker had to admit "he couldn't like." He became feared.

In 1995, he and Martha moved into a $5 million house in Brooklyn Heights.

Even though she knew it wasn't what her mother or any of her siblings wanted, Lara Pettit slowly got to know Dillman during this period. "I could see she made my father happy, and I didn't want him out of my life," she says.

But others in the office were less forgiving. They felt deceived by Pettit. "When we found out that this affair was going on, it was such a betrayal," says one former Lehman employee. "Part of the reason I loved being there was because I liked working for these guys. I feel like they at least had some sort of code. And that affair was a breach of the code."

Dillman was also divisive in the office because she was thought to be "Chris's spy." A former senior executive recalls that he and his peers were told by John Coghlan, a managing director in fixed income, to clam up whenever she entered the room, and as politely as possible, to leave. "We were told to tell her absolutely nothing," says one person intimate with the situation.

Pettit's troops resented her because she distracted him from his job—the two of them would disappear for hours.

Gregory played up all the tumult the affair created in the office. He had good reason. He knew Dillman loathed him, and he was still chafing with Pettit because of the peso fiasco.

Fuld largely kept out of all this. He did tell a few people, including Pettit, that he deeply disapproved of the affair. He expected Pettit to sort it out.

Eventually Pettit talked things over with Dillman and they agreed that she had to leave Lehman. In early 1995, Fuld sent out a firmwide memo saying Dillman was stepping down to spend more time with her family.

No one was fooled. Pettit, according to Lara, felt so bad about the whole thing that he set up a company for Dillman and put in some of his money. "He felt she'd given up her job for him," she says.

Dillman's resignation did little to silence Gregory, who told others that Pettit was still unhinged and that his private life was still affecting his work. Gregory also had another reason to pick a fight with Pettit. He felt his division, fixed income, which brought in the bulk of Lehman's revenues, should be better remunerated, and he didn't like the fact that Pettit was protecting the heads of equities and banking, which were not performing so well. (They were newer and weaker divisions.)

Gregory began holding secret meetings with people on the operating committee to explore ways to limit Pettit's power.

Gregory said he was doing this for the good of the firm. Tucker recalls that in early 1996, Gregory told him that Tucker had been a loyal friend to Chris, but now it was okay to let it go and not worry about the friendship. Pettit was too far gone. It would be better for the business, Gregory told Tucker, to relinquish the friendship. Tucker didn't say much in reply. He'd already decided that he was leaving Lehman. He'd seen quite enough of life on Wall Street. Unlike Pettit, he remembered the oath they took—and he wanted to keep it. Tucker still wanted to be a "good guy."

■ ■ ■

Pettit may have been distracted, but he clearly sensed that forces were aligning against him. Around this time, he told people to stop talking to John Cecil or Dick Fuld; he told them to come to him with their queries.

Chapter 9

The Ides of March

You think you would have liked Chris Pettit—but by the
end you would not have liked him. He became someone else.

—*John Cecil*

B y the start of 1996, both Lehman's equities and investment
banking units were still doing poorly compared to fixed income,
which was a weakness that Lehman needed to fix. Their
respective heads, Paul Williams and Mel Shaftel, were considered
overmatched by almost everyone save Chris Pettit, who repeatedly
defended them. He used to say to Tom Tucker, "Listen, managing
bankers is like herding cats" (in other words, impossible) and "Mel is
the only person I consider objective and reliable. I really can't think of
anyone better for the job."

Fuld wanted to hire Joe Perella, from the now-defunct Wasserstein
Perella boutique mergers and acquisitions (M&A) firm, to run banking.
Though Perella had interviewed with the firm and seemed very interested, Pettit was none too keen on him. "He will show up at 10 in the
morning and leave by three," Pettit complained to other senior executives. His frosty attitude had been clear to Perella during their interview.

Perella opted to join Morgan Stanley instead. Fuld would call him regularly, like a jilted lover, and ask, "Are you happy?"

"What the hell does it matter what hours Joe Perella works?" complained Mike Odrich, Fuld's bright chief of staff at the time. "He's the best M&A banker out there. We should have done everything to get him."

Deep down, Pettit must have known his heads of banking and equities were weak. He moved Tucker over to supervise Williams and help him fix equities. After several months, Tucker told Pettit: "Chris, he can't do it."

Williams's deputy, Leo Corbett, even went to Tucker and Pettit and said, "You have to fire Paul. He's just not up to the job."

But Pettit was very close to both Shaftel and Williams, who spent so much time at Pettit's house that many people, neighbors in particular, thought he and Chris were blood relatives.

Pettit held out against firing the duo even when the rest of the operating committee disagreed with him. "Show me better candidates," he kept saying.

When Joe Gregory started calling for Pettit's pals to be fired, an ugly confrontation was inevitable. Gregory told Fuld that if Pettit wouldn't fire Shaftel and Williams, then Fuld should fire Pettit—for the good of the firm, of course.

Gregory realized that the only way to convince Fuld—who was rarely willing to make the tough decisions—that he had the clout to win a fight with Pettit was to show him that Lessing and Tucker—Pettit's two best friends and very influential men in the firm—would back him.

Lessing obliged. Tucker simply told Fuld he thought Chris was making some wrong decisions and left it at that. He had no idea that a coup was afoot, and that he'd just cast the deciding vote.

Gregory then gave Fuld a plan: remove Pettit from the position of head of the operating committee, then create a smaller executive committee, and thereby limit Pettit's power. He knew Pettit would resist this shake-up.

Odrich warned Fuld not to have a showdown with Pettit until he had the Lehman board members on his side. Odrich knew Pettit would never think to court the board. He'd long ago ceded that ground to Fuld, and focused on managing his troops.

The board back then included Fuld, Michael Ainslie (president and CEO of Sotheby's), John Akers (former president of IBM), Roger Berlind (a theater producer), Thomas Cruikshank (CEO of Halliburton), Hideichiro Kobayashi (a general manager at Nippon Life Insurance), Henry Kaufman (the former chief economist at Salomon Brothers and the only person on the board with a background in finance), John Macomber (a real estate expert), Dina Merrill (an actress, daughter of the co-founder of E.F. Hutton), and Masataka Shimasaki (another Nippon Life head). They were all friendly with Fuld—and they'd never even met Pettit. The board endorsed his plan.

■ ■ ■

Even though he had made Fuld sign a $10 million severance deal, Pettit never saw the coup coming. It never occurred to him that his old friends would betray him. Why? Because he would never have done it to them.

As Mel Shaftel says: "Though he chewed Joe out, especially during the Mexican thing, it was like you'd chew out a child. He would *never* have fired Joe. Joe was 'family' to him."

■ ■ ■

On February 18, 1996, Lara Pettit organized a surprise 50th birthday dinner for her father in a private room at Gramercy Tavern, a swank American tavern in New York City's historic Flatiron building. She invited Fuld, Gregory, Lessing, and all the other members of the executive committee, and most of them came.

When Lara and her father opened the door of the private dining room for the big surprise, her father blanched. "Please stay," he begged his daughter.

"No, no. Have a good time," she said gaily.

The next day she went to the restaurant to pay the check, expecting it to be huge.

It wasn't. Judging by the receipt, the party had started at seven o'clock and was over by eight.

She asked her father what had happened.

He told her, "Oh we just had drinks—we didn't want you to pay for more than that."

The Ponderosa Boys had all carpooled together for decades, and now they couldn't even stand to be in the same room together.

■ ■ ■

Once Dick Fuld knew he had the support of Tom Tucker and Steve Lessing—"Chris's guys"—he knew that he had control of Lehman Brothers. He didn't want to fire Chris Pettit, but he did want to hobble him.

"It took a remarkable amount of push from me and Steve Lessing to get Dick emboldened enough," Gregory wrote later for the unpublished Lehman "Modern History." "He needed to believe that we, whom he viewed as Chris loyalists, would in fact be there for him."

Lessing and Gregory were in Singapore on March 15, 1996, on business when the plan to "force Chris into a box," as Gregory put it, was initiated. Fuld was going to tell Pettit he had decided to fire Williams and Shaftel, and that unless Pettit agreed, he'd have to strip Pettit of his directorship of the operating committee.

He would also tell Pettit the firm would henceforth be led by a small group known as the frontline committee, of which Pettit would be part—but not its head.

To the end, Fuld needed to be propped up for his confrontation with Pettit. According to Gregory, before calling Pettit into his office, Fuld asked Gregory and Lessing on the phone in Singapore, "How am I going to do this again?"

■ ■ ■

When Fuld summoned Pettit to his office and told him he needed to fire Williams and Shaftel, Pettit refused. In that case, Fuld said, he needed to ask Pettit to step down from running the operating committee. He laid out his plans for a small committee of six, and Pettit again refused.

So Fuld demoted him to "head of client relationships."

What happened next is known only by the two men who were in that room. All that anybody else knows is that there were raised voices and that Pettit then marched out of Fuld's office. Dave Steinmetz, Pettit's chief of staff, recalls seeing Fuld come out of his office right after he'd confronted Pettit. Steinmetz told colleagues Fuld was ashen-faced. Had he—completely unintentionally—done something irreparable with Pettit? Had he pushed him out?

For the better part of a week, Pettit tried to fight back, but once he realized that Tucker, Lessing, and Gregory were behind Fuld, he knew it was over. That Friday, he called Dan Pollack, the lawyer all senior Lehman executives used when they needed to fight over severance. He told Pollack he had to leave Lehman and there'd be a battle on his way out.

"Chris almost ate Dick but we didn't let that happen, because Chris was not a good guy," Gregory later wrote in his journals.

Pettit kept the news that he planned to leave to himself for as long as he could. His daughter, Lara, heard he'd changed job titles and went to seek him out. She found him in a new office on the 19th floor, which was known as the "dead zone." She was shocked at how small it was.

In the middle of their conversation, she saw her father weep for the first time. "He threw something across his office. And he started to cry, and he said, 'I have pride, I have pride.' It was horrible."

■ ■ ■

Tom Tucker announced he was leaving Lehman right after Pettit's demotion. He returned all but $1 million of his 1995 bonus, distributing it among his staff. He had always been interested in helping under-privileged children, and that's now what he set his sights on. He was dismayed about what was happening at Lehman.

"I wondered what we'd all become. All that money, that success. . . . Were we that brilliant, really? I was deeply troubled by what had happened to us."

He went to see Pettit in his office before it was public that Pettit was leaving. Tucker told his old friend that he couldn't bear to stay with Lehman any longer. He'd seen more than enough of Wall Street to last him a lifetime. Weeping, he told Pettit he wanted out.

He says Pettit was cold and defiant. "He looked at me crying like I was pathetic." Pettit said that he wouldn't come to Tucker's farewell party, because he was upset at the way Tucker—who was close with Mary Anne—had treated him and his kids in regards to his affair with Dillman. Pettit claimed that Tucker hadn't been a good friend, after all.

They had come so far from their days at Finnegan's, and the night when they made their pact that money would never change them.

Tucker recalls that the last thing Pettit said to him that day was: "In the end, the guy who coped best with money was you, wasn't it?"

Two weeks later, at Tucker's farewell party, in the partners' dining room at 200 Vesey Street, Steve Carlson passed Tucker a note that read, in part: "You are the heart and soul of Lehman Brothers."

Carlson felt that of all the firm's leaders—Fuld, Pettit, Hill, the Ponderosa Boys—Tucker was the only one, in the end, who really *had* meant to "do the right thing."

Pettit kept his word and didn't attend that farewell; neither did Lara. Her father had told her: "Out of respect for me, you will not go."

■ ■ ■

Pollack began the negotiations over Pettit's severance package, which he calculated was worth $40 million. Fuld wasn't eager to see that much money walking out of Lehman. It took eight months to sort out the mess.

Meanwhile, Shaftel was demoted and moved upstairs to the "dead zone" office next to Pettit's. "Bankers never die, they just change titles," he joked several years later. Pettit told him to hire Pollack, too. They weren't going down without one last fight.

Pettit had time to kill while Pollack fought with Bob Genirs over his severance. He put in some token hours at the office, and that summer he took Martha and Lara to Africa for a long vacation.

While in Africa, deep in the jungle, he was startled to receive a call on his cell phone. It was Jim Vinci, calling from a pay phone outside a ranger's station in the Adirondacks.

Vinci told him he had just been fired.

"That's not supposed to happen," said Pettit. But he was powerless to stop it.

Soon after, he got a call from his sister-in-law, who said that his brother, Rusty, had taken a turn for the worse. Could Chris come back and see if he could search for some miracle treatment?

Pettit cut his trip short and flew back to New York. He missed the planned highlight of the sojourn: He'd never seen a real gorilla in the wild.

Rusty died not long after Pettit got home.

■ ■ ■

When Pettit returned, he was able to watch the ascension of the man who had played a large part in forcing him out: Joe Gregory.

Fuld moved Gregory out of fixed income by the end of the year and asked him to head up equities following a presentation by Paul Williams to the new frontline committee that was considered "disastrous." Williams was fired. Gregory would be taking over for him at the start of 1997.

In less than a year, Gregory had changed from Pettit's acolyte to his Brutus. One person involved with the ousting says, "It's like the old lion and the young lions. Joe Gregory sees a weakness in Chris Pettit, something that he can grab hold of. He goes to Dick, and they push Chris out. He's killed a guy who was his boss, his mentor, his buddy. That speaks to Joe Gregory's character. It doesn't speak to Chris Pettit's at all."

Gregory was now a formidable force in the firm. Everyone knew that they were part of that "one firm" only as long as they followed the directives of Joe Gregory. His new nickname was "Joe the Wedge." Cross him, even on the smallest thing, and you were dead.

■ ■ ■

Bob Genirs, the chief administrative officer (CAO), on the verge of retiring, recalls walking into Fuld's office and seeing his CEO sitting there with John Cecil on one side and Tom Russo, Lehman's legal counsel, on the other. They were looking over Pettit's severance deal one last time. Russo and Cecil had both been hired by Pettit, and Genirs says he was suddenly infuriated.

It was an unusually generous agreement and allowed Pettit access to stock that wasn't fully vested. Genirs, who had drafted it, says he felt he'd done well by both Lehman and Pettit. But Cecil and Russo, according to Genirs, were trying to convince Fuld to scale it back.

"I had to say, right in front of Cecil and Russo—'Dick, these two guys want your position. And I'm telling you that's what's generating all of these comments,'" Genirs recalls.

"I said, 'So Dick, you're either going to believe what I'm saying, and go and sign this piece of paper, or you're going to believe these guys.' And he believed me, and he signed."

(Cecil says he doesn't remember this scene, though he does recall disputes over Pettit's severance package because of the fear that if Pettit gained access to stock that had not fully vested, others would want it too.) Genirs recalls, that Fuld phoned him at home that night. "Genirs, you've done a lot of things for me over the years. But how you got Pettit out, and what you did here, is beyond whatever I could do to thank you. This is the greatest thing you ever did for Lehman Brothers."

On November 26, 1996, Chris Pettit finally walked out of Lehman Brothers, the firm he could rightfully claim to have built into a behemoth with his brains and his indomitable spirit. He would not speak to Dick Fuld, Tom Tucker, Joe Gregory, or Steve Lessing—his old friends—ever again.

Chapter 10

Eulogies

Do I think that my father was so dispirited by what had happened that he was deliberately reckless? Not at all. He still had so much to live for. Martha wanted me to tell you: He was one of three people who died on the lake that night.

—*Lara Pettit*

On the evening after Chris Pettit's last day of work, Lara Pettit and her boyfriend, Bill Gilchrist, went to Brooklyn Heights to take him out to dinner. He'd been living there with Martha Dillman since 1994. Lara wanted to "take his mind off" of everything, as if that were possible. But when they got there, Martha asked that they all spend the evening with her children: John, 10, Sophie, 7, and Tom, 3.

The children were curious to know what the "special occasion" was. Chris Pettit looked drawn and embarrassed as he told them he wasn't going to be working anymore.

After dinner, Martha took the kids upstairs to bed and Lara and her father sat downstairs, not saying much of anything, and not needing to.

Over the next few weeks, Lara saw her father in tears several times. "I don't think he could figure it out himself—much less tell his daughter—how he had failed," she says. "I think it really hurt him because he had done so much for everyone there. . . . He felt like everyone had turned on him. He would just sit and cry."

Soon after, Pettit went on a job interview, and, according to Lara, was asked for his resume. "He'd been the *president* of Lehman Brothers," she says, "and he was being asked for a resume!" He walked out of the interview.

The last time Lara saw her father was on January 19, 1997. They were driving to a relative's christening in Connecticut and he insisted they stop at a bank, because he was determined to sell all the Lehman stock he held, which was now worth $6.8 million. Lara tried to stop him.

"I said, 'Are you kidding me? Why?' And he said, 'I can't—out of pride—I can't hold on to this.'" There and then, he sold all his Lehman shares.

Father and daughter spoke over the phone a few weeks later. Lara's sister, Kari, was going to come up and stay in Maine with Martha and Chris for the weekend before his birthday; Kari had not come to stay before. Kari, like the rest of the Pettit family except for Lara, had so far refused to visit with Martha. She was bringing a new boyfriend. Chris was lighthearted and excited.

(He had found his family's freeze-out of Dillman hard to bear since he had helped each of them in so many ways. He had gotten his brother, Andrew ("Andy"), a job as a director at Lehman. His aunt, Elizabeth ("Liz"), also worked at the firm. She traded commercial paper. According to Lara, he was also bankrolling three of his seven siblings' families, who repeatedly asked him for money. He appeared to give it gladly, so he was hurt by their sudden distance.)

Lara says that when she hung up the phone, she was smiling. It was good to hear her father happy again.

■ ■ ■

Dillman and Pettit spent a good deal of that winter in her cabin in Maine, where Martha had grown up. It was a modest home, and they were going over their plans to build a bigger house nearby so that they could host all their children.

They were thrilled that Kari, then a graduate veterinary student at Tufts, and her new boyfriend, Rich, who was a computer software engineer, had accepted Martha's invitation to stay on the weekend of February 15, several days before Chris's 52nd birthday. "It was a big deal, a turning point for Dad," says Lara.

For dinner Saturday they ate lobsters and drank wine. Kari recalls that her father was in excellent spirits, that they had a wonderful conversation.

It was Kari who suggested that they go snowmobiling after dinner—fun but dangerous in the dark. Kari knew, however, that Lara and *her* boyfriend had done it only a few weekends before and found it exhilarating.

She didn't know that Lara had also been scared out of her wits.

"There are stumps in the ice you just can't see. With four of us on the snowmobile at least we stopped him going too fast, but it was dangerous," recalls Lara.

Kari asked Rich and her father to not get on the snowmobiles until she made a quick drive to the local store for cigarettes.

When she returned she saw that they'd left without her. Martha was inside. And suddenly there was Rich in the driveway, covered in blood, calling for help. He and Chris had been snowmobiling and hit a stump. Chris had fallen, his helmet had been dislodged.

Kari told Lara what happened next. "When my sister's boyfriend went over to him, he was still alive, but he had a blunt head injury. Rich couldn't carry him . . . so he just left him and went running around to nearby houses. . . . He was covered in blood, banging on people's doors, trying to get someone to call for help. He couldn't get anyone to open their doors. He finally made his way back to Martha's cabin. He said, 'Come with me! Come with me! He's still alive!' But by the time the police came, it was too late."

Martha was questioned by the police since the accident occurred on her property and on her snowmobile. Rich was taken to the police station to give his statement and then released.

Kari was inconsolable. She blamed herself for his death.

Martha was asked if she wanted an autopsy. She rang Jim Sullivan, a lawyer who was an old friend of Chris's, and then Bill Pettit, Chris's older brother, and broke the news to them. She suggested to both men that if there was an autopsy, Pettit's blood alcohol levels would make for ugly headlines. They all agreed there was no need.

■ ■ ■

That Sunday evening Bob Genirs returned home and found 18 messages on his voice mail. He hit "Play," and heard Martha telling him Chris had died. She'd planned a funeral in Brooklyn on Monday. Four calls later there was a message from Mary Anne Pettit, saying a funeral had been planned for Tuesday in St. Patrick's Roman Catholic Church, in Huntington.

Mary Anne Pettit was livid when she heard of Dillman's plans. "It was like she kept his body hostage," she said. "Was there no end to her scheming?" (Dillman did not want to comment on anything to do with Chris Pettit.)

■ ■ ■

Two "wives," two funerals, but Lehman executives did not need to ask which funeral to go to. They all showed up for the Mass in Huntington on Tuesday, although there were several awkward moments.

The first was during the funeral procession—or rather, the two funeral processions. There were the Pettits, led by Mary Anne, and then there was Martha Dillman, with John and Sophie. Sitting at the front of the congregation at St. Patrick's were Dick Fuld and Joe Gregory.

Steve Carlson recalled seeing Tucker at the funeral. The two men had not spoken since that tearful scene in Pettit's office. It would be years before Tucker could forgive himself for not reconciling with his friend. "He had his arm around Mary Anne," Carlson said. "And we all knew that Tommy was part of the kerfuffle that took out Chris. We knew that he didn't feel good about this. He had this tortured look on his face."

The Pettit children were appalled when Martha's eldest child, John Dillman, took his position as one of the pallbearers. Chris Pettit Jr. turned to Mary Anne and said, "There's no way he's touching my father's casket." But no one stopped him. He was, after all, a child.

Tommy Tucker gave the eulogy as his friend was laid to rest beside his brother Rusty in Farmingdale, Long Island. As the coffin was lowered into the ground he said:

> When I look out at all of you, and think of all the lives that Chris impacted, the word that I focus on is *love.*
> I had a conversation recently that touched upon the subject of love. I learned that fear is the main obstacle in developing a loving persona. If you get through the fear, you can achieve wonderful things. Chris was the guy who removed the fear from all of us. . . .
> We were all better when he was around, because he took away the fear and gave us confidence. . . . Chris has made it easier for all of us to realize our full potential. He set the tone. He moved the obstacles. He made it fun. And he did it for all of you because he loved all of you.

Many of the Lehman people then went back to the city in their separate limos, back to their separate intrigues. Some left Pettit in the ground that day; some never forgot him. Tucker hasn't. He finished his eulogy that day with these words:

> Chris was my best friend. I loved him and he loved me. He always made me better than I was. I am sure his spirit will be with me for the rest of my life.

■ ■ ■

Which was, in some morbid fashion, true. Tucker was so haunted by Chris Pettit that six years after the funeral he visited a medium, James Fargiano, who is so heavily booked that he takes reservations a year in advance. Tucker says Fargiano was worth the wait. The medium, he says, summoned up Chris's spirit—after he had brought in the spirits of Tucker's parents to convince the skeptical Tucker this was no hoax—and the two old friends, or rather a spirit and a man, finally made their peace.

Tucker stayed close with Mary Anne. They were both shocked to discover that a codicil in Pettit's will left half his estate to Martha. The codicil was dated May 1994. "It was the date that horrified me," says Mary Anne. She does not understand why he would have done such a thing unless he felt guilty for making Dillman give up her job.

Steve Lessing always kept an eye out for Chris's children—he got Chris Jr. a job as a scout with the New York Giants. And he bought Finnegan's and gave the Pettit children a share of the investment in the place. It's currently one of the most popular pubs in Huntington.

There was no end to the enmity between the two "widows": The Pettit family was shocked to learn that not only would Martha Dillman be getting half of Chris's money but she had also taken out a $4 million insurance policy on Chris's life.

Why—and how—could she have done that? Mary Anne Pettit certainly didn't understand. She wanted to hold a wrongful death hearing, but refrained when she heard that Kari would have to testify.

Kari still blames herself for what happened. She rarely speaks about that night, and there was no way she could have made it through a trial.

Dillman also contested Mary Anne's claim to Chris's deferred compensation. Mary Anne appealed to Dick Fuld for help, and he assured her that Dillman would "get the money over my dead body." Legally, as Chris's widow, there was no doubt that Mary Anne had the right to the money, and Fuld kept his word. Mary Anne received Chris's deferred compensation—until, that is, Lehman filed for bankruptcy, and all deferred compensation checks stopped.

Dillman moved on quickly. In November 1998, the year after Pettit's death, she married Douglas Malcolm Schair; he had bought the large house in Maine she and Chris had built. They soon divorced, and in 2004 she married William Zeitz, vice president of the Maine College of Art. She is now separated from him.

Joe Gregory kept in touch with Mary Anne Pettit; they were, after all, neighbors and Lara was still working in the Lehman office. The Tuckers remained her best friends.

Perry Moncreiffe, who came over from Britain for the funeral, says that when he saw Joe Gregory that day he was struck by how his demeanor had completely changed. Moncreiffe says he was no longer the Ponderosa's "Little Joe." He was now a man ascendant, a man of power.

■ ■ ■

Not long after Pettit's death, Tom Tucker started a camp for financially deprived children who otherwise would never have a chance to escape the city.

He originally wanted to call it Camp Lehman Brothers and had gone in to meet with Gregory and Fuld to see if that was okay, since half the camp board was comprised of Lehman Brothers people. To his immense disappointment and frustration, Fuld and Gregory told him no.

"I think it would be great publicity for the firm to do this," Tucker argued. "That fell on deaf ears," he says. He does not know why.

The donations from Gregory added up to around $60,000, which was more than some former colleagues gave but a lot less than others. Fuld gave $10,000.

Over time, Tucker raised $3 million for the camp from many Lehman employees, including Steve Lessing and the former head of the Boston office, Bob Cagnina.

Tucker decided to name the camp the Fiver Children's Foundation. The subtext was clear: He was naming the camp after the runt bunny from *Watership Down* whose ambitions were pure and brave—what Chris Pettit once stood for, what they had all once stood for in a dim and increasingly distant past.

Richard Adams, the author of *Watership Down*, came with his wife for the camp's opening, and today, 500 children a year attend the camp in Poolville, New York. It is considered a huge success. In August 2006, it was featured in a segment narrated by Matt Lauer on the *Today* show.

Tucker, being the generous man that he is, never complained again about the lack of support from Gregory or Fuld—though he was very taken aback three years ago when he received a call from Nancy Hament, a former Lehman executive who had just had lunch with Gregory and had some surprising news. She said Gregory had told her he had never really liked Tucker. He felt they had different styles. While Tucker had never been as close to Gregory as he had been to Lessing or Pettit, he had believed they had a genuine friendship. He had even taken Gregory to lunch six months after he'd left Lehman because he'd felt like Joe was "slipping away."

When he heard what Hament said, Tucker felt like he'd been punched in the stomach. Joe? His carpooling buddy?

He called Lessing, who was more sanguine. Lessing told Tucker, "Joe's a phony, Tom. Haven't you worked that out yet? A complete phony."

Part Two

THE ECHO CHAMBER

Turning and turning in the widening gyre
The falcon cannot hear the falconer;
Things fall apart; the centre cannot hold;
Mere anarchy is loosed upon the world,
The blood-dimmed tide is loosed, and everywhere
The ceremony of innocence is drowned;
The best lack all conviction, while the worst
Are full of passionate intensity.
                    —*William Butler Yeats,* The Second Coming

Chapter 11

Russian Winter

It was us against the world. Because we went through that Shearson experience, it forced a group of us to be totally together.

—*Steve Lessing*

Toward the end of 1996, a Lehman proprietary trader in Japan got caught in a position that was plummeting and he was stuck there, overexposed. His department (fixed income) and his boss (Joe Gregory) would lose all the profits they'd made over the year. November, as every trader knows, is the worst time to make a mistake. This one cost Lehman $100 million.

Once again, according to sources, John Cecil believed that Gregory had not kept a zealous watch over all his employees.

The loss meant that Cecil, not Gregory, was the second-highest-paid executive in the firm that year.

Cecil earned more than $5 million—nearly $2 million in cash plus $2.3 million in stock and $1.1 million in restricted stock units (RSUs) and options—earnings that, according to sources, irritated Gregory.

He would "remind" Cecil "how easy it was for someone not running a division" to do well. He had never talked like this to Cecil before, and it was this kind of bonus envy that Fuld had hoped to eliminate when he reorganized senior management.

Fuld had replaced Pettit and the operating committee with six division heads who would be paid equally, which he called the frontline committee (the title was quickly dropped, according to Cecil, in favor of executive committee). Then there was a group of 20, known as the operating committee, which included the people who ran divisions like information technology (IT) and operations.

The reason Fuld came up with this idea of a committee of (supposed) equals, according to Cecil, was that he was tired of all the friction around him. It wasn't good for the firm. Fuld hated arguments, some of which concerned matters he was only barely familiar with, and he hated making management decisions—particularly concerning bonuses and drama between personnel.

He wanted to be left alone at the top, with the quiet and orderly Cecil behind him, but out of sight. (Cecil usually kept to his office on the 10th floor, and rarely appeared on the trading floor.)

Fuld meanwhile pushed to increase his visibility—and stature—outside the firm. The once taciturn trader suddenly and aggressively entered the New York establishment milieu: He became a member of the Council of Foreign Relations (Tom Hill was a member); he was named to the board of the New York Stock Exchange; he was a member of President Clinton's Advisory Committee for Trade Policy and Negotiation; and he became a member of University of Colorado Business Advisory Council.

The memories of Pettit faded fast. Articles about the firm's growing revenues (they were up 12 percent in 1997) never mentioned him, and by 2008 many people at Lehman had never heard of Chris Pettit. "We were all so relieved not to get any more memos signed TCP," says one senior person. (Internal memos were signed with initials, not names—hence TCP for Pettit.)

As for Joe Gregory?

He swept into his new role as the head of equities, fired 27 out of the 29 people in the department, and hired a fresh team. One of those fired was Craig Schiffer.

Many of the people fired by Gregory assumed it was because of their feelings for Pettit, not because of their job performance. "If Lehman held a Lehman court, they would have all testified for Chris, and so Joe didn't want them around," says one person close to the situation.

Years later when Schiffer met Gregory for breakfast, Joe told him blithely: "Never pick an argument with your boss, Craig, because the bigger title will always win. You lost your job because you didn't learn that." (Fuld later said about Schiffer, "Why did we let him go? I always liked him, always thought he was good.")

But some still remembered Pettit as the man who had positioned the company for its sudden rise. Jim Vinci says: "I can't tell you how hard I laughed when I saw that *Fortune* magazine article [in April 2006] about Dick." "So complete has Fuld's makeover of Lehman been that he is more like a founder than a CEO," it read.

"It was just ridiculous. I think a lot of us thought, 'How could they tell this story without Pettit? Like Dick did this all by himself?' It was nauseating."

■ ■ ■

Fuld, Lessing, Gregory, and the rest didn't have time to look back.

"It was a very exciting time in the marketplace. . . . We were competing aggressively with Goldman and Salomon Brothers . . . [and had] started to build out Europe and Asia . . . becoming more of global firm," Lessing wrote in the document commissioned by Gregory in 2003. "It was really an intense, once-in-a-lifetime opportunity to build something and bring back the Lehman Brothers name, which had a 150-year tradition."

The new frontline committee had Gregory (equities) and Vanderbeek (fixed income). Mel Shaftel was replaced by a banking troika—Mike Odrich's idea—comprised of Bradley Jack from fixed income and capital markets, Steve Berger from European investment banking, and Michael "Mike" McKeever from within banking.

The firm stayed on its upward trajectory. Standard & Poor's upgraded its outlook from "negative"—to which Lehman had sunk thanks to that $22 million first quarter —to "stable." Moody's had also downgraded the firm during the Mexican crisis, but by 1997 it had Lehman back up to single A.

Investment banking yielded record revenues, as did the real estate, mortgages, high yield, and emerging markets departments.

■ ■ ■

Two executives were crucial during this period.

One was Robert "Bob" Millard, an MIT graduate who was Lehman's biggest earner by far throughout the 1990s. His investment business had returns of around 15 percent per year—on no leverage. One of the most successful investments was in an aerospace company called L3 Communications where Millard was appointed lead director. "We invested $60 million; we ended up with a multiple of that many times over," he says.

Another MVP was Mark Walsh. Since 1991 Walsh, a very dynamic and well-liked executive, had run the principal investing activity for commercial real estate within the fixed income division's umbrella. This meant he made loans to both developers and buyers of commercial real estate. He provided the financing for an acquisition—like the $700 million purchase of the General Motors building (now home to FAO Schwarz and Apple retail stores) on Fifth Avenue and 59th Street in Manhattan.

Walsh would also invest in the equity of his deals. One of his most famous trades in the early 1990s was the purchase of a building in Times Square that was considered ugly and was being sold at a relatively low price. Walsh realized that its value was its position; you could make vast profits by sticking billboards on it. He rented out the wall space and then resold the building two years later at a far higher price. According to Cecil, that deal made Lehman $80 million, and cemented Walsh's reputation as Lehman's King Midas.

After that deal, Walsh was awarded increasing autonomy. Fuld was so confident in him, he often put the firm's balance sheet behind Walsh's deals. As interest rates declined and all asset values inflated, the values of buildings he had stakes in increased. Firmwide, Walsh was a hero. He seemed to have a knack for choosing properties that could be improved and would make a killing for the firm when they sold.

The trouble was that in doing this Fuld was tying the firm's balance sheet to illiquid assets. If something were to go wrong, the firm wouldn't be able to reduce its exposure. But in the meantime, his unit grew until reports said it generated more than 20 percent of Lehman's profits.

In 1997, the *New York Times* reported that Barry Sternlicht, the CEO of Starwood Hotels and Resorts, remembered Walsh bringing Fuld to his living room. Sternlicht was so impressed by the duo that he let them finance his $7 billion purchase of ITT Corporation, the parent company of the Sheraton Hotel chain, usurping a deal he'd already had in place with Goldman Sachs. From that moment on Fuld knew that Walsh was a key, if not *the* key, to Lehman's prosperity.

■ ■ ■

On April 6, 1998, the environment on Wall Street changed forever: The $83 billion merger of Citicorp and Travelers Group, which created the world's largest financial services company, was a watershed moment. It led to the repeal of the Glass-Steagall Act of 1933, which prevented bank holding companies from owning insurance companies and brokerage firms. And it opened the doors for a host of mergers and consolidations within the financial services industry.

Lehman's leaders could now entertain mergers with other houses, and they looked at hundreds of potential merger targets, including the retail brokerage PaineWebber. Lehman also looked at Prudential—again, in vain. Prudential didn't want to sell.

Lehman's real problem, however, was that its price-to-earnings (P/E) ratio was too low—around 11—while most booming Wall Street businesses had P/Es of 14. The P/E ratio is used for valuation—the higher the P/E, the higher the stock price. In order for Lehman to make a merger, it would have had to overpay to compensate for its low P/E, which would have been detrimental to its shareholders.

But all such dreams of expansion were postponed on August 17, 1998, when the pavement suddenly crumbled beneath Wall Street's feet, and all the securities houses heard rumblings of potential doom. Russia had devalued the ruble and defaulted on its government bonds—the first time any country had done this in the postwar era. Panicked investors sold emerging markets securities, while also selling Japanese and European bonds in favor of U.S. bonds, which were widely considered the safest currency and debt in the world. This in turn led to a drop in worldwide markets.

Cecil says, "Initially, it was a nonevent for the firm." Fuld had always been wary of investing in Russia. He often called the place "the world's biggest fucking crime syndicate."

Cecil knew that Lehman had some exposure through a money management group, III (Triple I) Offshore Advisors, which managed the High Risk Opportunities Fund (HRO). Lehman, he said, had $300 million of principle in jeopardy. According to Cecil, $300 million was a headache for the firm, but not life-threatening.

Tom Russo—general counsel and head of public relations—tried to go on the offensive and organize a collaborated response to the III crisis rather than let individual firms try to cut deals or seize the fund's assets.

Things were complicated, however, by the Securities and Exchange Commission (SEC), which decided to investigate Lehman's marks, or pricing.

Russo says the SEC alleged that Lehman's prices were higher than everyone else's, although the General Accounting Office—later renamed the Government Accountability Office (GAO)—would later show that Lehman's prices were accurate. In the meantime, the rumor mill went berserk. Lehman's stock price fell 60 percent.

The first Cecil heard about the rumors and the subsequent shorting of Lehman stock was when Bruce Lakefield, then the head of Lehman Europe, called during the second week of September to say there was a rumor swirling that Lehman had big exposure problems. Cecil told him not to worry.

While Lehman was being buffeted by this mess, a bigger one was unfolding for all of Wall Street.

In mid-September, the hedge fund Long-Term Capital Management (LTCM) fell apart, throwing the entire financial system into a panic.

LTCM was founded by John Meriwether—the former head of bond trading at Salomon Brothers—and led by a group of academics, including Nobel Prize–winning economists Robert Merton and Myron Scholes, who had, with Fischer Black, originated the Black-Scholes option pricing model. The complex mathematical equation proves, after a series of assumptions about the market, that "it is possible to create a hedged position, consisting of a long position in the stock and a short position in [calls on the same stock], whose value will not depend on the price of the stock," according to Black's paper about the topic. LTCM also included the highest paid trader at Salomon Brothers, Larry Hilibrand, and David Mullins Jr., a former Harvard professor and vice chairman of the Federal Reserve.

The fund was leveraged at 50 to 1, and until 1998 it had generated massive returns, supposedly because its mathematical geniuses had made these bets based on the historical relationships between various fixed income securities, such as U.S. Treasury bonds and risky corporate or emerging markets bonds. Almost every Wall Street firm was an investor, and even in a down year—1997—LTCM returns were 17.1 percent after fees.

But by July 1998, things had started to go wrong—and they only got worse once Russia defaulted and investors started to pull out of seemingly safe investments. On September 2, LTCM disclosed that the value of the fund's holdings, once $1.8 billion, had dropped by 44 percent.

Meriwether approached Goldman Sachs co-CEO Jon Corzine for help. Could they be partners? Corzine said he'd think about it, but only if the fund would be willing to accept risk controls and oversight. Meanwhile, the stock prices of all Wall Street banks sank because the market feared that securities firms would have to close out their LTCM positions at fire-sale prices.

Lehman stock plummeted from the mid-40s in August to the low 20s in September.

Warren Buffett agreed to put up $3 billion to shore up LTCM, and Maurice "Hank" Greenberg, the CEO of insurance giant American International Group (AIG), put up $700 million. Corzine led the Wall Street rescue by pledging that Goldman Sachs would put up $300 million—something his co-CEO, Henry Paulson Jr., disagreed with.

Corzine prevailed—at least for the moment.

On September 22, while LTCM was organizing a bankruptcy meeting, Todd Jorn—then Lehman's sales manager responsible for hedge funds—joined Fuld, Russo, Gregory, and Vanderbeek at the New York Federal Reserve at 33 Liberty Street in downtown New York, where each of the investment houses was asked to put in $250 million to shore up LTCM.

Jorn says Fuld didn't think much of the bailout idea, and was even "abrasive" about it. He had reason to be: Lehman was one of the very few houses to have turned down offers to invest in LTCM.

Earlier that summer Meriweather and some associates had come to see Fuld and Cecil and asked them to take 20 percent of the company for $1 billion. Cecil remembers that after the LTCM guys left, Fuld frowned at him and said, "Those guys look scared." To Jorn, Fuld growled, "I want to know what the fuck is going on, and I want to know yesterday." Jorn turned to analyst Ming Xu, who called every trading desk and every sales manager in the United States to try to assemble the firm's entire exposure to LTCM.

"Dick didn't feel like he should put in any goddamned money," Jorn says of the proposed bailout of LTCM. "One, because he didn't have exposure in LTCM, and two, because he thought by putting the money in, it would guarantee that everyone *thought* he had exposure."

David Komansky, then the CEO of Merrill Lynch, later told people that Fuld had said to him, "I'd rather reach into my pants, take out my dick and cut it off" before he would give anything to LTCM.

But Fuld did, eventually, fold. Lehman agreed to put in $100 million, while the others agreed to put in $250 million and formed an oversight board. Bear Stearns argued that since it was LTCM's clearing bank it was already overexposed. Bear Stearns put in nothing.

Jorn recalls: "After the first 24-hour session with the Fed, I went up to Joe Gregory and said, 'Joe, there is this consortium board. We've agreed to put in the $100 million investment. . . . Who is going to be our board member?"

According to Jorn, Gregory replied: "Why don't you just go hang out [at the Fed] and tell me what's going on."

Jorn says, "For such a serious, nearly cataclysmic event, there was a kind of cavalier attitude about it at Lehman."

■ ■ ■

Lehman actually emerged from this crisis stronger and richer. David Einhorn, the 40-year-old founder of the hedge fund Greenlight Capital, says that in 2008 he tried to figure out how Lehman had done so well in the bleak conditions of 1998. "I went back and I read their 10-Qs from May and August and November of 1998," he says, "and research reports from that period. And what struck me was that Lehman, who was rumored to be insolvent during that period, actually got through the entire period without booking any kind of a loss. How had they done it? They'd increased their bets as things got worse. And when the market came back, they made record profits in 1999."

Jorn says he believes that Einhorn is right.

He and Ming had suggested a series of hedges that Lehman could make if LTCM went to zero and was no longer a creditworthy counterparty. They calculated that Lehman had 460 trades (Merrill Lynch, by comparison, had around 5,000) and that this left them vulnerable.

They needed to buy $4 billion worth of 10-year notes, $4 billion of 10-year Treasuries, and options on another $1 billion of 10-year Treasuries to cover themselves. The purchase would be scaled out on a declining interest rate path, because Jorn reckoned that if LTCM collapsed, the Federal Reserve would inject liquidity and lower interest rates.

Jorn never knew if the trade—which he presented to the head of fixed income, Jeffrey Vanderbeek—got executed, but he believes it was. Events came to pass exactly as he and Ming had bet, and Lehman finished the year ahead.

The cruel twist is that Lehman's success in 1998 may have led to its spectacular failure a decade later. Einhorn explains how this experience hurt the firm in 2008: "Based on what they were saying publicly [in 2007], they thought the crisis would only last a couple of months. . . . The idea was in August 2007 not to take the write-down, to double down, and that way when the market comes back, they would make even more money."

In layman's terms: Lehman Brothers doubled down once, and made a killing. It doubled down again 10 years later, and got killed.

■ ■ ■

Despite coming through two harrowing crises with banner profits, Lehman was still getting hammered on the Street by rumors that fall. Gossip varied from the absurd to the sinister. One story said that the firm had invested $1 billion in a Russian satellite that had exploded in outer space; another claimed that the Federal Reserve was looking through the books and was about to take Lehman over; a third had it that Lehman was going to declare bankruptcy at exactly 11.30 P.M. on such and such date—and so forth.

" 'Wounded' Lehman Looks Like Next Merger Target" read the *New York Post* in November 1998. "The omens are ugly," a Lehman banker in London told the *New York Times*.

Cecil recalls that Rumor Storm lasted for about six weeks, and he noticed that the nasty bits of gossip usually appeared on Fridays. "We were now kind of in the Land of Shorts. And a classic trick, if you're shorting a stock, is to circulate some rumor of bad news about that company on a Friday, particularly in the afternoon. Nobody can do much about it, but the traders talk about it over the weekend, and everybody who's got exposure to the subject of the rumor gets nervous over the weekend— when they can't do anything about it, of course. And then they cut their exposure on Monday, driving the price down. And that seemed to be what was happening to us."

Since drops in the stock price are taken as an indication that a company might be in trouble, Lehman knew it was crucial that it calm investors and clients. "We started to get pressure on liquidity," Cecil says. "Basically people wanted larger 'haircuts,' wanted more secured financing, less unsecured financing. It became generally more difficult for us to get financing for certain kinds of assets."

Cecil says that both Jeff Vanderbeek and Steve Lessing, together responsible for all sales, equities, and fixed income, "did an absolutely wonderful job of keeping together the firm's funding base," and kept the firms' clients in place.

Lessing says, "I would spend 16 hours a day on the phone with clients. We'd say, 'This is where the firm is, we're fine, we're viable. We're going to have a profitable quarter. . . . ' At that point the whole executive committee worked extremely hard; we were all hunkered down on the client side, keeping the funding of the firm going. Those were the most intense days that I've experienced in my 22 years—the patch in '98 where there was a real thought that the firm could fail, and we actually ended up having a record year."

Fuld had his own uncharacteristic fix for this problem: he decided to go on the offensive and go out to the market, especially the equity market. He hit the road and visited client after client, along with Cecil and Lehman's talented risk manager, Maureen Miskovic, recently hired from Goldman Sachs.

What Fuld told the market was this: Lehman's credit exposure to hedge funds amounted to $447 million, of which $72 million was uncollateralized. The firm's potential jeopardy in regard to Long-Term Capital Management was $32 million, against $41 million of U.S. Treasury collateral. The firm's emerging markets risk was $305 million. Contrary to the rumors, the firm was in good shape.

This was the moment that all of Fuld's elocution and public speaking lessons paid off. Cecil says Fuld calmed his investors. "Clients were looking at us the way we'd looked at Meriwether—'Do they seem scared, or do they seem comfortable with their position? Do they have a good plan for the short-term period of difficulty and for the longer term?' In times like that, Dick can be very, very effective. And it's kind of a 'What makes you good makes you bad' kind of thing—he was very forceful about the firm. And it worked."

Fuld also worked with Cecil to placate the rating agencies, which wondered if Lehman's credit risk was going up because of pressure around liquidity. At one point Cecil feared Standard & Poor's wouldn't hold its rating. He went to Fuld and said, "We're dead." Fuld replied, "Can't be. Go back." He then lay down in the corridor outside of his office and looked up at the diminutive CFO.

"Do you just want me to lie down like this?"

Cecil went back to S&P and prevailed.

By November the fuss had died down. At the end of the year, the firm had $4.1 billion in revenue—an increase of 6 percent. Earnings per share rose from $4.72 to $5.19, meaning that Lehman shareholders received a 20 percent increase in their common stock dividend.

But Cecil took his time signing off on the balance sheet. He was concerned that as CFO he could announce earnings that spoke of the size of the balance sheet not just for the year-end, but for the future. He wanted to be sure the figures were correct and easily verifiable.

Cecil does not recall Gregory "or the guys in banking" having any involvement in any of this. "Joe had absolutely nothing to do with the financials," he says pointedly.

Yet Gregory's dictated notes in 2002 show that he went berserk over Cecil's hesitation.

"In 1998 John was both CFO and CAO at a time of great stress when everyone was dumping our stock and it got down to 22 and as low as 19 intraday," Gregory wrote. "We needed the CFO to say the firm is financially sound. John responded that he wasn't sure he could say that for threat of being sued. It happened on a conference call and I remember it like it was two seconds ago. We were all at home on the conference call and when he said that, we all went nuts. How could he say that? We were trying to keep the company alive—12 or 13 thousand people's lives were at stake."

Cecil points out that there were not 13,000 lives at stake, since the firm only comprised 7,500 at the time. He also says it did take him a while to get a detailed portrait of the balance sheet together and he wasn't going to rush something so important, nor was he going to tell investors things were okay without giving them solid proof. He has absolutely no recollection of Gregory's reaction, though he remembers the business heads were anxious to placate the market. He was, too, but he was going to make sure of his facts first.

Fuld, according to sources, shared Gregory's frustration with their CFO, who stood his ground. They felt this was a time for Chris Pettit's mantra of *team, team, team* and instead Cecil was holding out on the firm.

In the end—after two weeks of careful analysis, and only when he was truly happy with the financials—Cecil signed. He still believes he was absolutely right to take his time. He reflected recently: "I might point out that if the same care had been taken ten years later on the signing off on the financials, Lehman might have avoided all sorts of problems. It might even still be alive."

Following the earnings report, the SEC ended its investigation and things appeared to return to normal.

■ ■ ■

A colleague says that Fuld never forgave what he viewed as recalcitrance on the part of Cecil, and he made him pay for it down the road. Tom Russo says that although he believed Cecil was just being "meticulous . . . others thought that he was just more worried about himself than the firm."

Cecil thought the episode was over and just wanted to get on with his job. He was startled when he later heard what Gregory thought of him. Gregory wrote that "he was a man who thought he was going to be 'offered the keys to the city' but 'Dick didn't really want him in that job.' John made a series of mistakes and some really bad ones, especially in 1998, that made Dick very uncomfortable with John."

When asked what ultimately happened to Cecil, Bob Genirs wrote succinctly to a colleague: "Joe shot him."

■ ■ ■

Dick Fuld admitted to his senior managers that he had learned two things from 1998. Before the Russian crisis, he believed that talking to the press never worked out. "I was wrong," he said during one of the summer retreats he held for his executive committee. "It was one of the major lessons I needed to learn."

The other was that there was no time to lose.

Lehman could not stay vulnerable. Goldman Sachs was now finally going to float—offer its shares to the public on the stock market. He urged everyone at the company, whenever he could, to "bleed Lehman green."

"I want you to make money for this company," he said to everyone on staff. "Just keep thinking about ways to make money."

Lehman had already opened offices in Tel Aviv, Beijing, and Singapore in the mid-1990s. In addition to broker-dealers in Mexico, they had a banking license in Tokyo, a reporting dealer who was able to make trades in France, and a primary dealer closely monitoring the central bank in Italy. Fuld wanted Lehman's stock price to get up to $150 per share.

In 1999, Bradley Jack was promoted to be the sole head of banking; Cecil was still CFO and chief administrative officer (CAO); Vanderbeek was still head of global fixed income; Gregory was still head of equities; Michael McKeever was co-head of private equity; Lessing was head of global sales and research. Fuld was still growing into his role. He wanted people near him he could trust, but after the many power grabs that came after Pettit was forced out, he didn't know if the friends he trusted today would be enemies tomorrow.

By 1999, the front-runner to take over Fuld's throne was the young and popular Bradley Jack. He was beloved by Fuld and by all those who worked for him, even though some people thought that he was "in over his skis" running banking, because his background was in capital markets. Like Gregory, Lessing, Tucker, Pettit, and Fuld, Jack had grown up in Lehman Commercial Paper Inc. (LCPI). He was tall, blond, athletic, good-looking, and very charismatic. Like Pettit, with whom he was often compared, Jack was a natural speaker. But unlike the soulful, militaristic Pettit, he had a lightness about him.

Jack had met his wife, Karin, in the office. She worked for him, recruiting on the sales desk. After they were married in 1991, she became a housewife, but one who understood the ways of Lehman and never demanded anything of her husband that might interfere with his work.

■ ■ ■

Fuld still hadn't filled the COO spot vacated by Pettit. He just couldn't trust anyone to get that close to him—not even Jack. "The board wanted him to have a line of succession," recalls Karin Jack, "but it just wasn't ever planned."

This power vacuum was viewed as a weakness over at Goldman Sachs, Lehman's archrival. Fuld may not have known it, but Goldman Sachs viewed Lehman as merely a yappy terrier, snapping at its heels.

"Lehman always thought they were fighting Goldman Sachs, but we never thought they were even in our league," says a former member of Goldman's executive committee. "We didn't believe they had superior skill sets," he continues. "Risk taking was their way to distinguish themselves. We were a bit resentful, because we thought that they were overly risked, whereas we thought we were very management focused and very risk management focused." The Goldman guys also thought (not incorrectly) that Fuld ruled imperiously, that all the senior management people beneath him were mere court jesters telling him what they thought he wanted to hear.

In 1999, of all the senior management, only Cecil was ever a dissenting or even questioning voice; the rest were the equivalent of a sycophantic court, all jostling for power—led by Gregory, technically the head of equities, but also Fuld's buffer, his field general.

Sometimes, according to senior staff, Gregory would almost kneel in meetings to look up at Fuld as he talked. When Fuld made speeches to New York managing directors, Gregory could be seen sitting in the front row, almost falling off his chair to pay attention. "It was both funny and sort of appalling to watch the degree to which Joe sucked up to Dick," says one former senior executive.

Following the culling of both Pettit and the equities team, Gregory now had a reputation as a dangerous henchman. No one wanted to antagonize either him or Fuld. Gregory was notorious for being underhanded, for acting invisibly. "He'd stab you from the back, not the front," says one person. One executive recalls that Gregory told him he was doing fantastically well just two weeks before firing him.

From then on there was an in-house motto: "You never want to be told you are doing well by Joe." It was code for "You're fired."

Not surprisingly, Gregory's new role brought with it new nicknames. On top of "Joe the Wedge," he was now also "Uncle Joe," after the mass murderer Joseph Stalin, and "Darth Vader." Gregory never saw himself as anything like these caricatures. Even as he grew rich and acquired a domestic staff of 30, a fleet of boats, multiple houses, and private planes, he still saw himself as "ordinary Joe." "I'm a man of the people," he liked to say—and he told all incoming executives that Lehman men and women were *not* the sort of people who needed to check their bank balances regularly, insinuating that he never did that. In other words, though Lehmanites were bankers, they were not supposed to be interested in making money . . . at least not for themselves.

"Joe would be absolutely horrified if he realized how people came to view him," says Bob Shapiro. "At bottom, Joe is an emotional man, who deeply wants to be liked."

After Gregory, next in line to attend Lehman's King Richard was Tom Russo, the general counsel, widely considered Fuld's "intellectual shield." Russo was Lehman's public voice—before Congress, the Senate, and international financial panels. He loved to talk and share ideas, and he has a nascent passion for producing movies. Within Lehman, Russo was well-liked.

A few of the heirs apparent in the Fuld coterie came from outside the U.S. office. By 1999 Asia was headed up by Jasjit "Jesse" Bhattal, an immaculately dressed Indian who often sported a silk ascot. When the Asians videoconferenced in, many of the New Yorkers felt shabbily put together by comparison.

Bhattal was considered a huge step up in every way from his predecessor, Dan Tyree. Tyree weighed 350 pounds, spilled food on his clothes, and often slept through operating committee meetings. In the late 1990s, Fuld went with Tyree to a client lunch in Tokyo where local food—as in fish—was served. Tyree ordered a steak. He may as well have ordered an execution, since Fuld got rid of him as soon as he could.

Bhattal also won plaudits from his peers because he had a phobia about flying (which he never conquered), yet of all the Lehman executive committee members he probably flew the most. Watching him as the plane took off and landed, however, was a grueling experience, says someone who flew with him. "He'd grip the arms of the seat and hyperventilate noisily." Yet they had to hand it Bhattal, he was courageous: He flew.

He showed a similar commitment in the office. When he was made head of Asia, he did not pretend to understand the trading business. His background was in banking. "He went and sat on the trading floor and basically never left until he'd understood it thoroughly," says a New York–based colleague. "He was an inspiration to all of us."

The other overseas member of the Fuld circle was a young, ambitious British banker, Jeremy Isaacs, who was appointed head of all Europe in 2000. He was only 36 at the time. He had never gone to university. Every time Fuld landed on the tarmac in London, Isaacs was there to greet him. During trips throughout Europe, he almost never left Fuld's side— something some say Fuld would occasionally mock him for. "Jeremy, I don't need you to babysit me," he'd say as the Brit followed him into every meeting. Isaacs says, in fact, Fuld *asked* for him to be there.

As Isaac's influence in the firm grew, so did his girth. In 2003 he imported a five-star chef into Lehman's dining room in a penthouse in London's Canary Wharf, the new home of Lehman London (which he had gotten British Prime Minister Gordon Brown to inaugurate). In no time the Lehman dining room was labeled the best corporate executive dining room in town, which was an in-house joke in New York, as was the fact that Isaacs's London office was the only office in all of Lehman that was bigger than Dick Fuld's. Isaacs points out that he did not design it himself. Rather, Fran Kittredge, the New York–based head of philanthropy had.

Isaacs's weight gain became a cause for concern during a hike up Bald Mountain, at the Fulds' summer retreat in Sun Valley.

"We were seriously concerned that he might not make it," recalls a colleague.

Isaacs agreed. "It was a very unpleasant experience," he says. He hired a boxing coach when he returned to London. "I still have the trainer," he says. "Climbing up that hill gave me the kick I needed to get into shape." Isaacs also bought himself a home next to Russian billionaire Roman Abramovich in Cap d'Antibes and had himself a custom-made E-Type Jaguar. Stevie Wonder sang at his 40th birthday party in London.

He liked his surroundings to meet certain standards. In 2006, Isaacs arrived at the annual World Economic Forum at Davos, Switzerland, and found that his hotel room fell well below his standards. He berated the Lehman corporate staff for their shoddy organization.

Behind Bhattal and Isaacs came an influx of new Lehmanites. The firm started an aggressive hiring campaign for the brightest and best as the stock price got higher. The firm recruited primarily from 11 well-known business schools: Chicago, Columbia, Wharton, Tuck, Fuqua, Stern, UCLA, Kellogg, Harvard, MIT's Sloan, and Stanford. MBA candidates who joined the firm called the atmosphere one of "scrappy, friendly survivors."

Another commented: "People have been through a lot together, and they are very loyal to each other."

Another: "This place is as close to a meritocracy as it gets—I've been given more responsibility than I'd ever imagined."

"It's an aggressive firm that will let you take risk, if you can justify it," wrote yet another.

■ ■ ■

In April 2000, the executive committee was arguing about emerging markets, especially about whether the firm should open an office in South Africa.

"I thought it was a very bad idea, because we were never going to make money in these [emerging markets] businesses," Cecil recalls. "And banking's argument was that to be a global player you've got to do it, and banking is very revenue-oriented, not profit-oriented. And so we'd been having this debate forever."

The debate centered on the fact that trading in emerging markets necessarily meant taking on a lot of risk—four or five years of success could be followed by four or five years of loss. But that was the game. The problem was that every now and again a crisis (such as the Mexican peso fiasco, or the Russian default) would pop up and that risk might be enough to sink the entire firm. The debate, Cecil says, "came to a head in early 2000."

First, Fuld decided they were going to get Lehman out of emerging markets. As head of equities, this task fell to Gregory. He brought all his traders and salespeople in emerging markets together, told them what the new protocol was, and fired them.

Then, just hours later, Fuld changed his mind. He called a meeting of the executive committee and said, "We're going to stay in." According to Cecil, an exasperated Gregory stood up and said, "I quit."

He couldn't believe Fuld would do this right after he'd executed a mass firing.

Fuld hustled Gregory out of the room and the two men huddled in Fuld's office.

A few days later Fuld swung by Cecil's office and told him what had transpired. He then said that he wanted to "bring Joe upstairs with us. He will think differently. He will think about the business differently. I am going to make him chief administrative officer and you will be chief financial officer."

Cecil was surprised. At that time, he was both CAO and CFO. Cecil says Fuld told him, "You will still be the CFO—basically the two of you will be able to get things done and have your way with the rest of the executive committee, because you're the two most powerful personalities on the committee."

Cecil believed that Gregory was tired of running a business and had asked for the job and that Fuld, who hated infighting at the top, thought he could defer "senior staff management" onto Gregory. Cecil also realized he was being demoted, though Fuld—perhaps shrewdly—pretended not to notice.

"It'll be great; you'll be the CFO," he kept saying to a baffled Cecil.

"But I am *already* the CFO," retorted Cecil.

"I told him that Joe and I don't often see eye to eye," Cecil recalls, "and he said, 'When we bring Joe up here, he'll kind of adopt our point of view.'"

"He thought that bringing somebody up to corporate was kind of a cure-all—all of a sudden you think differently; you think about what's right for the firm, all the time," says Cecil. "It was hard on me, obviously, because I was giving up a big part of my responsibilities, which Dick just couldn't get. He kept saying to me, 'But you're going to be the CFO, and that's a huge job!' And I kept saying, 'But I *am* the CFO.'

"I said to Dick at one point that I thought this move was going to make life even more difficult for me, and I was tired and frustrated. And so I said that if he made Joe and me co-presidents, I'd do it, because then I still had to battle it out with Joe but at least I could turn around and tell the [executive committee] what to do. Dick basically said no, partly because I think he was very skittish about what had happened with Chris—he didn't want to be walled off from the organization again. He said no, and so I said, 'I quit.'"

Fuld acted as though this conversation had never happened. He kept appearing in Cecil's office, even after Cecil's notice had been given in April 2000, to the point that Cecil moved his office to a different floor in the building in June 2000. He hung around only at Fuld's request to make a smooth transition. David Goldfarb, the former controller, was eventually made CFO. Unlike Cecil, Goldfarb talked often and loudly.

"Goldfarb rubbed a lot people the wrong way," says a colleague. "He was very vocal and very critical of everyone else's divisions, which, of course, the division heads didn't like. They viewed him as just an overopinionated accountant. He had never run a division."

Fuld, however, liked the fact that Goldfarb didn't care if he undermined division heads in front of them. It was refreshing around that table to hear from someone not paralyzed with a fear of saying the wrong thing.

Chapter 12

Lehman's Desperate Housewives

On Wall Street, they pay you so much that they own you. You
know? So it's different. They have your soul. You gave it to
them for the money.

—*Karin (Mrs. Bradley) Jack*

Lehman senior executives were expected to have wives. And,
if possible, they were supposed to be happy with them—or
at least pretend to be. One of the things that troubled Dick
Fuld—openly—about Scott Freidheim, the young banker who was
appointed managing director, office of the chairman, in 1996 and then
became global head of strategy in 2005, was that he waited until he
was 42 to get married. Fuld wanted all his executives to be as settled
domestically as he was.

He hated to see signs of marital discord. During the annual
Lehman retreat at the Fulds' ranch in Sun Valley, it wasn't uncommon
for Dick to pull one of his guests aside and ask him numerous questions
about his home life to make sure everything was all right.

"Are you all having trouble?" he asked Bradley Jack, after over-hearing an argument between Jack and his wife Karin. "He *really* wanted to know," recalls Karin. "He didn't think Brad and I looked happy enough. It really worried him." (Brad Jack concurred with Karin's recollection.)

No one ever heard the Fulds argue—although Karin Jack says she heard Dick berate Kathy when she was 10 minutes late bring-ing the wives back from an expedition in Sun Valley. This was a rare occurrence. Within his own family, Dick had a rule. He told his children, "Disagree with me all you want in private. But never air your domestic grievances in public." The Fulds were, publicly at least, one of the happiest couples on the planet.

■ ■ ■

But, as the dramas played out in the Lehman offices, they also played out among the wives. Many of them were as competitive as their husbands, and they ruthlessly criticized or exploited any perceived weaknesses of their rivals.

The wives of executive committee members had to attend numerous Lehman functions, such as the annual induction of managing directors. They were expected to contribute to the numerous philanthropic causes Lehman supported (this number grew greatly once those endeavors fell under the purview of Gregory). Each couple was expected to make annual donations to the American Red Cross, Harlem's Children Zone, the American Friends of London Business School, and various hospitals—all of which often totaled more than $32 million each year in Lehman donations.

Over the years there were more and more corporate and social events that the wives were expected to attend—even ones that weren't directly related to Lehman.

Kathy Fuld collected modern art. She particularly liked Cy Twombly, Brice Marden, and Jasper Johns. In 2002, she was put on the board of the Museum of Modern Art (MoMA), and by 2007 was a vice chairman. Not only were the wives of Lehman's senior management expected to attend MoMA evenings (along with their husbands), but they also "were told exactly how much they had to donate," says one. There is now a wing of MoMA dedicated to Kathy and Richard S. Fuld Jr.

Whatever his influence and his success at marriage, not even Dick Fuld was powerful enough to abolish divorce. In April 1999, Teresa Gregory filed for divorce. No one was surprised. Joe'd often asked colleagues about their wives and exclaimed how beautiful they were. Teresa Gregory was athletic and fun, but according to one of Gregory's colleagues, "she didn't fit in at the Lehman dinners."

Karin Jack recalls one evening at the Fulds' apartment in the city when Teresa Gregory was left standing on her own. "She needed help, guidance, and Joe didn't give her any," Karin recalls.

■ ■ ■

By 2000, Joe Gregory had remarried, to a dark-haired Greek-born beauty named Niki Golod, who was recently divorced. Gregory and Golod had met through their sons, who were best friends at school.

"Isn't it great that now they'll be stepbrothers?" he used to say to colleagues.

Niki Gregory loved the clothes and the jewels that her husband lavished on her. She was known to take trips to Los Angeles just to shop. She gave the Lehman wives tours of her vast shoe closets in their Huntington home. One person taken on the tour described the closet as being "twice the size of the Jimmy Choo store in New York." It was filled with Christian Louboutin, Manolo Blahnik, and Chanel. It included every style imaginable: pumps, stilletos, boots of every height, ballet flats, strappy evening heels. "Many of them had never been worn," remarked one awed visitor.

Like her husband, Niki outsourced all her needs to a personal staff of about 30. "I don't think she ever set a table in her life for a dinner party," said one wife. "It wouldn't occur to her to do that."

After Niki was diagnosed with breast cancer and had a mastectomy, Lehman executives (at Gregory's request) were told to give like crazy to breast cancer awareness. "For the senior-level guys it was approximately 50 grand each; for the executive committee, approximately 100." Fran Kittredge, who was responsible for planning all Lehman's corporate events (even overseeing the details of the flower arrangements, which she had photographed and e-mailed to her before green-lighting them), told people what "their number was" each year.

The firm gave to political candidates as well. Fuld, say colleagues, was not loyal to either party; he went with whichever candidate he liked. The firm made sure it donated equally to both parties. However, since most of the executive committee, including Fuld, were Democrats, if a Republican looked like he might vault into the White House, Steve Lessing (a Republican) was designated to "handle" him. In 2007, after he'd retired as governor of Florida, Jeb Bush was made a private equity adviser and given an office on the 31st floor.

■ ■ ■

The executive committee members and their wives were all expected to attend the annual summer get-together at Dick and Kathy's ranch near Bald Mountain in Sun Valley, Idaho. One wife remembers, "It was this weird combination of business and then competition between wives and their husbands. Hiking was mandatory for all."

Karin Jack says that trip was always "an absolute nightmare for the wives to pack for." The evenings required pretty dresses, jewelry, and Manolo Blahnik shoes, while they needed hiking gear during the day.

The couples got there on the two planes owned by Lehman, known as "Lehman Air." The biggest—a G4 luxury jet—was known as LB1. That was the plane Fuld always used. Kittredge arranged for every person or couple to be met at the airport by a driver with an SUV. The waiting line of dark-glassed SUVs was almost comical to behold, according to one attendee. It was like a scene from a movie depicting the motorcade waiting for a landing president. Except this was not the president. This was just the Lehman Brothers executive committee and their wives.

Kittredge also flew in personal chefs to cook the meals. "Breakfast was sublime," says one diner. "It was the breakfast of your dreams."

The first meal of the day began promptly at 7:30 A.M. and ended an hour later. Then Fuld would sit in a hard-backed armchair beside the fireplace in his drawing room with the men in chairs and on sofas around him. Most of them would be wearing khakis and golf shirts. (The group would break at 12:30 for lunch and golf.) The women meanwhile shopped, biked, or went antiquing.

Everyone was supposed to be dressed appropriately.

This meant that men should wear khaki pants and either a golf shirt or a button-down. Steve Lessing almost always wore a shirt with the logo from one of the dozen country clubs he belonged to. Skip

McGee usually wore a button-down shirt and khakis. Jesse Bhattal stuck with his silk ascots.

But as the years went by, there were some nongolfers in the group who had no clue what the dress code was and didn't much care. This was a grave mistake—Fuld cared what people looked like, both in and out of the office. He always looked immaculate; he wore a navy suit to work, purchased from Richards department store in Greenwich, Connecticut, along with a white shirt, Hermès tie, and shiny black lace-ups in the British shoemaker Church's style. He had a tailor put matching stitching in each of his suit pants and jackets so he could easily see which tops went with which bottoms. "Sloppy dress, sloppy thinking" went his motto.

Lehman was the last of all the Wall Street firms to go casual on Fridays. In the late 1990s Fuld reluctantly called the operating committee to have a vote on whether they wanted it, and to his dismay they all did. He sighed, "I don't know what this means." He reinforced the point: "You know what? This democratic bullshit has gone on for long enough."

Gregory chimed in: "Oh, I don't want this either, Dick. We are a different generation. We don't believe in it, but we have to do this for the younger people." Fuld compromised by letting the entire firm go casual on Fridays except for the 10th (executive) floor. As he agreed to it he said, "It is a dark day for the firm."

In the summer of 2006, Roger Nagioff—a London-based co-head of equities, who owns a fleet of cars, including a Ferrari Daytona—arrived in Sun Valley and won the unofficial "worst-dressed prize" when he showed up in army cargo pants and a black turtleneck sweater. "I don't play golf and I do not apologize for that," Nagioff humorously explained. "My clothes were far too cool but Dick made me change because he was worried I would not be allowed on the course so I had to borrow some of those dreadful golf clothes."

"Dick didn't lay off, teasing him mercilessly all weekend," recalls one witness. Matters were not helped by Nagioff's atrocious beginner's golf. He was forced to play as part of the team spirit for the Lehman Brothers Cup (a silver trophy).

A member of his foursome recalls the agony of the 18th hole. Nagioff's group, despite the handicap of Nagioff, was in the lead. "All he had to do was to drive the ball. Now, if he'd just stood down and taken a bye [in other words, not hit], we'd have been okay. Unfortunately, he had a go, and touched the ball. . . . It went backwards way off the golf course, straight into the junk." Nagioff disputes that he had a choice. "As the worst golfer they had to count my best shot. I had to try." He does not dispute the outcome. It was a disaster. The team had to take another stroke penalty. They lost. (Nagioff might have done well to have followed the example of the inimitable Jesse Bhattal. Bhattal, too, had been a beginner at golf until very recently; but he believed that if one were to rise at Lehman, one took golf as seriously as work. Within a handful of years Bhattal managed to acquire a handicap of eight strokes.)

Nagioff's New York counterpart, the co-head of global equities, Rob Shafir, was similarly deaf to the importance Fuld attached to attire. In 2004 Shafir arrived at the Mark Hotel on Madison Avenue in New York for an off-site meeting. Shafir was five minutes late (Fuld was a stickler for punctuality) and as he looked around the room Shafir realized he was also the only person dressed business casual (no tie, Oxford shirt, and chinos).

"What?" Shafir asked as he caught everyone's horrified stares. "It's an off-site."

Fuld looked at him. "Rob: off-site, yes. Out of mind, no."

Karin Jack recalls hating the rigorous hike up Bald Mountain, so one year she arrived with a fake cast in order to pretend she had broken her leg. She was flummoxed when Niki Gregory arrived with a real broken leg and said she planned to climb regardless. "So I brought that stupid cast out there, thinking I could get out of the hike, and then Nikki shows up in one. I wanted to just die," Jack says.

"The competition between the men basically spread over to us," Jack continues. (She says she made sure she always arrived with a ready supply of jokes to keep Fuld amused. "I felt like a performing flea.")

When the women went shopping, there was always a pecking order. Usually, the spouses of the men holding the most senior positions in the company got to ride in Kathy Fuld's car. Karin Jack was the closest of all the wives to Kathy. Like Kathy, she had once worked at Lehman. Like Kathy, she was also blonde, pretty, and stylish. They used to go antiquing together. Dick liked Karin. Sometimes he would humorously push her from behind up the final stretch of the hike. Like Kathy, she understood the unwritten rules: If you were married to a Lehman god, you belonged to Lehman. Dick Fuld used to acknowledge as much when executives became managing directors. In a welcoming ceremony where spouses were present, he thanked them for all the "canceled dinners, weekends, and vacations" they were about to go through and no doubt already had.

"Lehman was his life," Karin Jack says of her husband. "I mean, Brad didn't do one single thing for 20 years that wasn't Lehman Brothers—not a postcard, nor a Christmas present, nor a phone call to his family. I did everything, unless it had a Lehman stamp on it. As a Lehman wife, you raise your kids by yourself. You have your babies by yourself in the hospital. And then you're supposed to be happy and pretty and smiling when there's an event, and you really would like to strangle somebody." Brad Jack agreed with Karin's sentiments.

One time, she had to manage the move to a new house on her own. She later received a card and flowers from Teddy Roosevelt (a managing director at Lehman and the great-grandson of President Theodore Roosevelt). The card said: "I know that all we do is steal your husband, and I'm sorry you had to move by yourself."

But that was just what was expected of all the wives. "I knew the culture," she says, "so I knew he couldn't come home if there was an important meeting. I was in labor with our daughter and had to lie there without him. . . . But I wouldn't get mad at him—he had called the entire Hong Kong office in for a meeting. We knew that it would have been used against him. If you made a personal choice that hurt Lehman, it was over for you." Brad recalls: "It's true. Karin went into labor. I got into the car but only made it three miles because the traffic was snarled up. I had to turn around and deal with the Hong Kong office who *had* flown in to see me. She was right. And she was very understanding. I had to be in that meeting."

Karin remembers the time one of her children had a seizure brought on by a high fever the day she and her husband were scheduled to look at the new McMansion Joe and Niki Gregory were building on Long Island. "It was just the six of us—Dick and Kathy, Joe and Niki, Brad and I. We were using Joe's helicopter. But I said, 'I have to take my son to the pediatrician.' So they landed the Sikorsky near our home and waited for me, and they were not leaving without me. Can you imagine the pressure? I have this really sick child, but I know that if I don't get on that helicopter, it's going to hurt Brad. (Her husband agreed.)

"[The Fulds] paid a lot of lip service to the importance of children and your family, but no one really cared."

Another executive who found this to be true was Shafir, who by 2000 had replaced Gregory as co-head of global equities, along with Roger Nagioff. By 2004, he was sole head. In 2005, according to Andrew Ross Sorkin's *Too Big to Fail*, Shafir discovered that he had a child with cystic fibrosis and he asked for time off. When he returned, he was demoted from the executive committee to run hedge funds. Several months later, Gregory asked him to move to Asia.

Shafir reportedly replied: "Asia? You have to be kidding, Joe. You know about my kid. . . ." Gregory didn't care, and didn't budge. In 2007 Shafir quit, moving to Credit Suisse.

■ ■ ■

Niki Gregory was as skillful a political operator as her husband—and just as ambitious. Some of the wives were a little intimidated by her, while others were just cautious.

One time in Sun Valley, both Brad and Karin Jack noticed that Niki Gregory was ignoring Martha McDade, the wife of Bart McDade, who was then running fixed income.

Martha was a civil engineer who had founded her own environmentally focused engineering company as well as a charity to help improve the lives of amputees. "She was a smart woman who was always herself, just a fabulous person," said one wife. On that Sun Valley trip, Martha asked some of the other wives: "Why will Niki Gregory not look at or talk to me?" Jack immediately interpreted the snub as a sign that Bart McDade was likely to be demoted or fired.

In early summer 2005, not long after the incident, McDade was moved from the position of head of fixed income to replace Shafir as the head of equities. Some saw the move as a demotion, but McDade was so successful in his new job that it simply increased his power base within the firm. Now two huge divisions respected him.

After McDade's demotion, the wives realized that their husbands' fates at Lehman would first become evident within their own circle: that, in fact, the social dynamics of the firm would initially play out among themselves. "The women can't hide their disdain for someone they know is on the way out. It's like the herd leaving someone with a broken leg behind," one says.

Chapter 13

The Young Lions

One of the great things about our firm is that if one of our people wants to get something done, such as finding the best doctor in the world, Lehman Brothers is small enough and flat enough that people are accessible where that can happen.

— *Steve Lessing*

In the 1990s Dick Fuld tried to make sure that at least one person in his entourage was whip-smart and unafraid to tell him the truth. The only way to do this was to appoint someone near him who would be content to remain under him, and be docile with regard to the rest of the senior team. "Dick was clever about this," says Tom Hill. "He found a young talent who wouldn't jostle the rest."

Until April 1996, Mike Odrich, Fuld's chief of staff, had been that person. Odrich was immensely likable, very bright, and completely loyal. He had attended Stanford and Columbia Business School. He had a single-digit handicap in golf. He had suited Fuld perfectly. But it was time for him to move on and build up Lehman's fledgling private equity division, which at that point consisted of little more than a merchant bank. Odrich's last big job as Fuld's chief of staff was to find his own replacement. Fuld asked Odrich to bring him the sharpest young brain in the firm.

Odrich sent him a redheaded graduate of Northwestern University with an MBA from the Kellogg School of Management named Scott Freidheim. At Northwestern, Freidheim had been the captain for the university's soccer team. He had been hired by Odrich and Hill in 1991.

Scott was the son of Cyrus F. Freidheim, the former vice chairman of Booz Allen & Hamilton and CEO of Chiquita. Freidheim was 31 years old at the time of his hiring, and was a senior vice president working in banking. He was, in many ways, like Fuld: a good athlete and intensely competitive—ruthlessly so, if need be—but he could also be charming. And he was extremely loyal.

When Fuld offered him the job, Freidheim immediately accepted. "Why don't you think about it overnight?" Fuld asked him. "Sure. I'll humor you," said Freidheim. "Then I'll come back tomorrow and say I want the job."

Fuld looked at him quizzically. Most people didn't speak to him like that. Fuld preferred it when people treated him like the scary gorilla.

Freidheim knew this promotion was putting him in a precarious but potentially life-altering position. Mary Anne Rasmussen, then director of human resources, met with him about the job and he mulled it over, and reportedly told her, "I suppose that if you want to let it rip, get close to the sun. But you had better be comfortable with knowing that it's either going to work out spectacularly well or it's going to blow up in flames. It will not be an average experience."

■ ■ ■

Freidheim struggled to engage with his boss for a while, and Joe Gregory was reportedly far from helpful. Colleagues say he considered Freidheim an obstacle—that he got in the way of Gregory's direct access to Fuld. But Fuld also wanted to test his chief of staff, and make sure he paid his dues and earned credibility. So Fuld never offered Freidheim a simple "How are you?" or "How was your weekend?"

Freidheim didn't respond well to this, and Fuld was growing wary of his latest chief of staff. "Is this guy really the right person?" he reportedly asked Odrich.

"Give him a chance," said Odrich. "You'll see."

Two years into his tenure, colleagues recall, Freidheim felt he needed to make a breakthrough. He thought about who Fuld really was and what would appeal to him. Freidheim considered the things that mattered most to Fuld. "Dick adored his family," he later told colleagues. "And he was just as passionate about work. When there was a problem, and when no one else could handle it, we'd wheel him in, and he'd take care of it."

Freidheim remembered a documentary he'd seen, *Eternal Enemies: Lions and Hyenas.* He brought the video into his next meeting with Fuld. As the meeting ended, Fuld was becoming aggressive about something, and ordered Freidheim to repeat something he had just said. Freidheim said, "Okay, Ntwadumela. Whatever you want."

Fuld leaned forward. "What?" he said.

Freidheim said again, "Whatever you want, Ntwadumela."

Fuld tipped back in his chair, took off his glasses, and looked at Freidheim. "This better be good," he said.

Freidheim described the documentary to his boss: Lions and hyenas go after a wildebeest, and in the confusion of the kill, one lioness finds herself on the wrong side of the territorial boundary, and she's surrounded by hyenas.

"And the hyenas are slowly—there must be 40 of them—surrounding the lioness. She's trying to fight them off, but they're all keeping their distance. But one by one, they dart in and bite her, then dart away. It's clear that they are winning, and she is going to die.

"Then, one of the two males—Ntwadumela—hears what is going on in the distance. He was sleeping, but he gets up, starts heading toward the hyenas at a trot. And then he starts running.

"As he gets close to the pack of hyenas, he picks up his pace, picks out the matriarch, and goes straight for her. The matriarch is the top dog in the pack of hyenas. Ntwadumela catches the matriarch, bites her on the back of the neck, throws her in the air, breaks her neck. She's dead. Everyone goes home. Game over."

Freidheim paused, then said: "*Ntwadumela* is Botswana for 'He who greets with fire.' And Dick, that would be you."

From then on, Freidheim called Fuld Ntwadumela whenever he could. And Fuld loved it.

Freidheim rose to become one of Fuld's most trusted confidants. Ten years later, he'd give Fuld a bust of a lion to put on his mantel.

■ ■ ■

The fact that Lehman's strength was in fixed income—namely as a bond shop—now worked to its advantage. Wall Street was slowly being taken over by capital markets guys: the same guys advisory bankers of yore had looked down their noses at. By the mid-1990s, Morgan Stanley (where John Mack was president), Goldman Sachs (Jon Corzine), and Lehman Brothers (Fuld) were all led by men who had started in capital markets. The high-stakes gamblers were now in charge of the casino.

"This was the time that people's balance sheets grew significantly," says Bob Steel, a retired vice chair of Goldman Sachs and former undersecretary of the U.S. Treasury. "I don't believe these things are accidents."

Leverage became an important word. So did *mortgages*. As the housing market grew, mortgage-backed securities became the devil's dice—and no one was more aggressive in this field than Lehman, under the leadership of its longtime real estate guru, Mark Walsh.

"Walsh had a lot of credibility because he had a very good long-term track record investing in commercial real estate," John Cecil says. "And so when Dick and others decided to improve firm performance even further, by taking proprietary risk, he was one of the guys that they wanted to see go . . . and he did. Ramping up to the end, you probably see a rapid growth of the assets under Mark's control."

In 2000, Fuld rewarded Walsh for all the money he had been making in real estate by naming him co-head of a new private equity group that invested in real estate. Walsh raised $1.6 billion in pension funds and delivered an internal rate of return of more than 30 percent over the next few years. He raised $2.4 billion for a second fund, which generated 15 percent until it closed in 2005. Lehman owned just 20 percent of the funds, but if outside investors passed on a deal, the fund managers could use Lehman money.

If they won—and until 2006 they were winning big—they got huge bonuses. Walsh's commercial real estate department was not the only one to rise within Lehman. So too did the residential housing, namely mortgages—which Lehman both originated and securitized (that is, diced up and sold off as financial pieces to clients) under its fixed income group. It was so prolific in this area that a senior member of the Federal Reserve would later say, "A lot of people thought of Lehman as a bond shop; but really it became a mortgage shop."

Lehman was slowly transforming itself from an operation that survived deal to deal into a more streamlined, multifaceted shop. In 1999 it lead-managed Qualcomm's $1.1 billion initial public offering (IPO); served as Olivetti's adviser in the $34 billion acquisition of Telecom Italia—later hailed by *The Banker* magazine as "the deal of the year"; advised MediaOne in its $63 billion merger with AT&T (*Institutional Investor's* M&A deal of the year); and assisted US West in its $48 billion deal with Qwest Communications. The firm was also an adviser to Honeywell International in the acquisition of Pittway Corporation—the deal of the year for *Investment Dealers' Digest.*

That year Lehman also announced an agreement with Fidelity Investments to offer its research and a host of products to the company, a leading force in the mutual fund industry. It acquired Delaware Savings Bank to leverage online technology by providing a consumer bank. In 2000, to bolster one of its top moneymaking divisions, Lehman hired ex-Salomon Chief Equity Strategist David Shulman as the senior real estate investment trust (REIT) analyst.

On the UK banking side it hired John Williams, the sought-after investment banker who led the demutualization of Abbey National—transforming it into a joint stock company—and was an adviser to National Westminster Bank. It also hired Will Draper, a widely respected analyst from HSBC Bank, to strengthen Lehman Europe.

Another notable hire that year was Holly Becker, from Salomon Smith Barney, who was brought in to cover Internet equity research. At 43, Becker was the top-ranked Internet research analyst on Wall Street, according to *Institutional Investor,* and was married to Michael Zimmerman, one of the rising stars at Steve Cohen's hard-charging hedge fund, SAC Capital.

With all its new hires, Lehman continued to prosper. One person who worked at Lehman then says employees who had been asked to buy stock in 1998 made eight or nine times their investment "within three years."

By the end of 2000, Lehman had opened offices in Rome, Stockholm, Amsterdam, and Munich. The firm brought in revenues of $7.7 billion—and a net income of $1.78 billion. It even joined forces with nemesis Goldman Sachs to lead a $3 billion global bond offering for the World Bank, the first international bond offering to be marketed, sold, and traded through the Internet to both retail and institutional investors.

On July 16, 2001, *Business Week* wrote a laudatory piece under the headline: "Lehman Brothers: So Who Needs to Be Big?" Lehman was proving that despite its smaller size, it could compete with the titans of Wall Street—as Pettit had once dreamed. According to an in-house history, senior management believed that Lehman's size was a chief selling point: All aspects of the bank could service a client without conflict. The bankers didn't contend with the traders. The "one firm" motto translated into profits. A corporate video made that year shows an unusually relaxed Fuld boasting, "There are no walls here."

That year, as Lehman celebrated its 150th anniversary at a black-tie gala in the Museum of the City of New York, it joined the S&P 500 index and its stock price rose above $100 for the first time.

Like the rest of the country, Lehman was prospering, and feeling mighty good about itself.

Chapter 14

9/11

When you're in one of these tragedies, people just do what they have to do, whatever that is. Some are brave; some are not—they just do what they've got to do.

—*Joe Gregory, "The Modern History"*

Joe Gregory, watching the markets at his desk, thought he saw a plane streak across the sky. He looked again out the window of his office and across the Hudson River, and saw nothing but the glint and glare of the Hoboken skyline in the morning sun. Then the floor beneath his feet shook with a terrible boom. It was 8:47 A.M.

Down the hall, on the 10th floor of 3 World Financial Center, Scott Freidheim's assistant, Marna Ringel, rushed to the window in the offices of Lehman's headquarters and screamed: "It's a bomb!"

Paul Cohen, a senior vice president who had been at Lehman longer than just about anyone else, was in an office facing the Twin Towers. He went straight to Gregory and said he thought a plane had hit the World Trade Center, maybe a twin-engine Cessna. Dick Fuld's assistant, Marianne Burke, sat slumped at her desk, doing her best to remain calm. As the phones began to ring all around her, Burke went to the window and saw a terrifying confetti cloud of metal and dust rising from the ground.

Her boss was five miles away in midtown, having a Tuesday breakfast with clients.

■ ■ ■

When American Airlines Flight 11, a Boeing 767 that was supposed to be en route from Boston to Los Angeles, slammed into 1 World Trade Center on September 11, 2001, Brian J. Bernstein was at his desk on the 38th floor. The tall building shook violently, and Bernstein jumped out of his chair. He went to the window and saw a sheet of paper, metal, and glass debris raining down. Bernstein was one of Lehman's 780 employees who worked in the North Tower. The firm's technology development group occupied floors 38, 39, and 40.

Bernstein grabbed his wallet, keys, and Palm Pilot and headed for the fire escape stairwell—already filling with panicked people fleeing the building, and by the time he reached the 20th floor the stairs were so jammed that no one was moving. Smoke was filling the elevator shafts and the stairwells. The people on the stairwell started moving again, slowly. At the landing of the ninth floor, firemen rushed by, heading up.

Bernstein heard running water and saw, floors below, a veritable river. Clearly something had hit—and burst—a water main. He crossed to the northeast corner of the building, near the fourth floor, to reach an alternate stairwell. He had been in the stairwell for 20 minutes, but it felt like seconds—and hours.

He went down another couple of flights of stairs and got to the mezzanine, where he was able to leave the building. Outside, the ground was covered with fallen debris, and people were yelling, screaming, and looking up with terror in their eyes. "Get out! Get out!" they cried to friends, co-workers, and strangers who couldn't hear them.

■ ■ ■

Across the street, on the 10th floor of the World Financial Center, Tom Russo, Gregory, Freidheim, and Jeff Vanderbeek gathered in Fuld's office. (Bradley Jack was in San Francisco that morning.) Gregory led

Lehman's management team in 1989 (*clockwise from top*): Richard S. Fuld Jr., Robert A. Genirs, Paul Williams, Robert A. Shapiro, Steven Gott, Bruce Lakefield, Thomas H. Tucker, Theodore Roosevelt IV, Jeffrey Vanderbeek, Joseph Gregory, John Coghlan, T. Christopher Pettit.

CREDIT: Sherry Lane Caricatures, www.sherrylane.com.

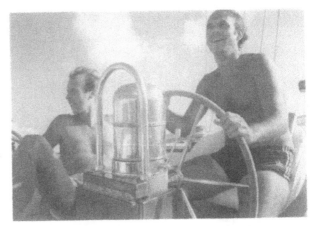

Tom Tucker (*left*) and Chris Pettit (*right*) on holiday in Little Dix Bay, Virgin Gorda, 1984.

Happy times: Chris and Mary Anne Pettit, Virgin Gorda, 1984.

(*Left to right*) Mary Anne Pettit, Chris Pettit, Tom Tucker, Heather Tucker, Virgin Gorda, 1984.

Chris and Mary Anne Pettit play tennis on Virgin Gorda, 1984.

Chris Pettit (*right*) and Tom Tucker (*left*) shoot the breeze, Virgin Gorda, 1984.

Chris and Mary Anne Pettit, Virgin Gorda, 1984.

Joseph and Niki Gregory at the GLSEN (Gay, Lesbian and Straight Education Network) 2005 Respect Awards' New York Gala.
PHOTO CREDIT: Desiree Navarro/Getty Images.

Lehman CFO Erin Callan poses for *Portfolio* magazine while the company faces rocky markets (March 17, 2008).
PHOTO CREDIT: © Jeff Riedel/Contour by Getty Images.

Scott Freidheim speaking at
the opening plenary session of
the World Economic Forum
annual meeting in Davos,
Switzerland (2006).
PHOTO CREDIT: Photo World
Economic Forum/swiss-
image.ch.

The Museum of Modern Art honors Richard Fuld Jr.
(shown with wife Kathy) with the David Rockefeller Award
in February 2006.
PHOTO CREDIT: Matt Carasella. © Patrick McMullan.

(*Middle left*) Steve Lessing, Jeffrey Vanderbeek, and Joe Gregory; (*bottom right*) a young Dick Fuld.

John F. Cecil, the chief financial officer
(later chief administrative officer) who
should never have been allowed to leave.
PHOTO CREDIT: Julie Beers.

Former CEO J. Tomlinson "Tom" Hill:
The Lehman co-head who should not
have been fired.
PHOTO CREDIT: Courtesy of J. Tomlinson
Hill.

Robert E. "Bob" Diamond Jr.,
president and CEO of Barclays
Capital, orchestrated the deal of the
century.
PHOTO CREDIT: Barclays.

Nancy Dorn and George Walker at the Whitney fall party (September 2005). PHOTO CREDIT: Matt Carasella. © Patrick McMullan.

Peregrine Moncreiffe in Scotland (1993). PHOTO CREDIT: Mungo Meehan.

U.S. Treasury Secretary Henry "Hank" M. Paulson Jr. briefs the press on September 15, 2008. He later said, "I didn't want to stand up and say, 'Guess what? We're sitting here naked. The United States of America is powerless.'" PHOTO CREDIT: Brendan Hoffman/Getty Images.

the conversation, with Fuld on speakerphone. They debated whether they should evacuate their floors immediately—Gregory said they didn't have all the facts and he was concerned that employees could be hit by falling debris outside. He suspected that a commuter plane had accidentally hit the tower. Gregory decided that they should stay.

Freidheim walked back to his office. He could see on a TV screen that large crowds were evacuating lower Manhattan. Before he returned to Fuld's office, he found his assistant of 10 years, Ringel. She recalls Freidheim telling her to leave. She objected, but Freidheim cut her off. "If you stay, I will fire you." Ringel left.

Two minutes later—at 9:03 A.M.—United Airlines flight 175, heading from Boston to Los Angeles, hit the South Tower. The same group of senior Lehman officials gathered again in Dick's office, which faced the building, and as they looked up they could see the fireball as the plane exploded.

Jeff Vanderbeek's voice cracked. "Oh my god!" he said, and buried his face in his hands and started to quietly weep.

They called Fuld back. Gregory said, "Dick, something just happened. We're not sure. We're going to look into it. We're going to get the facts." Freidheim looked at the TV in Fuld's office, and saw again that everyone was fleeing from the towers and the surrounding buildings. He looked around the room and saw that Tom Russo, too, looked very concerned.

Freidheim pulled Russo into his office and argued that they were taking a huge risk by staying. Russo then called Fuld, who told him to call another meeting in Gregory's office. This time, Fuld told Gregory to "get everyone out. Now."

Gregory relayed the order. He, Lessing, Vanderbeek, Goldfarb, Russo, Anthony "Tony" Zehnder, Fran Kittredge—the head of philanthropy—and a few others swept the building, floor by floor, to make sure all their people had evacuated. Fuld's assistant, Marianne Burke, was still frozen at her desk. Gregory leaned over her and shook her.

"Marianne, we are going—now!" She got up and went with them.

Lehman's 7,000 employees in the World Financial Center building quickly took the stairs to the lobby and then left. The last group, the 15 sweepers, ran for the street, now covered in dust. They then headed west, for the Battery docks, where they got on a ferry that would take them across the Hudson River to Hoboken, New Jersey, where Lehman had a backup facility.

They were halfway across the river when suddenly there seemed to be an extra blast of light. It was like an eclipse had just lifted. Then came a grating roar, as a cloud of smoke and dust slowly bellowed up from lower Manhattan.

Gregory said, "One of the towers is gone."

Someone pointed and said, "No, it's right there."

"That's the other tower," said Gregory. "One tower's down."

No one spoke for the rest of their trip across the Hudson.

■ ■ ■

Freidheim got separated from the others, Marna Ringel says her boss later told her.

"He stayed on the 10th floor, in the office of PR chief Bill Ahearn after I left," she says.

"I was walking up the West Side Highway and I stopped to speak to the Channel Four news team on the corner of Vesey Street. They had a zoom lens so what they could see was horrendous. It was people jumping from the top floors and the crowd below screaming: 'Don't jump!'

"I was explaining to the crew who I was and where I worked. I didn't know at the time, but Scott was watching me on TV.

"I was midsentence—that's when the North Tower fell. The ground shook, there was this rumble, and then a huge plume of smoke that went south. I screamed 'Omigod!' I only learned later that that's when Scott rushed for the fire exit. He told me he had to vault down the stairwell to make it out in time.

"I was still standing at the corner of Vesey Street when I saw him suddenly sprinting past me—in his Gucci loafers—on the West Side Highway. He stopped to tell me he was fine. He was on his way to see Dick."

Freidheim knew Fuld would be at Lehman's broker's offices at 48th Street and Park Avenue.

When Freidhem got there, Fuld was watching the horrible scene unfold on the television. He pelted Freidheim with questions about personnel, equipment, the buildings—everything and anything he could think of. He was worried sick. Freidheim told him: "Dick, there's no going back there. We have to find our people. We've got to rebuild the company, like *now*. We have to find our people. We have to start from scratch."

Fuld told him to "get everyone together and meet at the backup facility in New Jersey."

■ ■ ■

That night, over dinner with a friend, Freidheim pulled out a notepad and started to create an agenda for Lehman.

One: Find people.
Two: Real estate.
Three . . .
Four . . .

On and on it went.

He was not the only person thinking ahead. That night Ian Lowitt, a South African–born Rhodes scholar and then the treasurer of Lehman, did something incredibly brave that probably saved the firm. He slipped behind the police lines and secretly reentered the Lehman building. He knew he needed certain computer files to be sure the firm could fund itself again the next day from Hoboken.

The next afternoon, Lehman's senior executives met in New Jersey. They had been unbelievably lucky—they had lost only one person: Ira Zaslow, a financial analyst who had been stuck in an elevator in the North Tower. A former colleague remembers that Zaslow, who worked on the 38th floor, preferred the coffee on the 40th floor and had been on his way to get it when the plane struck.

Lehman's technical staff had carried computer servers down 29 flights and brought them across the river to Hoboken, where a facility that accommodated 800 people was adapted to serve 3,000 — including 1,400 traders and support staff. Jonathan Beyman and Bridget O'Connor, then in charge of information technology, had also organized for the sufficient technical equipment to be trucked in within 48 hours.

On the afternoon of September 12, there were dozens of tractor-trailers parked outside the facility, hauling servers and equipment from as far away as Denver.

When the debt markets opened on Thursday, September 13, Lehman was prepared to trade every asset class.

Anyone who could get any kind of phone service got in touch with Lehman's clients and told them, "It's business as usual."

The firm's relationship with Barry Sternlicht of Starwood Hotels would now pay huge dividends. Lehman Brothers arranged temporary office space for hundreds of employees in the Sheraton Hotel in midtown. They got 1,000 laptops from IBM and 10,000 phone lines from SBC.

The rest of Lehman's 6,200 employees were scattered to 39 locations throughout New York and New Jersey.

If ever there was a time for the people of Lehman to pull together—to be "one firm"—it was now. And they did.

Peter Thal Larsen later told the *Financial Times* that the hotel rooms in the Sheraton—two people to a room—"resembled a campaign headquarters on election night or an elite university during final exams. The sense of purpose was tangible."

Four weeks after 9/11, Lehman purchased a new 38-story building at 745 Seventh Avenue, where the company would move as soon as possible. It would also lease space at 399 Park Avenue. This time Joe Gregory would make sure the company was invincible in the face of terrorism. The new Lehman buildings were the first in New York to have nuclear fallout sensors and training programs in the event of bioterrorism. If there were a bioterrorist threat, the buildings would become hermetically sealed at the push of a button.

Worldwide, all Lehman windows were shatterproof. Gregory even commissioned iris scanners—before the airports did. Lehman also bought disaster recovery sites in Jersey City and deeper into New Jersey. And 745 Seventh Avenue had four policemen on duty and two bomb-sniffing Labradors, each with their own ID tags. Lehman led the first post-9/11 initial public offering (IPO), for Given Imaging Ltd, and the first multibillion-dollar debt deal, for General Electric Capital. Its return on equity jumped to 26 percent from 15 percent the prior year.

It also committed $10 million to humanitarian causes related to 9/11. That year it was the only securities firm not to lay anyone off. In fact, its head count rose 16 percent worldwide—to 11,326 employees by the year's end. It was also voted investment bank of the year by Thomson Financial. Lehman had not only survived, it thrived.

The media stopped portraying Lehman as a small bank waiting to be acquired; it now was clear the firm could carry its own weight. In 2002, *BusinessWeek* magazine voted it the 23rd best company in the S&P 500.

Several years later, Roy Smith—a professor at New York University's business school, Stern, and a former Goldman Sachs partner—said this about Lehman and the firm's response to 9/11: "An awful lot of people are surprised that Lehman is still alive. These guys are survivors. They have defied the world, spit in its face."

■ ■ ■

After surviving 9/11, two things consumed Dick Fuld and Lehman: Getting the stock price to 150 and beating Goldman Sachs.

The Goldman and Lehman battle was not restricted to their respective offices. One former Goldman executive committee member recalls that if he saw a Lehman employee at a cocktail party, he'd ignore him. "It was childish," he says, "but it was also war." (Lehman was just as petulant when it came to mixing social life and the competition. Elton John sang at a concert hosted by Lehman for the World Economic Forum in 2002 when it was held in New York. Joe Perella, at the time working for Morgan Stanley, arrived at the venue, the Four Seasons Restaurant, uninvited. Fuld politely escorted him out.)

Fuld started to shake up his management, adding three members to the executive committee: Rob Shafir, the head of equities; Bart McDade who headed fixed income; and David Goldfarb, the CFO. Most significantly, Fuld overcame his paranoia and appointed Brad Jack and Joe Gregory co-COOs. "Cocoa puff," Gregory liked to joke in the office.

A colleague recalls that Fuld made those appointments because of pressure from the board to implement a succession plan—but Fuld held off naming a president. He was still not ready for anyone below him to have that much power.

He felt safe appointing Gregory COO because no one thought he was a future CEO, in part because he kept saying he was about to retire. Brad Jack, in contrast, was CEO material. Tall and charismatic, he was similar to Chris Pettit—except that most people did not think he had Pettit's intellectual breadth. Jack confessed that he found business trips with Fuld exhausting, whereas Pettit had had the stamina of an infantryman.

In fact, in 1998, Jack, then head of training, had been diagnosed with cancer and had to take some time off. When he returned, there was a massive scar on his torso, from his back to his front, as if a shark had bitten him. People would see it when he worked out in the Lehman gym and be shocked. Because of the surgery, he was on strong pain medication for months. Jack says he came back to work much sooner than he was supposed to for fear that Gregory would somehow impede his job. "I even had the staples in my stomach when I went back to the office," he says. "But I was so afraid that if I stayed at home to recuperate Joe would somehow find a way to unseat me."

Gregory meanwhile set to work on his new passion—building a culture for Lehman that was groundbreaking in its emphasis on diversity and inclusion. As Lehman opened in two new locations it was undergoing an internal makeover. Fuld used the relocation as an excuse to reinstate his "no casual Friday" policy.

An in-house memo from 2002 noted that there was no female or minority representation on the executive committee. No one doubted that Gregory would change the situation as soon as he could, and he immediately put himself in charge of the in-house group, the Gay, Lesbian, Bisexual, and Transgender (GLBT) Network. There was also an Asian League, a Women's Initiatives Leading Lehman (WILL) organization, and others. Gregory then hired a group of executives—as many as 30—to run inclusion and diversity programs and to make sure that recruitment extended to minorities.

At Gregory's behest, all senior employees took the Myers-Briggs typology test, a personality assessment that sorts people into psychological types. (Enron had also used Myers-Briggs to help evaluate senior personnel.) Gregory wanted to do this so that people could understand their own strengths and weaknesses and learn to work better with their colleagues. Some executives complained that the test—part of a larger "cultural induction course" that was held over the course of a few days—was a "waste of time."

Gregory's diversity program was derided in part because it was as big and expensive to run as some of the revenue-producing divisions. It was more expensive and had more employees than all of risk management. Behind his back, senior executives called the program "Joe's social science project." Someone nicknamed him "the Oprah Winfrey of Wall Street."

Gregory wasn't dissuaded by such grumblings; he knew the attention and money that Lehman spent on diversity made for good public relations. Indeed, Harvard Business School would even publish a paper on Gregory's diversity program and its accomplishments.

Gregory was not a target for mockery because of his big-picture cultural goals for Lehman, which were laudable. He became a target because he had a smallness about him; he was man who was emotional and had instinctive likes and dislikes that sometimes seemed to inhibit common sense. He also seemed to grow increasingly distant from the business he was meant to be supervising.

■ ■ ■

One anecdote illustrates Gregory's shortcomings. In Lehman's lore, it is called "the glass door story."

Bob Millard had always irked Gregory. Millard was extremely bright—a well-educated and self-described intellectual. He quoted, with ease, Richard Dawkins, Charles Darwin, and William Shakespeare. He had an MBA from Harvard and a degree in architecture from MIT. His returns on his investment business, now named Realm Partners (which was funded by Lehman), were legendary. His compensation was even greater than that of Fuld or Gregory since he took a percentage of his fund's profits, rather than the firm's. He was also widely liked within the firm, and he would talk as often to assistants as to senior executives. Yet he was not on the executive committee, in part because he also didn't want to have his compensation lowered to the same level as the other executives. Millard's revenues had been lifesaving for Lehman during the 1990s, and he was somebody Fuld was careful to cultivate. He was definitely not someone Fuld wanted to offend.

Millard believed Gregory disliked everyone who, like Millard, had a direct line to Fuld. (This had been part of Gregory's problem with

Goldfarb, who was directly reporting to Fuld when he was appointed CFO.) The two men were also pretty dissimilar. Millard is a cultured, cerebral man; Gregory was a self-made man who, many felt, still couldn't believe he had made it. There was always tension between them.

After Lehman relocated, Millard was given a small corner office at the 399 Park Avenue location, next to a conference room. He asked the architect if he could have a glass door installed so that he could see into the adjoining conference room. A while later the answer came back: The glass door would violate the building code. Millard, who had a degree in architecture, knew that was not true. He suspected Gregory's handiwork, and called Fuld to complain.

Fuld laughed at him. "You are paranoid," he told him. "Don't be ridiculous. Of course Joe has nothing to do with it. But I will look into it for you and see if I can get you your glass door."

A few days later, Fuld called Millard back. "Well, I have to say it—and I cannot quite believe it—but you were right. It was Joe. Joe wants to talk to you. And you will, of course, get your glass door. I am very sorry for having doubted you."

A few minutes later, Millard's phone rang again. It was Gregory. "I will come and see you," Millard said.

"No, no, I will come to you," said Gregory. The episode swiftly descended into farce. Millard found himself stuck listening to Gregory for an hour as Gregory's apology meandered on and on. "I know I haven't behaved well toward you in the past," Gregory said.

From then on the two men stayed distant but cordial.

■ ■ ■

Fuld's efforts to cultivate the press were starting to pay off—though not without much pain in Lehman's PR department. If ever a story appeared that was remotely negative, Fuld would give the press officer responsible a grilling—or worse. One by one, over the years, the most senior Lehman PR executives—Bill Ahearn, Tony Zehnder, Hannah Burns, and Andrew Gowers—were fired because of stories Fuld had not liked. Only Scott Freidheim (who was in charge of them all) survived, along with a hire of his, Rose Shabet, a former chief of staff for Henry Paulson, John Thornton, and John Thain, the former gods of Goldman Sachs. (Shabet resigned in April 2008 and moved to the hedge fund Viking.)

By 2002 Moody's had improved its outlook on Lehman's long-term debt from stable to positive, which the rating agency said reflected "the disciplined risk controls, posture and culture that Lehman has installed throughout the organization and its people in recent years." Fuld was named one of the "Top 25 Managers of the Year" by *BusinessWeek*. The fixed income division had a record revenue year, and the European mortgage business was expanded through the purchase of SPML—a subprime mortgage lender in the United Kingdom. Lehman's business in Europe slowly started to improve under Jeremy Isaacs, as did their prospects in Asia, thanks to Jesse Bhattal.

By now it was time to get rid of all weak links, so Gregory turned his knife on the last remaining Ponderosa Boy: Steve Lessing.

Gregory believed that Lessing had hung himself by bringing too many friends into Lehman who were not up to the job. Lessing had been running all capital market sales, but, according to many sources, he was not respected by younger employees. In 2002, he was made head of client relationship management, a title that was meant to save face while he looked for another job.

Lessing's move was never announced publicly—that would have been too humiliating for a man with so much tenure. To many, Lessing was synonymous with Lehman, so his demotion was kept an internal secret. Still, everyone who knew about it expected Lessing to quit.

But he did not. Instead, he turned the client relationship job into such a success that within a year he rejoined the executive committee. Unlike most people who interpreted the title "head of client relationship management" as "time to find a way out," Lessing actually did what it asked of him—he built client relationships. Furthermore, he got one of three corner offices on the 31st (executive) floor of 745 Seventh Avenue. (Dick had one, and Fran Kittredge gave herself the other.)

"Dick never quite got over how Lessing turned this bad situation to his advantage," said Cecil, who had remained close to Lessing. "It really impressed him that he hadn't quit. He'd stuck and made the job work."

Lessing had one huge advantage: As had been proved with the Russian crisis, thanks to both his popularity and his vast Rolodex, there were not many clients—or potential clients—Lessing could not get on the phone.

As Doug Ireland, a former Lehman managing director, recalls, "He's a natural sales guy. He knew the guys at Met Life, and he knew the guys at Federated, and he knew the guys at Black Rock. And when we needed favors, during [the Russian crisis], Steve was Johnny-on-the-spot, calling every single one of them, saying, 'What do you need? How can we help? We're going to be okay; stay with us.' And he was absolutely, in my mind, the MVP."

Lessing was also the liaison between Greg Maffei, then the CFO at Microsoft, and Fuld—which was a precious relationship for Lehman. Unlike his contemporaries, Lessing was also able to "eat crow," as one peer put it, and get back into Gregory's good graces. This was a feat no one else in the history of the firm managed to pull off.

Jeff Vanderbeek was not as lucky. He was demoted from the position of head of all capital markets to office of the chairman, "responsible for risk, strategy, and private equity."

Vanderbeek was not respected by many of the people who worked under him in fixed income, including Bart McDade and Mike Gelband. Vanderbeek was expected to find a graceful exit strategy.

■ ■ ■

The following year—2003—was a big one for Lehman. Its price-to-earnings ratio was now finally up to 14, which meant it was in a position to buy a valuable investment without diluting shareholder value. On July 22, 2003, it bought the investment management business NeubergerBerman for approximately $2.625 billion—which brought Lehman's assets under management to $116 billion. Neuberger became known as "the crown jewel" at Lehman.

Fuld was enjoying mountains of good press, and he was named the top CEO in fixed income sales and trading by *Institutional Investor*. Lehman's brand of fixed income sales and trading, equity research, and fixed income research were all ranked first on the *Institutional Investor* list. There were no such accolades for banking. As usual, this was Lehman's weakest spot.

So Fuld again decided to shake up personnel. He promoted a former Texas high school football player turned formidable Houston energy lawyer, Hugh "Skip" McGee, to global head of investment banking; Mark Shafir, from Thomas Weisel Partners, was hired as head of mergers and acquisitions (M&A). Other strong hires included a young German, Christian Meissner, who was recruited to run banking under Isaacs in Europe, where the firm still had not broken into the top 10. In private equity, Charlie Ayres was hired from MidOcean Partners to head up global merchant banking.

Fuld and the executive committee prodded Walsh to work harder than ever. Walsh now had several funds under management, aping Goldman Sachs's model, the so-called Whitehall Funds—but Fuld and Gregory wanted to keep using the firm's balance sheet for his lucrative deals. Walsh was happy to oblige. "When Mark was keen to do a deal he didn't want to know about obstacles or risk; there wasn't much stopping him," says John Cecil. One major New York City realtor recalls that at this time, "Lehman's aggression was just startling in [real estate]. They were determined to beat out absolutely anyone to every deal."

Goldman Sachs was envious, but wary. "We stuck to ensuring that the maximum we had exposed of our own money was only 20 percent—the rest was put out to a fund," says a source at the company. "You just couldn't assume the real estate market would continue to go up."

But Walsh, Fuld, and Gregory did.

By 2008, the firm had at least $30 billion of commercial real estate on its books, the result of 2,500 different line items (deals). Cecil watched this from afar and shook his head. "It needs to be $5 to $10 billion at most," he believed. No matter how lucrative Walsh's deals were, they were illiquid—if trouble hit, he wouldn't be able to get out of them and shrink the balance sheet. It was an appalling risk.

But if anyone said to Gregory, "Shouldn't we be careful?" they were given this answer: Got to beat Goldman Sachs.

Gregory continually talked about "building a better brand than Goldman." He gave speeches saying Lehman needed to surpass Goldman Sachs in the next five years. Meanwhile he continued to build his diversity program. He hired Anne Erni as chief diversity officer in the United States, and Fleur Bothwick as head of diversity for Europe. Mentoring and inclusion programs started to attract positive press—and, as mentioned, even a Harvard Business School report—which was a useful counterweight to the press reports on star Internet analyst Holly Becker, whom, it emerged, the Securities and Exchange Commission (SEC) had been investigating since 2003. The agency thought Becker might be giving her husband, Michael Zimmerman, a stock trader at the hedge fund SAC Capital, inside information on Lehman research reports. (Becker left Lehman that year, and the SEC eventually dropped the investigation without charging her.)

Several senior executives told Fuld they were concerned that the firm's focus on diversity was taking up too much of Gregory's attention—and too many resources. Fuld talked to Gregory about the concerns but nothing changed. It was clear that Gregory was no longer interested in running a business. In executive committee meetings he talked about his tremendous wealth. He was also obsessed with cleanliness and personal hygiene. He kept a ready supply of Tic Tacs on his desk that he offered around, and he swilled Listerine at least twice daily. Like Fuld, he did not like slovenliness in others.

It was commonly known among the senior executives on the 31st floor of 745 Seventh Avenue that Gregory's personal annual spending budget was $15 million a year. "I never did understand why he bought a vast house in the Hamptons for just two weeks each year," one colleague noted dryly. He also had both a seaplane and a helicopter ready for his daily commute.

Another employee says: "Joe always stayed in Huntington rather than moving somewhere more affluent because he wanted to be a big fish in a small pond. He wanted to be the richest man in town."

■ ■ ■

In 2004 Gregory pulled off his best political move yet. He persuaded Fuld to get rid of Brad Jack on the grounds that he had not been sufficiently focused on work since his illness. Jack says this is nonsense.

On May 24, 2004, Jack was demoted to office of the chairman, with responsibility for overseeing all of the firm's investment banking relationships. Soon he was out—with an $80 million severance package. In 2008, Brad and Karin Jack divorced but remained great friends. They speak daily. Jack says, "The truth is that if it had not been for the years of long hours and pressures, Karin and I would still be married. But we had drifted apart."

In 2004 Vanderbeek had left, too. He knew his career was over when he was demoted; an avid hockey player, he had seized the chance to buy the New Jersey Devils for $175 million.

Fuld so trusted Gregory now that he did something that would have been unthinkable a year before: He anointed him president. It was official: The ghost of Chris Pettit had been vanquished.

This move was not universally hailed in the office. The problem with Gregory, many said, was not so much what he was, but what he was not: He was not on top of the numbers and the businesses. A few months later Peter Cohen idly asked Fuld, "Why did you make Joe president?"

Fuld replied cavalierly, "I don't know. He will probably be my undoing."

Chapter 15

No Ordinary Joe

I think if Joe had been in some other job—say, head of diversity—there would have been no problem. But he was president of the firm and all he appeared to be interested in was diversity. That was the problem.

—Lehman executive committee member

Joe Gregory and Skip McGee never got along. McGee was completely unlike Gregory—he scored an "I" for introvert on the required Myers-Briggs personality-type tests, whereas Gregory was an "F" for feeler and an "E" for extrovert. In executive committee meetings McGee said as little as possible—a marked contrast to the loquacious Gregory.

Gregory didn't trust the taciturn McGee (or anyone else who seemed to keep to themselves; he once complained that Mike Gelband, the head of fixed income from 2005 until 2007, looked down at the ground too often). Even though banking under McGee had brought Lehman its second best year in firm history—2004—with revenues of $11.6 billion (34 percent ahead of 2003), Gregory grumbled that it wasn't good enough, and pointed out that the firm's global fee share still had not cracked the top five, which was one of Fuld's goals.

Hope Greenfield, who worked for Gregory in human resources beginning in 2001, told McGee that he'd "gone as far as he would at Lehman Brothers." She'd heard this from Gregory, who was reportedly hoping to assign McGee to a commodity trading business in Houston—where McGee lived, and commuted from every week via NetJet. According to a source who encountered McGee right after his talk with Greenfield, he was "crestfallen."

One of Gregory's complaints against McGee was the long hours his bankers put in. Gregory got a time sheet each week, and he wasn't happy with what he read, according to colleagues. The bankers worked far longer hours than employees in the other divisions.

Partly this was cultural. The banking analysts and associates would throw footballs around the office and even hit golf balls—precisely because they *wanted* to still be at work and sending e-mails from the office at 3 A.M. It looked macho. But Gregory abhorred such practices. He viewed them as unhealthy.

■ ■ ■

Workaholics and introverts weren't the only people who annoyed Gregory. Now topping the list of people he wanted to fire was chief financial officer David Goldfarb, who rivaled Gregory as Fuld's top sycophant, and kept a perennially bullish outlook, which he attributed to the market's decoupling from the fundamentals of the American economy. He also had a habit of referring to the firm as "the Bros." One person joked, "You may only guess at Joe Gregory's reaction to this."

But when Gregory told his boss he planned to fire Goldfarb, the CEO took the unusual step of intervening. Instead of being sacked, Goldfarb was "promoted" to the position of chief administrative officer (CAO).

Goldfarb, ignorant of the behind-the-scenes machinations, took the new position as a hearty endorsement.

He went out and immediately bought snappier suits and a St. Regis condo in Fort Lauderdale. "His shirts had a sheen," says a colleague, and he wore booties, or ankle boots.

The condo became Goldfarb's albatross: He'd told the rest of the executive committee how he had invested $4 million in renovating the property, only to have some mix-up on the deeds keep him from finishing the job. He kept droning on and on until his audience lost his thread of thought. He even called Jeb Bush, the governor of Florida, and Mark Walsh for help. Some on the committee snickered secretly at his meandering tale of woe and apparent ineptitude. However, someone close to Walsh felt that the people who belittled Golfarb over this were petty and mean-spirited. "The developer died right after David bought the property," someone close to Walsh points out. "That's a pretty unusual thing to have happen."

Fuld's efforts might have been better utilized sparing some other underlings from feeling Gregory's wrath—namely, Bart McDade and his deputy, Mike Gelband, a duo Gregory disparagingly called "Fortress FID" for the fierce loyalty they commanded over the traders in Lehman's fixed income division. They were too "isolated," too cut off from Lehman's "one firm" culture, Gregory complained. This was why he had been able to convince Fuld to let him move McDade over to run equities, even though McDade didn't have the usual experience required for that job.

■ ■ ■

Fuld increasingly left the firm's management to Gregory, whose general directive was to "do as much business as you can; take risk." He argued with Madeleine Antoncic, the risk officer, that she was out of line and being too fussy when she suggested in 2006 that falling house prices might mean the balance sheet should come down. She was gradually sidelined, kept out of meetings, ignored, and asked—constantly—to leave the room.

Fuld, meanwhile, was out of the office a lot, visiting clients. Few employees ever caught a glimpse of him, including the executive committee. Fuld routinely skipped the Monday morning meetings, leaving Gregory in charge. Fuld wasn't missing much: Gregory's agenda generally centered on what he'd done over the weekend and how much he had spent. As one exasperated former committee member recalls: "Not once—in, say, 20 meetings, for argument's sake—did he ever ask about the business or the numbers or risk, or anything else."

In one memorable Monday meeting, an executive committee member asked what the firm's China strategy was. "I don't have a China strategy," Gregory blithely replied. "That's for you guys to work out."

In 2005, Joe Perella once again came knocking on Lehman's door. He had left Morgan Stanley and formed his own advisory boutique, Perella Weinberg Partners, and Fuld wanted an exclusive deal with the outfit. He and Perella (who had been a mentor of Skip McGee) even drew up a contract. The idea was that Perella would give Fuld exclusive advice. Since he was on the outside, he could bluntly tell Fuld the kinds of things his own staff might not. Then, Perella met Gregory—and according to someone close to Perella, "the idea sort of died." Nobody inside Lehman was surprised. The last thing Gregory wanted was Fuld having a direct line to somebody of Perella's stature, with zero input from Gregory.

■ ■ ■

Gregory liked to remind senior executives that they should not confuse life with work. "I'm a little concerned about this group of guys who are very tight in fixed income," Gregory once told Alex Kirk, then the head of the high yield business. Kirk would be well advised, Gregory implied, to learn some lessons from the Lehman history books. He bemoaned what had happened between Tucker and Pettit and the rest of the carpool guys—it hurt the firm, he said. "Rick Rieder, Mike Gelband, and Bart McDade are good friends. They play golf together and they vacation together. If there's a time when you think that personal closeness is interfering with business decisions, I want you to let me know."

Rieder—who ran a proprietary hedge fund for Lehman, R3 Capital—was once given a pep talk by Gregory, who told him that if Goldfarb ever got in his way, Rieder was to talk to "Uncle Joe."

In 2006, McGee was still on Gregory's hit list. The investment banking group had advised on three of the five largest mergers and acquisitions (M&A) transactions of the year, pulling in record revenues of $3.3 billion. But the department still ranked only ninth among its peers—underscoring perhaps more than anything else the feverish pace of the deal flow at the peak of the bubble—and Gregory, according to colleagues, tried again to use it as an excuse to fire McGee—or in lieu of that, undermine him as often as possible.

Gregory kept a rotating roster of teacher's pets, and he liked to dangle the CEO carrot in front of them. According to multiple sources, he independently told Bart McDade, Scott Freidheim, and Roger Nagioff they could all be the president of Lehman one day.

In 2004 both Freidheim and Ian Lowitt, the former treasurer, had been promoted to the title of chief administrative officer. Freidheim's golden boy moment had come in 2004 when he gave a presentation to the board on Lehman's strengths and weaknesses around the world. It was the first time, one board member said to him, that they'd heard the "unvarnished truth" about where Lehman was weak, and the board loved it so much he ended up giving them two more presentations.

Fuld was proud of his protégé's performance. He increasingly called on him to present at corporate retreats. He would introduce him with a snippet of Shakespeare he reserved for a favored few: "Lay on, Macduff." Freidheim obliged.

Jeremy Isaacs, believed that he too was a candidate for the seat of president. "Jeremy thought he was the rightful number two," explains a former colleague who was close to Isaacs. "If anything happened to Joe, he thought he should be number two. He had reason to believe this. . . . He says he had said to Dick in May 2007: 'I've been running Europe and Asia now for eight or nine years. I've done what you asked. Europe now contributes 50 percent of Lehman's revenues. I need to have an idea of where I'm going next. So, if you can give me a signal of that forward pathway, good. If not, let's have a conversation about how I can gracefully move on.' According to Isaacs, Dick basically said, 'Oh, you are wrong. Give me a year. If I can't work something out, I will give you $500 million to start your own firm, but give me a year.'"

But Isaacs did not help himself when he gave an interview to the *Daily Telegraph* at the end of 2006 in which he stated that the following year Lehman planned to open an office in Russia. The plans had not been finalized (even before the 1998 default, Fuld mistrusted the Russians), but Isaacs had been involved in two years of discussions on the matter and thought he'd expedite matters if he went public with the plan. It was not a move Isaacs could get away with, and the new public relations chief, former *Financial Times* editor Andrew Gowers, knew it.

"Jeremy," he asked gently during the interview, "are you sure you are now off the record?"

"No," Isaacs insisted. "It's on the record."

As soon as the interview appeared, Gregory called Isaacs and tore him apart. Isaacs later told Gowers, "You were quite right to try to stop that story. . . . I had myself a new asshole ripped by Joe Gregory."

■ ■ ■

Gregory installed another golden boy in 2006, hiring George Walker away from Goldman Sachs, where he'd been the CEO of Hedge Fund Strategies and then Alternative Investment Solutions. Walker, a relative of President George Bush, was made head of investment management and immediately put on the executive committee. Gregory told the understated, likable Walker that he was a future candidate to run the firm. That year investment management had its third record-breaking year in a row, with revenue of $1.7 billion.

But Gregory's most successful—and divisive—teacher's-pet project was yet to come. She was a young blonde banker named Erin Callan, who—with a push from Gregory's hidden hand—was vaulting up Lehman's ranks. He planned for her to be the most visible symbol of his cultural remake of Lehman Brothers.

■ ■ ■

In 2004 Erin Callan was one of three Lehman executives to deliver a keynote speech before the annual dinner of Lehman's group for women executives, Women's Initiatives Leading Lehman (WILL), at Avery Fisher Hall in New York's Lincoln Center. Diane Sawyer was the paid keynote speaker; 1,500 Lehman employees were in attendance. It was an event that got the blonde banker noticed by all the senior management.

Gregory was pleased.

"It was never clear if [Callan] took the position at WILL to get noticed by Joe, or if Joe gave her the position to make sure she got noticed by everyone else," one of her peers, a banker, noted wryly. (Callan's ex-husband, Michael Thompson, says Gregory asked her to make the speech and she spent a great deal of time preparing it.)

Whatever the case, it was soon widely understood within Lehman that Callan was Gregory's newest diversity initiative. Senior executives who were privy to who got paid what in banking noticed that Callan's compensation was always "bumped up" way above that of her peers.

When, in 2006, *BusinessWeek* spotlighted the enterprising work of Lehman's finance solutions team in an article on the boom in so-called hybrid securities—complex securities blending attributes of stocks and bonds so as to maximize tax benefits and minimize the appearance of risk—the magazine quoted only one executive at the firm: Erin Callan. Only one executive's photograph appeared in the magazine: Callan's. The decision was, of course, *BusinessWeek*'s, but the rest of the team took it as a slight. To them, the real innovator on the team was John Curran, who left for Deutsche Bank the month before the story appeared.

After the *BusinessWeek* article appeared, Callan was promoted to run Lehman's hedge fund group, where she threw herself into the high-profile initial public offerings (IPOs) of the hedge fund Fortress Investment Group and a bond offering for the hedge fund Citadel Investment Group. A June 2007 *Institutional Investor* profile depicts Callan pitching Citadel founder Ken Griffin on the $500 million debt issuance as a cautionary measure she encouraged after expressing "amazement" that Citadel, like most hedge funds (and indeed, like the very firm that employed her), relied so heavily on overnight loans that "banks could pull at a moment's notice."

Callan had the ideal blend of fancy and scrappy credentials when she joined Lehman in 1995. Raised in Queens, she was a New York City cop's daughter and a product of the Catholic school system—but she was also an alumna of Harvard, New York University Law School, and the prestigious corporate law firm Simpson, Thatcher and Bartlett. And she was family—she'd been married since 1991 to Michael Thompson, a former Lehman investment banker, who now trades for himself. The couple made extra money renovating and flipping houses. She used to refer to her husband as "my CFO."

Unlike Callan, who found her passion at the bank and truly "bled Lehman green," Thompson was miserable at work. "I was struggling to find what I wanted to do while she was zooming ahead," he says.

Callan used to ask her husband why he wasn't happier at the firm. "I think she found [my uncertainty] very frustrating," he says. He filed for divorce in 2007, but the two remained on friendly terms until 2008, when he told people, "She's cut me dead."

Before the divorce, Thompson says, she'd worn pretty much one designer: Chanel. But Callan underwent a gradual makeover after the split.

The hair became blonder, the gym routine intensified, and what she considered suitable work attire increasingly played up her femininity. She occasionally came to work in an ensemble that "would have been fine for a cocktail party but not for the office."

"She really played on the fact that she was a woman," says one member of Lehman's executive committee. "She always wore low-cut dresses and short dresses, and she was always very flirty and almost girly. And I always thought it was pretty inappropriate."

"The whole time I knew her, she was always a sharp dresser," another colleague says. "I had heard that she would occasionally show flashes of poor judgment—see-through things, leather things . . . but the really far-out, flashy stuff really happened after she joined the hedge fund group—when she was single."

Callan's new look was often the subject of morning interoffice e-mails, until suddenly there were infinitely weightier matters to discuss. The markets had started to turn. For the first time in 20 years, the housing market looked like it might crash.

■ ■ ■

Since 2006, it was clear to most observers that home mortgages had become preposterously easy to get, with millions of Americans moving into luxury housing they couldn't afford and millions more using the bubble-addled housing prices to turn their homes into personal ATMs by doing cash-back refinancings and taking out home equity loans. Yet for a full year, Wall Street continued to make mortgage-backed securities the hottest commodity around, and rating agencies in turn continued to brand them triple A.

In many ways, Lehman was no worse than any of its peers. But what was peculiar was one of its reasons for staying bullish on the housing market. A senior executive said, quite seriously, that part of Lehman's push in the mortgage space stemmed, according to his observation, from Joe Gregory's desire to encourage a protégé, the mortgage chief Ted Janulis. Janulis had sold his New York apartment to one of Fuld's daughters. Gregory always talked him up. (In the Myers-Briggs typology, the senior executive further explained, Janulis was the only senior manager besides Gregory who tested "F" for "feeler.") In 2006 Lehman's subprime mortgage arm employed nearly 4,000 people.

As early as 2005, the so-called smart money—namely Deutsche Bank, JPMorgan, and Goldman Sachs—had started backing out of the business and scrambling to hedge its remaining exposure, while the dumb money—Bear Stearns, Lehman, Citigroup, and Merrill Lynch—all seemed to be pursuing a strategy best summed up by former Citigroup CEO Charles O. "Chuck" Prince in June 2007, when he told the *Financial Times* that "as long as the music is playing, you've got to get up and dance. We're still dancing." ("Music" was Prince's metaphor for liquidity—which anyone with a Bloomberg terminal could have told him by that time had dried up.)

Lehman Brothers, however, had even bigger problems on its balance sheet than subprime mortgage collateralized debt obligations (CDOs)—it had some massive mortgages of its own, leveraged loans and in 2006 Mark Walsh still wasn't finished investing in commercial real estate.

Walsh had unparalleled access to the firm's balance sheet, which he used to directly invest in thousands of commercial real estate deals—something that made Lehman unique among its peers. Fuld loved Walsh's strategy, many of his former colleagues speculate, because it mirrored that of a private equity firm and put Lehman in direct competition with his old rivals at Blackstone Group—and also, obviously, because during the boom it was immensely profitable. Former colleagues estimated that Walsh's real estate investments accounted for 20 percent of the firm's record profits of $4 billion in 2006. But this success came at a horrible price. When the housing market began to turn at the end of 2006, and as foreclosures began to spike across southern California, investors wanted out of a partnership Walsh had previously struck with Boris Elieff, the founder of SunCal Companies, which invested in undeveloped land in southern California. Walsh returned the investors a small profit and transferred $2 billion in SunCal to Lehman's balance sheet.

But Walsh was not yet leery of the commercial real estate sector. In 2007, when some property developers were skeptically referring to Lehman as "the lender of last resort," Walsh spearheaded a deal—along with Barclays and Bank of America—to finance Tishman-Speyer's $22 billion buyout of Archstone-Smith, a massive portfolio of East Coast rental properties in May 2007.

It was a controversial move. Walsh did it partly because he believed, along with leading research at the time, that a fall in the residential market can be good for rental apartments. But within the firm there was dismay at yet more billions of illiquid assets being moved onto the balance sheet to pay for it. The voices of dissent within Lehman got louder. Bart McDade, whose equity division had closed out the year with a record annual revenue of $4 billion, was scared by the large amount of debt piling onto the firm's balance sheet. He knew that the facts behind the housing bubble were troubling, and he was deeply worried by the firm's exposure to commercial real estate, mortgages, and loans.

So too was his former deputy, now the head of fixed income, Mike Gelband, and technically Walsh's boss who had issued his first dire warning about the coming housing crash to "Fortress FID" almost two years previously.

Subsequently, in the summer of 2006, Gelband's deputy, Alex Kirk, had made a presentation before 150 of the firm's senior managers, warning that if they continued to grow their leveraged businesses, they could lose billions of dollars.

Fuld heard the presentation with Gregory, but shrugged off the warning. He believed that "the more business we can do, the better," says Kirk.

As one attendee puts it, "Dick had this idea that for every dollar of revenue you earn in doing an LBO [leveraged buyout] you earn five more dollars of follow-on business—which, by the way, when you do the math, is actually two times. And you have to take a lot of risk to earn all those dollars. So Dick and Joe didn't like being told to be risk-averse."

Also troubling: By 2006 David Goldfarb had been moved out of the CAO spot and made head of strategic partnerships and principal investments, essentially giving him control over $50 billion of Lehman's balance sheet with instructions to invest it at the very peak of the market. (Again, according to a member of the executive committee, most of them—except for Goldfarb—realized this was because Fuld was inventing a way for him to stay at the firm, while Gregory wanted him gone.)

By 2007 Treasury Secretary Hank Paulson had begun warning all the securities houses to recapitalize, by slashing dividends and scaling back their balance sheets. But Lehman ignored Paulson, too. Among Treasury staffers, Dave Goldfarb acquired the nickname "Planet Goldfarb," because, as one of them explains, "the things he said could only be true on Planet Goldfarb, because they weren't true on Earth."

Lehman spent most of 2007 on an otherworldly buying spree. In May, the same month the Archstone deal closed, the firm also acquired Eagle Energy, a Houston-based energy company, for $400 million, against the advice of Mike Gelband. Sources say Fuld boasted that Eagle Energy, which was run by a friend of Skip McGee, would turn a billion-dollar profit for the firm within 12 months. But over the next 12 months, Eagle Energy would come to owe Lehman $664 million in outstanding loans. In October 2008, the French utility giant Electricité de France SA (EDF) bought Eagle Energy out of bankruptcy court for only $230 million, under the condition that Lehman forgive $433 million in outstanding loans. And then there was Grange Securities, an Australian CDO distribution house Lehman paid $100 million for on the advice of Jesse Bhattal. The acquisition happened just as "CDO" was entering the public lexicon as shorthand for the insanity that characterized the mortgage boom of the prior few years. Gelband squawked, but he was told to be quiet. Grange Securities was another bust.

The danger in buying up whole businesses this way, especially when it required Lehman to pile on billions in debt, was that if the profits failed to meet the rosy projections, Lehman could have a tough time making the payments. And unlike other firms, Lehman made few attempts to get anyone else in on the action by securitizing its deals so investors could buy in. Lehman kept all the risk for itself.

■ ■ ■

Gelband spent the year in constant conflict with Fuld and Gregory. Fixed income had made $9 billion in 2006; Gregory told Gelband that he and Fuld expected $12 billion the next year. The tension, former colleagues say, had much to do with the intellectual disconnect between them. "Mike would say something and Dick would argue with him because he didn't understand what Mike had said," says one observer at executive committee meetings. "A lot of people didn't understand what Gelband said."

In May 2007, Gregory fired Gelband. "You wanted to make changes. Well, I'm the change," Gelband reportedly said to Gregory.

Steve Lessing e-mailed Tom Tucker to say that Gregory had fired Gelband without even giving the executive committee the opportunity to discuss it, adding that he could not believe Gregory had been so stupid and jealous as to push Gelband out. He told Tucker that everyone was now so terrified of Gregory that he feared for the survival of the firm.

Soon after Gelband left, an exasperated Alex Kirk reportedly went to Fuld and complained that he, Fuld, hadn't been listening to Gelband properly—largely on account of the "guy down the hall" (Gregory) whom "nobody believes," and "who just tells you what he thinks you want to hear, not what is actually going on."

Fuld told Gregory what Kirk had said. Kirk promptly became Gregory's next target.

In a classic Lehman maneuver, instead of replacing Gelband with Kirk, who knew the business inside out, Gregory promoted Roger Nagioff, the former head of European equity derivatives, who lived in London and who had zero expertise in fixed income, to run it. Isaacs says he saw Nagioff's promotion as a sign that Fuld was raising the profile at the European business. In fact, many people thought Nagioff had been chosen only because Gregory liked him and didn't think he posed a threat. Gregory did not even mind that Nagioff said he wanted to stay in London, but he told Nagioff he would have to spend two weeks per month in New York and presumed him to buy an apartment in the city.

"That was the trouble with the whole philosophy of the place," says a former managing director and head of global recruiting, who worked at Lehman for 20 years before leaving in the late 1990s. "Instead of going out and finding the best, they'd find someone loyal."

■ ■ ■

After the Lehman holiday party in 2007, word got around the firm that Alex Kirk had taken a company-chartered bus home and asked the driver to drop him off first, ahead of the first scheduled stop.

The man he jumped ahead of was far junior to him, but he was a member of the Gay, Lesbian, Bisexual, and Transgender (GLBT) Network headed by Gregory.

"Do you know who I am?" Kirk had reportedly asked the driver when he had at first demurred. When Gregory heard what had happened, he was furious, according to colleagues. He docked $1 million off Kirk's bonus.

In early 2008, Nagioff told Gregory he was exhausted from the transatlantic commute and he was quitting. Instead of appointing the obvious successor—Kirk—Gregory chose Andrew Morton, a Canadian who had met Fuld just twice, to run the fixed income division. There are reports that Kirk either quit and was fired. Either way, he was gone.

Plenty of Lehman employees, including Tom Russo and Freidheim, gave speeches warning that a bubble was coming and how imperative it was to manage risk. At Davos in January 2008, Freidheim was quoted in the *Financial Times* saying, "We don't have to wait to find out whether there is a recession or not. . . . We're in a credit recession and we have to deal with it."

Russo gave a speech to the G30 in November 2007, later updated for the 2008 World Economic Forum in Davos, called "Credit Crunch: Where Do We Stand?" the highlights of which were bullet points such as: "Household net worth will likely start to decline on a [year-on-year] basis in the first half of 2008"; "Signs of a softer job market are starting to emerge . . . contributing to a decline in consumer confidence"; "Meanwhile the consumer is very levered"; and "Mortgage market problems and the contagion into credit markets and banks pose an additional challenge to consumers."

So why wasn't Lehman taking its own advice?

By 2007, Lehman's real estate commitments had sprung in just one month from $20 billion to $40 billion. Gregory was annoyed, executives say, that Lehman had lost out to Wachovia and Merrill Lynch for a deal financing Tishman-Speyer's $5.4 billion acquisition of Stuyvesant Town, a huge apartment complex in Manhattan. Fuld, too, was irked; he was close friends with Jerry Speyer, the chairman of the real estate developer, and those relationships were supposed to lead to contracts. Speyer and Kathy Fuld were board members of the

Museum of Modern Art. Gregory and others urged Walsh to get the next major deal.

And so to the surprise of many on Wall Street, Walsh spearheaded a deal with Barclays and Bank of America to finance Tishman-Speyer's $22 billion buyout of Archstone-Smith, a massive portfolio of East Coast rental properties, in May 2007.

At first Fuld and Walsh were thrilled with the deal. They agreed with a report from leading industry analysts, *Greenstreet Advisors*, that Lehman had actually *underpaid* for Archstone. They simply had not foreseen how quickly and severely the market would turn.

The timing was so atrocious that Speyer even called Fuld, according to the *New York Times*, to see if Lehman wanted out. Of course not, Fuld said. He was a man of his word. He'd put $4 billion on the Lehman balance sheet.

"Archstone would have been a good deal if there had been time to hold on to it," says a member of the executive committee. "But the timing was terrible, especially given how Lehman funded it. The market completely collapsed right at the time when they were supposed to move all this stuff out, and so Lehman got stuck with it."

Steve Berkenfeld, chief investment officer for private strategy and formerly one of Lehman's attorneys, later explained why Lehman was so willing to take those risks: "How do we compete in a balance-sheet-driven business when we are half the size of Morgan, Merrill, and Goldman, and a fraction of the size of Citi? . . . We go in to a client, and they want $15 billion of financing. They don't want to hear that $5 billion is too big for us. Do we get more active in the real estate area, which is a way for us to do it? Yes. These are our ways of competing."

Perhaps, but these were also a way of dying.

Erin Callan later told *Fortune* that in the minds of Fuld and Gregory the gamble was nothing more than a rerun of the Russian crisis; they thought they were playing high-stakes poker. In her words, "The commercial real estate portfolio really was the albatross of the firm."

■ ■ ■

Late in the summer of 2007, just as investors were beginning to panic, realizing that the subprime mortgage meltdown might have much broader consequences, Gregory decided to make more personnel changes. At this,

Madeleine Antoncic, the head of risk, who was already heading out the door (sources say she had been demoted to a seat in charge of government relations), threw up her hands. She says she couldn't believe the stupidity of what she was seeing—and she had seen a lot. She left.

Gregory went ahead with his plans, which were implemented a few months later. CFO Chris O'Meara was demoted to chief risk officer (replacing Antoncic)—and the new CFO was Erin Callan.

Skip McGee—who, as Callan's boss, had to make the announcement— deliberately moved it to the bottom of his agenda during a managing directors meeting in London, because he dreaded the incredulous reaction he knew it would elicit. Callan had zero accounting background, even though Lehman was about to head into the worst financial crisis in decades.

"When Skip McGee announced that she had become CFO and that she would join the executive committee, it was as close to sort of open rebellion [as] I've seen at the firm," says one attendee.

"Some people who'd worked for her for a long time were basically shouting, and it was just pandemonium," remembered a former member of the executive committee. "A detached view is that she had worked for some of the guys in the room, and if somebody gets promoted one or two steps ahead of you, you're not going to be too happy, almost regardless of the circumstances. So I guess you have to discount some of it. But basically, people thought that she was a bad person." Or maybe not bad, but a political person who dealt with male colleagues in an inappropriate way and was not qualified.

"She had zero clue about accounting . . . and she had never run a team bigger than 50 people. So the combination of no external experience, no finance background, no management background, and this, the most difficult market ever, doesn't exactly strike you as the most qualified individual to get that job," one colleague said. It was a cry that echoed around the firm.

Some members of the executive committee complained to Fuld. Ros L'Esperance, arguably the second most senior woman in the investment banking division, told Fuld point blank that Callan did not have the right skill set to be the CFO, and that this was the worst possible time to experiment. They were courting disaster. Her arguments fell on deaf ears.

Gregory was thrilled—he had put a woman on the executive committee. To celebrate, a dinner was given in Callan's honor at La Grenouille, something that hadn't been done for anyone else promoted to the big table.

Callan was given three months to get up to speed, which meant that Chris O'Meara put out the earnings call in November 2007 announcing yet another record year, with revenues reaching $19.3 billion, along with the boast that the firm had "maintained a conservative funding framework to mitigate risk."

The company's liquidity pool had grown by $7 billion in the last year. All divisions had record revenues. Marquee transactions had included work on the Blackstone IPO, the Fortress IPO, Man Financial IPO, Citi, and Ochs Ziff. Banking got its first significant advisory assignment for General Electric, which was for the sale of GE Plastics. Standard & Poor's rated Lehman at A+, while Moody's had it at A1 and praised the "scale and breadth of the franchise."

The other big banks were mystified. How could they all be suffering while Lehman was doing so well?

■ ■ ■

Lehman held a dinner for its alumni in 2007, at the suggestion of Scott Freidheim, who had taken it upon himself to copy Goldman Sachs and McKinsey—both companies found that an alumni network was a useful ecosystem of relationships that often spawned new business.

Fuld was a gracious host all evening. He was thrilled to greet successful men such as Steve Schwarzman, Peter Solomon, and Peter Cohen, who all came to toast Fuld and the extraordinary story of a phoenix rising from the ashes—in this case, literally, after 9/11.

A cocktail reception was also held for the so-called A-minus list in the pool room of the Four Seasons restaurant. Fuld spoke to a packed crowd.

Not everyone was blinded by the bonhomie. Steve Carlson, the former head of emerging markets, who was now the chairman of Provident Group, had a question for Steve Lessing: "Stevie, aren't you worried about the real estate?"

Lessing, careful not to ruin the spirit of the night, raised his glass in toast, and said, "Oh, don't worry—we're hedged."

Chapter 16

The Talking Head

I guess you could argue that Erin Callan was an interesting idea—and at a different moment in time might have been a brilliant choice. But it was the worst moment to put a rookie in the seat—very unfair to her.

—*Peter A. Cohen*

In the middle of a bank run, perception is reality. In the early spring of 2008, Bear Stearns was perceived to be the Wall Street firm most vulnerable in the mortgage crisis—and as soon as one big client began asking questions about its solvency, it was fighting for its life. Erin Callan, a new species of CFO (Conspicuous and Female) was perceived to be one of Lehman's biggest assets, and was, to some, a welcome change from the old way of doing business.

She was tall, five feet eight inches, blonde, and had dimples. She was confident and voluble. She looked and sounded like a straight talker. Meanwhile, Bear Stearns CEO Jimmy Cayne's marijuana habit had been news since the *Wall Street Journal* first reported it in November— the sort of gossip that corroded the image of the firm as it slouched toward the abyss.

Bear Stearns's stock lost more than half its value the week of March 10, closing at $30 on Friday, March 14, after JPMorgan agreed to facilitate a Federal Reserve maneuver to keep Bear afloat while they could look at the implications of its demise.

That weekend JPMorgan CEO Jamie Dimon and about 150 of his employees descended upon Bear to begin scouring the books, and by Sunday, March 16, he had determined that about $30 billion of the firm's securities were too risky to take on without government help. Much to the horror of the Bear board, the Federal Reserve agreed to guarantee the loans—as long as Dimon offered shareholders more than the initial offer of $2 a share. (The offer would be raised to $10, but not before the $2 figure sent panic through the market.)

On Monday, March 17, Bear Stearns died—and Lehman looked like it might follow the firm into the grave. Fuld had rushed home from a business trip in India the weekend that the deal was hammered out under the direction of Treasury Secretary Henry "Hank" Paulson, who knew that Lehman's exposure to the distressed real estate market was similar to Bear's. He had also seen Lehman narrowly escape ruin in both the 1995 Mexican peso crisis and the double whammy of the Russian crisis and the implosion of Long-Term Capital Management in 1998, so he was worried. He wondered, he said later, whether Fuld was "like a cat with nine lives."

■ ■ ■

The near-overnight collapse of Bear was stunning. Until that fateful week in March, few but the most sophisticated investors appreciated the magnitude of the risk inherent in the prevailing Wall Street business model.

"No one expected an institution that was 85 years old and had relied on wholesale funding . . . could just vanish because of a run on the bank," said a senior Fed official. "Everyone was doing business with them—until they weren't."

If Fuld had any doubt as to which firm the market believed would be the next to fall, it was erased when the market opened at 9:30 A.M. Lehman stock plummeted 48 percent in the first hour of trading.

That same Monday, the April issue of *Condé Nast Portfolio*, an issue devoted to "Sexism in the Workplace," went on sale with a profile of Callan (aka "The Most Powerful Woman on Wall Street").

Accompanied by a two-page photograph of her stepping out of a gleaming black limousine in a short dress and high heels, the article seemed wildly inappropriate. "I don't subordinate my feminine side," she told writer Sheelah Kolhatkar. "I have no problem talking about my shopper or my outfit." Even during booming markets, this might have seemed strange, but given Lehman's situation, the article and photograph were incongruous, bordering on the suicidal. It was no time for flattering and flirting. Lehman was fighting for its life.

The next day, however, Tuesday, Callan lived up to the hype during the firm's scheduled conference call to announce first-quarter earnings. She exuded confidence, competence, and, seemingly, candor. When the call was over, the bearish banking analyst Meredith Whitney complimented her performance—and Callan got a standing ovation from the trading floor. The investment bank's net income had fallen by more than half from the year earlier, but times were tough, and Lehman had still booked nearly a half-billion dollars in profits. After closing Monday at $31.75, Lehman shares roared back to $46.50 per share on Tuesday. Gregory led the executive committee in a round of applause for Callan at its next meeting. Like the dinner at La Grenouille, this was unprecedented. But Callan was a hero. She had overnight become the public face of Lehman Brothers.

Still, some were puzzled. Those earnings just didn't make sense. What about Lehman's huge exposure in real estate and mortgages?

Chief among the skeptics was Hank Paulson. The Treasury secretary was aware of Gregory's toxic influence at the firm, in part because he had talked to Lehman's former fixed income chief, Mike Gelband, who had come to interview at the Treasury after leaving Lehman. The Treasury team didn't have a job for him, but they were impressed.

They were vaguely aware that Fuld was cut off from people at the firm who had the intellectual firepower to handle this crisis, says a member of the Treasury team. So, while Gregory assured his old buddy, Fuld, that the firm would pull through, just as they had done before, the Treasury secretary was trying to send a different signal. "Hank was consistent in emphasizing to Dick, 'You've got to have a plan B and C. Hope isn't a strategy,'" says Paulson's then deputy, Bob Steel.

When Paulson called later that week to encourage Fuld to consider raising capital, he was gratified to learn that Lehman was already working on it, and by April 1 the bank had raised $4 billion in convertible preferred shares. On April 12, at a G7 dinner in Washington, D.C., Paulson took Fuld aside. "I congratulated him on his capital raise," Paulson says. "I encouraged him to do more." Paulson was trying to use positive reinforcement to get Fuld to be even more cautious and even consider selling the firm, but that's not what Fuld heard. Later that night, he e-mailed Tom Russo the following memo:

> Just finished the Paulson dinner.
> A few takeaways//
> 1-we have huge brand with treasury
> 2-loved our capital raise
> 3-really appreciate u +Rieders work on ideas
> 4-they want to kill the bad HFnds + heavily regulate the rest
> 5-they want all the G7 countries to embrace
> Mtm stnds
> Cap stnds
> Lev + liquidty stnds
> 6-HP has a worried ed view of ML [Merrill Lynch]
>
> All in all worthwhile.
> Dick

■ ■ ■

No doubt emboldened by her home-run earnings call, Callan began appearing more often on television—particularly on the business channel CNBC—to brag about Lehman's huge brand and its many successes. There was a personal benefit to this as well: She told colleagues that a former high school friend, now a fireman, had contacted her after seeing her on the network, and they were dating.

On April 1, as Fuld dealt with Paulson, Callan was talking to longtime CNBC anchor Maria Bartiromo about the capital raise. She hedged expectations ("pretty solid results, [but] not on an absolute basis") and kept with her line about transparency: "We're happy to open the kimono and let everyone see the story." It was another articulate, confident performance.

"As you know, Maria, we're in a market where perception trumps reality," she said.

That would not be the case for much longer, thanks to the 40-year-old hedge fund manager David Einhorn.

Einhorn hadn't applauded when he'd heard Callan's earnings announcement. He increasingly suspected the firm had been resorting to accounting fraud to juice its earnings, and he said as much in various investor conferences. He even said he believed that the Securities and Exchange Commission (SEC) was letting it slide to avert a bigger crisis. (Einhorn had been badly burned by the foreclosure crisis as a major shareholder and director of the subprime mortgage behemoth New Century Financial, which had gone bankrupt almost overnight in 2007.)

Einhorn figured the only way Lehman could be reporting profits was if it was vastly—and illegally—overvaluing those assets. And he had some convincing evidence: a $1.1 billion discrepancy between the results posted in Callan's March earnings call—in which she said the bank had written down the value of its Level 3 assets to the tune of $875 million—and those in the quarterly report filed with the SEC a few weeks later, which claimed the bank's Level 3 assets had actually risen in value.

He asked Callan to call him—via e-mail. And, against the advice of the executive committee, who felt Einhorn was best ignored, she did. On the call, Einhorn challenged Callan to explain how the firm had come to write up its assets during a period when everything, from equities to fixed income to real estate and private equity, had lost value.

He reportedly asked Callan about the rejiggering of the Level 3 assets, and how the firm could justify its minuscule $200 million write-down on a $6.5 billion pool of collateralized debt obligations (CDOs), when the value had plainly collapsed in the past few months.

Einhorn claimed not to have gotten a single straight answer from Callan, but the phone call gave him plenty of material for his next public anti-Lehman diatribe—at the Ira W. Sohn Investment Research Conference on May 21st.

Among other things, he said: "Now, given my experience with . . . the SEC, I have no expectation that Lehman will be sanctioned in any material way for what we believe it has done. I suspect that some of the authorities applaud Lehman's accounting ingenuity." But, he cautioned, "If there is no penalty for misbehavior—and, in fact, such behavior is rewarded with flattering stories in the mainstream press about how to handle a crisis—we will all bear the negative consequences over time."

Lehman's stock price fell a dollar from $29.50 and slowly drifted lower.

■ ■ ■

Lehman's executive committee was squirming. "She's been caught in her underwear," one of them later griped. But Callan, "spiraling out of control," according to someone on the executive committee, continued her media blitz, shilling for Lehman, and herself.

Around this time David A. Viniar, Goldman Sachs's 53-year-old CFO, picked up the phone and called Callan. He was concerned for his young rival, who seemed to be on CNBC every time he turned it on. Viniar had held his seat for nine years and no one had ever seen *him* on TV. He wanted to pass along some friendly advice: He didn't think the young CFO was helping herself or Lehman by taking on Einhorn or the short sellers in the open like this.

According to Callan's colleagues, she wasn't overly receptive to the call. When he suggested they meet, she said she didn't have time. "I think she may have thought he was the enemy, Goldman Sachs," says Michael Thompson, her ex-husband, in her defense. But even Fuld always took the calls of his Goldman Sachs counterpart, Lloyd Blankfein. A couple of years back, Fuld's son Richie even went to work for Goldman Sachs. Callan seemed to think she was too good to speak to a rival CFO. What had happened to the smart young banker? Where was her judgment?

"We didn't know she would turn into a rock star," Tom Russo said later.

And that was just the beginning. In the Saturday edition of the *Wall Street Journal* on May 17, right before Einhorn's devastating speech, a long profile on Callan concluded with a snippet about her personal shopper at Bergdorf Goodman. Her colleagues were appalled. She was now the most senior woman on Wall Street, Lehman was fighting for its life, and this was how she was presenting herself to the most important business paper in the country?

Callan had been given little or no guidance on this stuff by Gregory, according to Russo. She had just done her own thing.

"She wanted the limelight. As smart as she was, she should have been smart enough to know her own limitations," says one of her former colleagues, adding that she should have known enough to turn down the job of CFO when she was offered it, "and she didn't."

■ ■ ■

During the buildup to George Walker's June wedding, Callan stayed out of the limelight. She knew that this time there could be no gloss on the earnings she had to sign off on. Lehman was about to report a $2.8 billion loss for the second quarter, its first quarterly loss as a public company. She needed to prepare the market for this very bad news.

But on June 4, three days before the Walker wedding, an article appeared in the *Wall Street Journal* by Susanne Craig, breaking the news that Lehman was considering a "capital raise." This was technically incorrect, and it made Lehman look like it was running scared. Freidheim, who kept a tight lid on the communications staff, went ballistic when he read it. Sources say he went through the Lehman phone records to find the leak.

"Lehman had been looking for a strategic partner for the past three years and equity in the open market—not a capital raise," he told people at the time. The distinction was important—a capital raise would dilute the stock and therefore lower its price, while an open-market purchase of equity from a strategic partner would not.

In the logs, Freidheim found calls from Callan's office to the *Wall Street Journal*. Fuming, he reported this to Fuld and Gregory, telling them, "We should consider all options, including firing her."

"We can't," Gregory said. "She's under a lot of pressure with the earnings coming up. We don't want her distracted right now." Fuld deferred to his deputy. Callan was Gregory's domain, his project.

Over at the *Wall Street Journal*'s offices, Craig got a call from Fuld telling her "she was "no longer considered a friend of the firm."

Startled, Craig phoned Kerrie Cohen in Lehman's press office. "I just got off the phone with Dick," she told Cohen. "You tell Erin to call me immediately."

Meanwhile, Andrew Gowers, the *Financial Times* veteran who now was a senior PR executive for Lehman, quietly went behind Fuld's back and put in a call to his buddy, Robert Thomson, the managing editor of the *Wall Street Journal.* The two men had a long history together, since Thomson had preceded Gowers as editor of the *Financial Times.* "I told Robert to ignore what Sue had been told. I'd make sure they had access," Gowers says. "I felt, at least from my narrow corner of the thing, that proprieties were preserved, no matter what idiocies were being pronounced from the top floor [of Lehman]."

But tensions in and around the press department spilled over into George Walker's wedding. As they danced to the band, Skip McGee found himself in a heated discussion with Freidheim—there with his pretty French fiancée, Isabelle Dufour—over Lehman's recent press. McGee had not agreed with a recent decision to fire a press officer, Hannah Burns, whom others had felt to be too "emotional" when dealing with the press.

In fact, McGee hadn't agreed with much he'd seen recently, and he was dreading the earnings results.

The next morning, Sunday, the day before the earnings announcement, McGee walked into Fuld's office, shut the door, and insisted that Gregory, who was sitting there, leave. McGee then told Fuld that Gregory had to go. The market needed that much; Fuld had to fire him. "You need to do this," he said.

Fuld told him, "I'll never do that. We've been partners for 30 years."

■ ■ ■

On June 9, Callan released her earnings report. As insiders feared, the market was horrified by the mammoth losses. Immediately, Lehman stock started to free-fall from $30, falling 7 percent by Tuesday evening and another 14 percent on Wednesday.

Everybody was anxious and unhappy. On Tuesday, June 10, in an executive meeting, Fuld asked everyone at the table to take a turn airing their suggestions about "restoring confidence." McGee spoke first, at Fuld's behest, in part because McGee had received—and forwarded to Fuld—an e-mail dated June 9 from Benoit D'Angelin, a former Lehman employee who had left just months earlier for the hedge fund Centaurus Capital. It read:

> Many many bankers have been calling me in the last few days.
> The mood has become truly awful in the last few days and for

the first time I am really worried that all the hard work we have put in over the last 6/7 years could unravel very quickly. In my view two things need to happen very quickly.

1. Some senior managers have to be much less arrogant and internally admit that some major mistakes have been made. Can't continue to say "we are great and the market doesn't understand."
2. Some changes at senior management level need to happen very soon. People are not and WILL not understand that nobody pays for that mess and that it is "business as usual." We also need to hire a few very senior guys VERY quickly to bolster confidence.

Sorry to be so blunt but a serious shock is needed to allow the firm to rebound quickly and aggressively.

Keep it up and good luck.

At Fuld's prompting, McGee summarized the contents of the e-mail.

He told his fellow executives, "Morale has never been worse. . . . "Somebody in very senior management has to be held accountable. I think we're supposed to stand up and say that we've made mistakes, and we're going to change things. . . . "

Gregory glared at him. McGee knew that some people sitting around that table agreed with him—he'd spoken to McDade, among others—and he was hoping that one of them would back him up. No one did.

The meeting continued, almost as if he had not spoken. If anything, he was attacked. Gregory talked about the importance of "sticking together" in times like this.

Under the table, McGee typed a two-word e-mail to Jeff Weiss, a banker who was not present: "I'm dead."

■ ■ ■

But by now, like a sleeping giant just awakened after a 30-year slumber, Fuld was slowly coming to grips with the turmoil inside his firm—and outside. Over the next couple of days he attended executive committee meetings in different divisions and made it clear that he wanted to hear the truth. He *wanted* to know what the troops thought of Lehman's senior management.

On Wednesday, June 11, he had lunch with the people in McGee's division, and solicited their opinions. He didn't eat a thing—highly unusual for a man with a voracious appetite—and as he got up to leave, he asked one last question: "What would you say if I wasn't here?"

Their answer came back as if from a Greek chorus: "You are not listening."

But, for once, he was.

Chapter 17

The Sacrificial Ram

I don't know what you've been told, but absolutely I was not
fired.

—*Joe Gregory*

L ate in the afternoon following McGee's executive committee
lunch with Dick Fuld, Tracey Binkley, head of human resources,
informed Scott Freidheim that Joe Gregory was "looking at his
stock holdings." The obvious inference was that Gregory was looking
to bail out. At the time, he had over $260 million worth of Lehman
stock; records show that since 2003 he had taken home $40 million
in compensation and sold over $260 million worth of Lehman stock
($70 million of which was used to pay taxes on the stock sales).

How quickly things had changed.

Two days earlier, right after the earnings call, Freidheim's press
department was besieged; there was a rumor that Gregory and Callan
were leaving. Was it true?

This was a story Friedheim had never heard before: Joe Gregory
leaving the firm? In shock, Freidheim walked down to Fuld's office
and asked if such a thing had even been considered.

"No," Fuld had said. "It's not under consideration."

Gregory had been even more emphatic. "Absolutely not," he told Freidheim.

But that was before Fuld had gone around the firm, division to division, and heard the resounding cry: Joe must go!

What actually happened next is known by only Fuld and Gregory, who had a closed-door conversation.

"Falling on his sword for the good of the firm" was how Gregory would later explain his abrupt departure, according to sources.

Not many people inside the firm were fooled. "He was fired," Lessing later told people. But Gregory had one last card left to play. He realized the dramatic media coverage of the fall of "The Most Powerful Woman on Wall Street" would eclipse his demise.

Erin Callan was manning the phones with analysts and investors, running damage control on Monday's cataclysmic earnings announcement that Wednesday afternoon, when Gregory told her he was stepping down and that she was, too.

She was shocked but she dutifully went into Fuld's office and said, "I think I've lost my relevance." His terse response, a source says, was: "I think you have." Just minutes later, she was seated in a conference room listening to her mentor, Gregory, tell the executive committee he was stepping down.

"She's resigning, too," he said, and motioned to Callan. Tears began rolling down her cheeks.

Later Callan would tell *Fortune* magazine a rather different story. Had just Gregory stepped down, she said, "it would have mattered a lot internally, but I didn't think it would have a big impact on the market" because Gregory "was not known to the outside world."

Callan characterized her resignation as something she and Gregory had decided to do together, for the good of the firm. What she did not say was that both of them had agreements drafted that specified they would be paid until the end of the year. (Gregory moved to a nearby office on Sixth Avenue to justify the paycheck.)

Gregory had calculated correctly. The resignation announcements went out on Thursday, June 12. The next day's business press was dominated by the riveting tale of the humbling of Wall Street's most senior female executive. In a typical headline, the *London Independent* wrote: "Wall Street's Leading Woman Pays Price for Lehman's Losses." Gregory was scarcely mentioned.

■ ■ ■

Now Fuld needed to do something he had never done before. He needed to hire a new president, and for the first time since becoming Lehman's CEO, he had to choose ability over loyalty. He had to hire someone shrewd and powerful enough to protect his life's work, even if that person might very well unseat him. In one of life's most bitter ironies, he realized he needed Chris Pettit—12 years too late.

There was an obvious successor: Bart McDade. The former boss and business school roommate of Mike Gelband was the dissidents' favorite to replace Gregory.

A veteran of the fixed income market who had chaired the bond market association, he was, thanks to Gregory's eccentric human resources maneuverings, now also an expert on the stock market; he had the chops.

No one doubted that McDade, who had joined the firm in 1979 as an intern, bled Lehman green. If he lacked for anything, he perhaps lacked Pettit's charisma. But he was, in the words of one colleague, a "businessman's businessman."

McDade was quietly, fiercely intellectual. "He had the brilliance of being able to look at things complicated, break them down in a way and reimagine them imaginatively, and move the business forward in a way that makes sense," says one colleague. "One example: It's now common on the Street for everybody to do equity transfers—CSAs, commission sharing agreements. Bart came up with that idea, pioneered it with Fidelity." Basically, CSAs allow the transfer of commissions on a trade from a broker to a third party.

He kept his body and his mind sharp. He worked out religiously, and when not at client meals, he ate Special K for breakfast, lunch, and dinner. He was extraordinarily thin and he dressed in sharp suits. He had a military bearing, which was enhanced when he suddenly— surprisingly—shaved his head upon hearing that he'd been appointed president.

On June 12, Fuld called the executive committee and announced that McDade was his man. The committee approved heartily of the choice, as did most of the people at Lehman, past and present. When Tom Tucker read about it, he e-mailed McDade immediately. "I hope you can right a great wrong," he said.

One of the few who objected to McDade was Jeremy Isaacs. Echoing the complaints about Pettit, Isaacs considered McDade a "Marine" type.

When McDade got the job, Isaacs handed in his resignation, but Fuld pleaded with him to stay. He knew that losing Isaacs so soon after the jettisoning of Gregory and Callan would play disastrously in the press and in the market. Isaacs agreed to stay on to help see through a merger with the Korea Development Bank (KDB), a Korean government bank that had expressed interest in purchasing Lehman. But in all but name, Isaacs was quietly replaced as head of Europe by the young German Christian Meissner and Benoit Savoret.

■ ■ ■

By Friday, June 13, as news of the shakeup hit the press, Fuld was ready to move on. McDade's appointment was officially announced to the firm the next Monday at the Sheraton Hotel, close to Lehman's midtown offices on Seventh Avenue, where both Fuld and McDade made a grand "do the right thing" gesture by announcing that they would forgo their bonuses that year.

Fuld had told McDade he wanted to have Gregory attend the ceremony, as if he were passing the torch. McDade objected—he wanted all traces of the man many blamed for Lehman's reckless risk taking expunged as swiftly as possible.

In fact, when he was shown Gregory's office—where most assumed he'd take up residence—he declared that it had bad "feng shui." Instead he moved into Tom Russo's office and had it professionally redecorated. He quickly installed an oriental figurine he called "the Money God," which he'd always kept for good luck. Russo moved into Gregory's old office.

McDade quickly began making staffing changes. The Tuesday following Gregory's ouster, he met with his old friends—and Lehman exiles—Mike Gelband and Alex Kirk at Kirk's apartment and persuaded them to rejoin the firm. By late June, the two were back on the trading floor, where they were greeted with deafening applause.

McDade also brought back John Cecil. He said, "John, I need you in a meeting." It had been several years since Cecil had looked over the Lehman balance sheets. When he saw roughly $40 billion in commercial real estate and a further $25 million in residential real estate, he was appalled. It struck him as he looked around the Lehman executive floor that even though the mood was grim and determined, everyone seemed exhausted. "There was no sense of sufficient urgency," he says.

McDade rapidly dismantled Gregory's costly human resources department. At long last, co-CAO Ian Lowitt, a Rhodes scholar and McKinsey-trained polymath who had been widely considered a shoo-in for the CFO spot before Callan nabbed it, got the job. (One reason Lowitt may have been passed over, according to one executive, was that Gregory considered him to be a "sloppy" dresser.)

Jerry Donini, the head of American equities, took McDade's old job as global chief of equities, and an Italian banker named Riccardo Banchetti was tapped to be Christian Meissner's partner heading the investment bank's European and Middle Eastern operations, the post vacated by Isaacs. Two new fixed income chiefs were also named, Asian capital markets head Hyung Soon Lee and global credit products chief Eric Felder. In short order, Fuld's band of loyalists had been almost wholly marginalized.

McDade split senior management into teams to divide the considerable labor of executing his game plan to save the firm. His major objectives included selling the firm by the next quarter, which was less than three months away. The eight specific tasks at hand were, in summary:

1. Get the toxic assets (the commercial real estate loans) off the balance sheet and spin them off into a separate vehicle—which would come to be dubbed "SpinCo"—that would be disbursed to shareholders. The idea was that if SpinCo could somehow be deemed exempt from the requirement to mark all of its 2,500 commercial real estate investments to market, it would eventually ride out the bear market and generate a profit for shareholders.

2. Raise at least $3.8 billion by selling an equity stake in the newly sanitized "CleanCo" to a partner, an endeavor that was named "Project Blue." Skip McGee and the bankers were put in charge of "Project Blue," and worked off a document that outlined a possible merger with the Korean Development Bank (KDB, Korea's national bank), which, Lehman hoped, would own 55 percent of Lehman's investment management division, which included NeubergerBerman, which had no debt and was worth perhaps as much as $9 billion (some insiders even thought $10 billion). Aside from KDB, there were also merger talks with Bain and Hellman, Kohlberg Kravis Roberts, and Blackstone.

3. Reduce "less liquid asset exposures in mortgages, commercial real estate, and high-yield acquisition finance"—in lay terms, stop plowing money into risky real estate ventures.

4. Reduce head count and expenses.

5. Make multiple management changes to improve performance and risk management.

6. Finalize a restructuring of all "securitized product origination platforms." (Translated into English, this generally referred to finishing off the mass purge of Lehman staffers involved in the mortgage business.)

7. Slash nonpersonnel expenses by $250 million.

8. Reduce the common dividend to $1.25 per quarter.

By now an emissary from the government—either Treasury, the New York Federal Reserve, or the Securities and Exchange Commission—was inside Lehman (and most other Wall Street firms) daily. Paulson had even persuaded his old Goldman Sachs buddy, Ken Wilson, to act as a liaison with Lehman.

Paulson was prepared to help Fuld try everything, but the SpinCo venture—which the folks at Treasury quickly renamed "ShitCo"—worried him.

"They came up with this goofy idea of the SpinCo," he recalled a year later in a room in Johns Hopkins University in Washington, D.C., his brow furrowing with puzzlement. "I just kept questioning Dick: 'Why do you think you can raise equity in your bad real estate if you can't raise it in your company?'"

In other words, how could they expect to raise the money to pay ShitCo's prodigious bills without committing securities fraud? The only remotely viable option the firm had floated was through the sale of the asset management firm NeubergerBerman. But the bankers had made clear that selling that was considered their funding option of last resort.

Essentially, what Lehman and/or SpinCo needed in the short term was an unlimited line of cheap credit at the Federal Reserve discount window.

"Main Street" banks, with depositors, bank branches, and ATM machines, have access to the discount window because their depositors are insured by the Federal Deposit Insurance Corporation (FDIC), which in turn has the authority to seize, take over, and sell off banks whose managers get too sloppy with the books. It was a long shot, but within a matter of months both Goldman Sachs and Morgan Stanley would be scrambling to do the same thing. So, with the help of a Sullivan & Cromwell lawyer, H. Rodgin "Rog" Cohen, a Lehman team drafted a proposal called "The Impact of Becoming a Bank."

■ ■ ■

Lehman's SpinCo team—Fuld, Russo, McDade, Lowitt, Freidheim, Lessing, and Lehman treasurer Paolo Tonucci—floated the idea on a conference call in July with the president of the New York Federal Reserve Bank, Timothy Geithner. He instantly vetoed it.

On the fly, one person on the call remembers, Russo stepped in. "If you don't want us to convert to a bank holding company," he pleaded with Geithner, "then let us make a one-time election, where we move certain assets, our mortgages and commercial real estate. Move those assets to our Utah bank. We then can post to the window. And it's over. It's over."

"You can formally apply," Geithner said tersely, according to someone on the call.

But there was little doubt that Lehman was light-years from meeting the qualifications required to become a bank holding company. Approving the firm's application would have hurt the Fed's reputation, according to a senior source there.

(It didn't help that Russo wasn't taken particularly seriously by government officials, who called him "Radio Tom" for his penchant for babbling. "He transmits but he doesn't receive," said one former Treasury official, who remembers holding the phone at arm's length during some of Russo's more tedious monologues.)

Lehman applied, but the whole thing "was theater on their part," someone close to Federal Reserve Chairman Ben Bernanke later said. Their application was rejected.

With the benefit of hindsight, however, Russo's idea looks pretty smart, concedes a former Treasury staffer. "He was absolutely right to want to become a bank holding company." But the Fed wasn't in the mood for such "outside-the-box" thinking just weeks after the Bear Stearns bailout. What it really wanted Lehman to do was the same thing Paulson wanted Lehman to do: Sell. Now.

But they also knew there were few, if any, buyers. Who would want to take on those toxic assets?

"They went around the whole world, trying to find investors," Paulson said a year later. "I essentially knew that they had been to everybody you could think of. No one wanted to invest in them."

"If there *were* buyers for an investment bank, there were other firms with more attractive franchises. With Bear Stearns, we had been very fortunate to have JPMorgan there as a buyer.

And even if a buyer miraculously appeared, would Fuld actually commit to a deal that he thought undervalued Lehman? Paulson was not sure that he would.

"Although Lehman was a storied old firm with a rich heritage, Dick was the guy who had, in many ways, founded the new Lehman when it spun out of American Express. So, his ego was tied up with the company, with the price of the stock," Paulson said. "He was very focused on the price of the stock."

On the other side of the Atlantic, Peregrine Moncreiffe ran into a friend who worked for hedge fund king John Paulson. "Fuld told us he's deliberately going to keep the balance sheet big," he told Moncreiffe. "He thinks that this way, the government will have no choice but to save him."

Chapter 18

Korea's Rising Sum

One problem with the Korean deal was that Dick forgot
E. S. Min was not still his employee. He treated him as though
he was.

—*Lehman executive committee member*

There were only a handful of potential buyers strong enough
to purchase Lehman. The list included the United Kingdom's
HSBC Holdings PLC, Germany's Deutsche Bank AG, Japan's
Nomura Securities, and Spain's Banco Santander SA. There were also
the sovereign wealth funds in China and the Middle East that had
invested billions in Citigroup and Merrill Lynch earlier in the year.
But the Chinese were still smarting from some major losses its state-
owned China Investment Corporation had taken investing in the crew
of ex-Lehman guys who founded Blackstone Group. Negotiations in
the Middle East went nowhere.

Behind the scenes, the U.S. government was contemplating that if
the worst happened, there might be two major buyers. One was Bank
of America, which, Paulson felt, might be interested in acquiring an

investment bank. That was his first choice. In the back of his mind there was the British investment bank BarCap, the investment arm of Barclays PLC, which Paulson would not have thought of were it not for his friend Bob Steel, the outgoing undersecretary for domestic finance at the U.S. Treasury (who would later briefly helm the ailing Wachovia until its speedy government-brokered takeover by Wells Fargo at the end of 2008).

In May, Steel had told Paulson that Robert "Bob" Diamond Jr., the CEO of BarCap, wanted to move back to the United States from London. "I suggested to Hank that Barclays was an excellent route to go; they wanted a much bigger U.S. business. Bob Diamond knew investment banking and capital markets cold, was an excellent leader, and was keen to return to the U.S.," Steel says.

But Paulson was skeptical. "When Barclays came to me the first time, I was thinking, first of all, do they know how to complete a deal? They'd lost out to RBS and ABN Amro."

■ ■ ■

Meanwhile, Lehman had spent the summer hoping to pull a rabbit—and its corporate backside—out of a hat with "Project Blue."

The Korea Development Bank (KDB)'s Capital Corporation was interested in purchasing a minority stake in Lehman to give itself a global platform. Lehman took this seriously, and the executive leading KDB's talks was a former Lehman employee—their chairman and CEO, Min Euoo-sung (E.S.).

In late July, Fuld, McDade, Isaacs, Russo, McGee, Kunho Cho, and Bhattal flew to Hong Kong to meet with Min, a passionate and bright financier. The deal they imagined was a "significant but non-controlling investment . . . coupled with three joint ventures," says someone with knowledge of the discussions, and included various agreements to possibly integrate Lehman's and KDB's investment banking operations in Asia.

Min clearly wanted to make a deal, but he had to contend with a continually shifting backdrop. The South Korean currency was beginning to crumble in the summer of 2008. By summer's end, the South Korean won had lost nearly 20 percent of its value since the start of the year, and reached a four-year low. There were serious issues concerning the South Korean current account deficit (which had reached $12.59 billion between January and August), South Korea's dollar reserves, and the general state of its domestic economy. Further, because KDB was owned by the South Korean government, government officials, according to a source involved, from "various agencies and political factions . . . wanted the ability to review any transaction" before giving their approval. They told Min that they wanted a formal "management consultant" style study performed on the merger before it could be approved.

Fuld arrived in Hong Kong ignorant of all this. The night before their meeting, Min called Fuld at his hotel and dropped three bombs: First, KDB was working in a consortium with, among others, the South Korean Hana bank as well as an assortment of other players, all of which would have to support the deal. Second, the South Korean government was involved, and wanted the aforementioned study of the deal before approval. Due to this, there was no way there could be any announcement of a deal before August 22. Further, should a deal take place, it would have to be structured so that if Lehman underperformed and the merged entity started to suffer massive drops in share price, there had to be a way the South Koreans could transform their minority stake into a controlling majority stake—they would take over Lehman's management. (Structuring an investment like this—allowing a minority shareholder to assume control of a company without paying a control premium to the shareholders—could be illegal.)

Fuld was shocked. He thought he'd come to finalize the deal; now he was practically starting over.

Min was being advised by three parties: C. K. Lee, the president of South Korea's Hana investment bank; Victor Lewkow of the New York law firm Cleary Gottlieb Steen & Hamilton; and a tall dark-haired American banker from the New York boutique advisory firm Perella Weinberg. His name was Gary Barancik.

Fuld asked Min if they could at least announce they were in discussions to do a deal. When Min made it clear that his government approval process wouldn't allow an announcement prior to August 22, Fuld asked whether KDB would at least be willing to announce the following week that discussions between the parties were taking place. Min, though he had initially indicated that he would consider this, subsequently concluded that it would be "unwise" to announce discussions before receiving the government's blessing. He told Fuld no.

Nonetheless, arrangements were made for talks to continue in New York City on August 5, in order to hammer out a term sheet and begin the due diligence on Lehman's business units, though some on the Lehman team were beginning to doubt that this deal was viable. "It was just too complicated; it had too many parts," one member of the executive committee said later.

Min was also starting to have doubts. When the South Koreans landed in New York on the night of August 2, Min's concern about Lehman's real estate portfolio had grown exponentially—he wouldn't proceed with the deal until those assets were shipped elsewhere. As a result, Min turned the proposed agenda for the New York meeting on its ear, asking that the time be spent reviewing Lehman's real estate assets on the first day, rather than doing the planned term sheet negotiations and general due diligence. He'd proceed only if what they found satisfied him.

A representative from KDB called McGee and asked if the Lehman team could bring Mark Walsh to the next day's meeting to walk Min's team through the valuations.

Walsh obliged. Min, however, was not satisfied. He expressed his concern about the real estate marks to market at the end. Fuld was not present during this meeting, but Bart McDade suggested a way around Min's objections. What if Lehman offered him a stake in a "CleanCo" that had none of Lehman's commercial or residential real estate? Min liked this idea. He even said that KDB would pay 1.25 times the book value, so long as the real estate was removed.

The two groups planned to meet again, at 6 P.M.—without Walsh—and go over a term sheet for such a deal. That afternoon, however, Fuld called Min twice. Both times he told him that the original deal was better, that it made more sense for Min to keep the businesses together. He said, in effect: "There's tremendous opportunity here, given how depressed market prices are for these assets right now. If you invest now and buy the whole thing, you're going to look like a hero."

Min was put off by Fuld's calls, and was alarmed at his continued insistence on dumping the toxic assets on him, but nonetheless showed up for the 6 P.M. meeting, along with his bankers and lawyers.

Fuld kicked off the conversation by reiterating that he believed KDB was missing an opportunity by not taking on the whole company, all real estate included. It was the third or fourth time that day he had tried to persuade Min, and the pitch was wearing thin.

One person in the meeting says, "Everyone in the room other than Dick looked increasingly concerned" as Fuld talked. "Dick's going through this whole thing, trying to sort of key up the same exact deal again to buy the whole company. And E.S. kept raising objections, politely reminding Fuld that KDB was uncomfortable with the amount of exposure, and Dick kept arguing with him. It was sort of incredible.

"KDB had already met with the whole Lehman team earlier about CleanCo, and had reached a conceptual agreement. The Koreans thought they were all there to talk about, 'Are you prepared to accept our offer and move forward on a CleanCo deal?' Dick comes in and tries to change tack."

Finally, Barancik spoke up, and tried to make it clear that KDB was concerned that the real estate had not been appropriately marked to market. "KDB has already made the decision that the only basis on which it is prepared to move forward is on the CleanCo structure," he said bluntly.

Fuld fired back: "Have you really looked at this real estate and what it's valued at?" he asked, incredulous. "If our marks aren't accurate, what should they be?"

Barancik said he was not commenting on the marks or drawing any conclusions. He simply wanted to concentrate on the deal his client wanted to do: CleanCo.

To everyone's relief, McDade leaped in and produced a term sheet drawn up by the lawyers.

"Look, Dick, we do have *this* term sheet—let's talk about the deal that we came here to talk about," he said, and the term sheet was passed around.

Min looked at it and was surprised. It was a one-page document. And it was selling a different CleanCo than the one they'd agreed to buy.

A person on Min's team recalls, "CleanCo wasn't totally CleanCo. In fact, CleanCo was going to have some amount of assets . . . between, like, $5 billion and $15 billion of real estate assets, that would be chosen by mutual agreement, some of which would remain with

CleanCo because they were nontransferable, and some of which the Lehman team proposed be cherry-picked as providing attractive value to CleanCo."

The tension in the room was palpable. Fuld sat silent but scowling. Min was confused. There were small clauses to haggle over, but the main problem was the elephant in the room: namely, that CleanCo was no longer CleanCo. Until this was resolved, negotiations could not continue.

Min and his advisers asked if they could step out for a minute to confer. In private, Min made it clear that he'd had enough, that he felt Lehman was hiding something and attempting to pass its problems to him. He said he was getting on the next plane to South Korea. As far as he was concerned, the deal was dead.

But Barancik persisted: Would Min be willing to proceed with a deal that was truly clean? One that resembled the deal discussed earlier in the day with McDade and McGee?

Min said he was, then reentered the room and told Fuld and the others that he was flying home, but that Barancik had been instructed to work with Lehman on coming to terms on a deal.

Min rose to leave the table. Fuld was, at this point, slumped in his chair. He didn't try to hide his anger. He said to his former employee, "So what do you mean, E.S.? You mean you're just walking out? You're going to give up now? After all the work we've done and after all the time we've been talking? You're just going to walk out the door?"

There followed an excruciating pause. Would Min walk out in a huff? He didn't. As the group disbanded, he chatted with Fuld at the door. Min politely stuck to his position and Fuld seemed to calm down.

■ ■ ■

The Lehman team decided to exclude Fuld from further talks. From that point on, Lehman became far more cooperative—perhaps out of desperation. With the Perella team, they modeled spin-off structures, and sent newly furnished financial information to KDB to encourage a definitive proposal.

In late August, KDB drew up a term sheet offering to invest approximately $6 billion into a CleanCo Lehman. Lehman would be paid 1.25 times book value but at a significantly written-down book value. The offer worked out to $6.40 per share. At the time, Lehman stock was trading around $13. The Koreans demanded two board seats and control if Lehman didn't meet performance targets in terms of stock price and return on equity. Lehman would also have to keep its single-A credit rating.

In Lehman's eyes, the offer was untenable. According to its valuations of the real estate, the stock should be priced at $17 or $18 a share. The South Koreans countered that they might be prepared to pay more if after 18 months it looked like they had undervalued the company. But Lehman wasn't interested. In fact, no one seems to know if Fuld even showed the term sheet to the Lehman board. Tom Russo, under whose purview such matters fell, said he "could not recall" if Fuld ever produced the document.

Given Lehman's ultimate fate, such an omission would have been a grave deviation from standard operating procedure.

On September 1, Barancik asked McGee what Lehman's reaction to the term sheet was. McGee said it had been rejected, but that Min was welcome to come to New York and talk further. In the meantime, Kunho Cho, a member of the Lehman team requested that KDB not reveal that there had ever been any talks. A leak like that would negatively impact Lehman's already depressed stock price.

■ ■ ■

Five days later, on September 6, Freddie Mac and Fannie Mae imploded. The U.S. government had to seize the two mortgage giants and pledge as much as $200 billion of taxpayer money to save them. On Monday, September 8, there were press leaks that the deal between Lehman and the South Koreans had fallen apart. It was widely assumed within Lehman that the South Koreans were the ones responsible for the leaks, terrified that their involvement in talks would be made public. In any case, the leaks spelled disaster. They further undermined the credibility of the firm, and reinforced the idea that—for all the rumblings—Lehman was just blowing smoke about having a buyer.

By Tuesday, Lehman stock had dropped 45 percent, to $7.79.

Barancik called McGee and asked if Lehman would be willing to reconsider KDB's offer. McGee, staring into the abyss, said Lehman would consider it.

But he was too late.

On September 10 a South Korean government official told Reuters they were walking away from the deal. The stock fell 9 percent to $7.25. Hours later, a KDB official told the news agency the two were still in talks and that the bank had made an offer—only to concede a few hours later that prospects looked grim. Lehman stock fell another 60 percent the next day to $4.22.

Bob Steel summed up those failed negotiations this way: "It takes nine months to make a baby, and they didn't have nine."

Chapter 19

The Wart on the End of Lehman's Nose

The trouble was that by the end they believed their own press. They were in la-la land. They really did believe they were omnipotent. It just never occurred to them they couldn't get away with that balance sheet.

—*Former senior Lehman executive*

Fannie Mae and Freddie Mac, the two teetering giants that kept the multitrillion-dollar housing market churning with cheap loans, officially collapsed on September 7, 2008. Although the two companies were technically publicly traded capitalist entities, they had been founded by the government during the Depression and were still called government-sponsored enterprises. They were also flat broke. After warning Congress that they might need government assistance in July, Hank Paulson officially nationalized them six weeks later, estimating that the cost of bailing them out would run around $200 billion.

It was finally clear even to the most casual observer that the housing and asset bubble had burst—and that the damage would in no way be, as Federal Reserve chairman Ben Bernanke had predicted a year earlier, "contained."

Observers had initially feared for Main Street's smaller community banks, but Fannie and Freddie were also massive buyers and sellers of the mortgage-backed securities weighing on the balance sheets of every Wall Street firm. If the two firms could go from getting a clean bill of health from regulators in July to needing $200 billion six weeks later, what did that foretell for everyone else with billions of dollars in mortgages on its books?

The question spooked James L. "Jamie" Dimon, the 53-year-old CEO and chairman of JPMorgan Chase. Dimon learned first-hand the type of risk his more aggressive competitors had piled on when he took over Bear Stearns in March. As the leader of Lehman's official clearing bank—meaning cash and securities exchanges arranged by Lehman actually took place at JPMorgan Chase—he was also partially privy to Lehman's books.

Dimon had two disturbing conclusions: One, that Wall Street was so dependent on short-term financing that any one of them could become the next Bear Stearns, and Two, that he didn't have any more room on his balance sheet to rescue the next victim.

On Tuesday, September 9, right after the government seizure of Freddie and Fannie was announced, Dimon reportedly sat down to lunch with Bernanke and warned him that he was done bailing out banks. Dimon wanted to know if the Fed was ready to step in to save Lehman.

"We're working on a number of initiatives," Bernanke said vaguely. "We're just trying to stay ahead of this thing."

Dimon took the hint. If Lehman were to fail, JPMorgan would be stuck with those securities and a massive loss of cash. So as a precautionary measure, it was going to need to ask for more collateral from Lehman Brothers.

Dimon understood that any potential acquirer of Lehman would want at least some of the potential losses subsidized by the Fed—what had come to be known as a "Jamie deal" since he had gotten the central bank to guarantee $30 billion in Bear's bad loans back in the spring. What few on Wall Street realized was that another Jamie deal would be impossible to put together. The hole in Lehman's balance sheet was vastly bigger than Bear's, and while the criticism of Paulson and Bernanke over the Bear Stearns deal had largely come from the populist left, the Fannie-Freddie bailout had won them the enmity of the right. (Their role in housing policy has long associated them with left-leaning advocacy groups like ACORN.)

In other words, Hank Paulson was out of friends on Capitol Hill.

On the Tuesday afternoon after Dimon's lunch at the Fed, Dimon instructed his investment banking chief, Steve Black, to call Dick Fuld. The gist of the call, Black later said, was to gently warn Fuld that unless he could find a buyer fast, Lehman had to start thinking in terms of arranging a Long-Term Capital Management style rescue.

And by the way, JPMorgan Chase was going to need another $5 billion in collateral.

■ ■ ■

When Lehman's senior management heard about JP Morgan's collateral calls they went berserk. After consulting with McDade, Fuld decided there was only one way he could survive: He would preannounce Lehman's earnings results and launch SpinCo into the world in hopes of placating the market.

One person involved explained it this way: "In terms of capital, the feeling was that we would have a capital hole at the time we did SpinCo, which would have been in the first quarter of 2009. But we had the time between then and the first quarter of the next year. . . . We could either fill it with the sale of Neuberger, which nobody wanted to do, . . . or get people to put money into the firm. So we sort of felt we had a fallback position on someone saying, 'Ah, but you won't have enough capital if you do SpinCo.' We thought SpinCo may take $8 billion. So when the plan was put together by Bart, there was a feeling that 'Boy, it sounds pretty good.' And the theory would be that at the time of our earnings in September, we would go through the whole plan, and people would say, 'Wow.'"

On September 10 at 8 A.M. Eastern time, Fuld delivered his announcement in a conference call to investors. From around the world, Lehman's 25,000 employees listened in with countless others, and knew this was a historic moment. "I heard his voice and it was so tired, and it was cracking—and I just knew this is over," said a London-based managing director who was listening in on his cell phone while waiting for a flight.

"So today, we're taking a number of necessary actions," Fuld began. "Here's the summary: We put a concrete plan in place to exit the vast majority of our commercial real estate; we are reducing our residential and leveraged loan exposures down to appropriate operating levels; we are in the final stages of raising capital with sale of a majority stake in IMD [the investment managing division], strengthening our capital base—as we strengthened our capital base in June, protected our liquidity, and are cutting our dividend; we reshaped our human capital and product [set expense base] to these changing markets; lastly, we implemented a series of management changes, some of which you saw in the last couple of days. Taken together, these actions have quickly derisked and resized the firm. Let me just go through each in more detail:

"Today we announced a plan to separate a vast majority of our commercial real estate assets from our core business by spinning off those assets to our shareholders and to an independent, publicly traded entity which will be adequately capitalized. The spin-off improves our balance sheet while preserving value for our shareholders. The spin-off entity will be able to manage its assets for economic value maximization over a longer time horizon, given the fact that it will not be a mark-to-market entity, but rather use held-to-maturity accounting. This will preserve economic value for our shareholders."

Then, Ian Lowitt laid out the details of SpinCo, while the banking analysts on the call waited for someone to ask the obvious question: Since Lehman had not sold NeubergerBerman (talks were still ongoing with the private equities firms Bain Capital and Hellman & Friedman), how was SpinCo going to be financed?

Within the firm's senior management there had been debate— throughout the night, right up to the moment of the call—as to what Lowitt should say when asked this inevitable question. Lowitt had not got much sleep because of the continual back-and-forth over *exactly* what words he should use. McDade had insisted it would be disastrous to convey to the market the lack of certainty over the execution of their plan, even though the reality was that Lehman hadn't yet tied up all of SpinCo's numerous loose ends.

After Lowitt had laid out the company's plans and opened the call to questions, Deutsche Bank analyst Mike Mayo asked the big question: "To the extent you might need $7 billion to capitalize that entity and [assuming] you will get $3 billion with the spin-off part of IMD, how would you get the other $4 billion?"

Lowitt replied: "We don't feel that we need to raise that extra amount to cover the seven because you will have less leverageable equity in core Lehman than in, you know, where you are at the end of this quarter."

In other words, he didn't have a good answer.

The market's response was indeed "Wow!"—just not in the way Lehman had hoped.

A close friend of Dick Fuld, who does not want to be named, shook his head when he heard the announcement. "Dick's just highlighted the wart at the end of his nose," he said to himself.

■ ■ ■

Mayhem ensued. As the *Wall Street Journal* later reported: "By the following day, Sept. 11, the price of Lehman's credit-default swaps—the cost to protect against losses on $10 million of its debt for five years—had soared to $800,000 a year, from $219,000 at the end of May. Clients began calling and emailing Lehman to get their money out. Lehman scrambled to comply so as not to betray weakness."

JPMorgan Chase was worried about holding lending positions with Lehman if the firm collapsed. For the past week, Morgan had been advancing collateralized lending to the tune of at least $100 billion a day, so that Lehman could stay in business. By the night of September 11, though, Morgan froze $17 billion of Lehman's cash and securities. Jane Buyers Russo, head of JPMorgan's broker-dealer unit, phoned Lehman's treasurer, Paolo Tonucci. She told him that Lehman would have to turn over the $5 billion in collateral that Morgan had asked for days earlier. The amount was big enough to temporarily freeze Lehman's computerized trading systems; it nearly broke the firm's trading arm.

A run on the bank had begun, and there was nothing Fuld or McDade could do to stop it.

Once Wall Street CEOs heard that Dimon was asking for more collateral, they started calling each other—and the government—to get a sense of how badly they would be hit if Lehman went down.

■ ■ ■

By Thursday afternoon, Bank of America CEO Ken Lewis had soured on Lehman. Earlier in the week, Bank of America had come to Christopher Flowers, whose private equity firm J. C. Flowers & Company was always on the hunt for failing banks, and asked him to partner on the deal. Flowers, a math genius, had spent 24 hours poring over Lehman's books with a team from Bank of America and found the firm's $32 billion portfolio of commercial real estate assets highly questionable—to say nothing of Lehman's exposure to residential mortgages. The team didn't value the firm at anything close to Lehman's self-valuation of $600 billion.

Lewis called Paulson and said, "We've looked at it and we can't do it without government assistance. We just can't get there." He wanted out of this deal. Instead, he wanted Merrill Lynch.

"Tell us what you need help on, and we will come up with a way to get there," Paulson told him.

Meanwhile, Lehman thought Bank of America was neck deep in the deal: An acquisition by BofA made sense. Bank of America was a retail bank. Why wouldn't it want an investment bank?

Fuld believed that by Thursday afternoon it was all but done. He mentioned to a colleague that Lewis had even said to him Thursday night, "You know, we're going to do this deal." Lewis had given him his home phone number in Charlotte, North Carolina, and signed off with "We will need to stay in touch over the weekend."

Fuld was optimistic.

Over at Lehman's offices at 745 Seventh Avenue, Steve Berkenfeld put in a precautionary call to Stephen Dannhauser, head of Weil, Gotshal & Manges, asking him to start preliminary work on bankruptcy papers. Dannhauser conveyed the message to Harvey R. Miller, the country's leading bankruptcy attorney and a member of the firm. Miller understood this was an important client (the firm's largest) and started in immediately.

■ ■ ■

Meanwhile, sensing Lewis's nervousness, Paulson finally called Bob Diamond in London and asked, "Are you serious?" He says Diamond told him he was. Very.

"That's what made me so optimistic—they kept saying they couldn't stand to get to the altar and be topped by someone again," Paulson recalled.

Before Diamond left, Paulson told him, "Don't come unless you are serious."

■ ■ ■

Bob Diamond and a team got on a plane to New York.

Diamond *was* interested in buying Lehman—but only its U.S. assets, and at a distressed price. Diamond and his boss, John Varley, the CEO of the parent company Barclays, had been chewing the idea over with the Barclays board in the United Kingdom and with their regulator, the Financial Services Authority (FSA), all summer.

"Lehman was number one in equity research for six or seven years, number one in fixed income research; the Greenwich survey said they had the deepest, highest quality of penetration of U.S. institutional clients," Diamond explained later.

"So all of a sudden we realized that as proud as we were . . . of our strength in the UK and Europe, the biggest strategic issue we faced was, 'How do we get into the equity business without a U.S. franchise? And how do we become a scale player in the U.S.?'"

The consensus was that if Barclays could get Lehman cheaply, according to Diamond, "the U.S. franchise was worth the pain of integrating the rest." Provided, of course, that due diligence did not throw up any surprises.

But BarCap had a major obstacle.

Diamond believes he had warned Paulson that the other key player in a deal with Barclays was the British regulator. The Financial Services Authority (FSA) would never sanction the deal unless Barclays got a guarantee for funding when markets opened Monday morning. Under British law, Barclays had to have a shareholder vote before it could stand behind Lehman's liabilities. It could not hold a vote in time and "the FSA would not waive that requirement." The funding would have to come from the United States, either from a third party, such as Warren Buffett (a rerun of the LTCM scenario) or from the Fed, which would, of course, mean U.S. taxpayer dollars were at stake. The British were not going to put their taxpayers' money at stake for a private deal by Barclays.

Diamond says he told Hector Sants, the CEO of the FSA, that he would explain to the U.S. Treasury secretary and to Tim Geithner of the Federal Reserve Bank of New York that the UK regulator should not be called for help that weekend. He and the Americans would find a way around it.

But was he conning himself? Even as Diamond and his crew flew over the Atlantic on Thursday night, the staff inside the British regulator was skeptical that Barclays could pull of a deal that met their requirements.

A source inside the FSA says: "We just thought, 'Oh, God, there go the Americans . . . Diamond and Paulson and all their buddies thinking they can make us be part of their deal with all their big talk.'"

But Diamond believed he could make it work.

■ ■ ■

Around lunchtime on Friday, September 12, Diamond entered the Lehman building through a back elevator, so no one could see him.

He was meeting with Fuld, and the conversation was going to be brief and delicate.

According to Diamond, Fuld asked if he could be involved in the new company once Barclays bought Lehman. "It was a really difficult conversation," Diamond says. "But I had to have it. I had to say: 'If we're able to do this, whether I wanted you to be a part of it or not, the regulators are not going to allow it. And we should just get this off the table now.'"

Diamond then left for the midtown law offices of Simpson, Thatcher and Bartlett, where his team was waiting. He was surprised to see that no Lehman executives were there.

"We had an army of people," Diamond recalls, "but we couldn't find Bart McDade. We couldn't find any of [Lehman's] senior people. There was absolutely no data for us. The reason was, they were with BofA."

He was irked partly because Paulson and Geithner had told him to rush over to get a head start on due diligence and partly because both men had also assured Diamond that if he was serious, they wouldn't hand Lehman to another suitor. And Bank of America was a particular thorn for Diamond since he'd recently lost the La Salle bid to BofA in the takeover battle for the Dutch bank ABN Amro.

But Diamond would not stay angry for long. He would soon discover that a deal between Lehman and Bank of America was all but kaput.

Fuld called Ken Lewis's home number three times that Saturday. Every time, Lewis's wife Donna picked up and told him that her husband wasn't there. Fuld kept apologizing: "I'm only calling because Ken gave me this number. . . ."

Eventually, she said to him, "If he wanted to talk to you, he would."

■ ■ ■

Friday evening. Desperate times screamed for desperate measures. In an echo of the Long-Term Capital Management rescue 10 years before, Paulson told Geithner to summon all the heads of Wall Street to the Federal Reserve, where he laid out the situation.

Paulson wanted to figure out a way to save Lehman—but with the criticism over what had happened with Fannie and Freddie still burning in his ears, Paulson was determined to do it without spending a cent of taxpayer money.

"Remember, there was no public policy issue," Bob Steel, Paulson's erstwhile deputy, said many months later, "so he [Paulson] had to deal with the political issue, which was: 'So let me get this straight—you're going to bail out Lehman Brothers so that the clowns who live in mansions with long driveways can continue to send their kids to private schools?' That's how people think."

Paulson agrees. He owns a modest house, wears socks with holes, and is a very moderate Republican (his wife Wendy is a registered Democrat). Paulson would never suggest, even in jest—as Lloyd Blankfein, his successor, later would—that bankers do "God's work." Far from it.

Paulson later said, somewhat jokingly, that when he ran Goldman Sachs, "I used to say to bankers, 'Listen, people don't like bankers, and that means you. I know your mother loves you. If you're lucky, your wife and your kids like you. And your clients may like you individually. But they hate bankers. And so, why are you building these huge homes? Why are you pulling up to a client's office in a limo? Why are you doing this? It is harmful. It's hurting all of us.'"

■ ■ ■

Even as he landed in New York and rolled up his sleeves to get to work, Paulson was making some key phone calls. One was to Warren Buffett. Could Buffett be the third party to help finance Lehman's sale?

But Buffett had read Lehman's 10-K (the company's annual report filed with the SEC) back in April and decided he wasn't interested.

Even so, Paulson went back to the Oracle of Omaha and, according to Buffett, "gave me his thoughts. Though I'm sure he would have been pleased if I had done so, he did not urge me to make the investment."

Paulson also called Alastair Darling, the British chancellor. How helpful were the British going to be? Could Barclays get any backup from its government if they could get a deal going?

The conversation was not a pleasant one. According to Paulson, Darling "was very nervous." He knew exactly what the implications of Lehman failing would be. Nonetheless he wasn't going to let British money backstop an American deal. It would have been voluntarily moving the U.S. cancer overseas.

Paulson recalled that Darling said that the notion of Barclays as a buyer was "of some concern" and he (Darling) wasn't hopeful that Barclays could pull it off. "I forgot exactly the words he [Darling] used, but I was hopeful that maybe, you know, the British regulators were independent," Paulson said months later.

Even so, Paulson had reportedly said to Darling: "Your regulators are asking a lot of questions." Darling shot back: "They are right to."

Paulson now knew he was relying on Bob Diamond's zeal. Maybe the banker really could win over his regulator. "When Barclays . . . started going through the different assets they were going to take, it sounded pretty bad, but they were a motivated buyer," he says. "So the deal seemed challenging—but doable."

■ ■ ■

Saturday morning, Diamond and his team entered the New York Federal Reserve at 33 Water Street, a vast lobby chockablock with lawyers, and were funneled into a room on the fourth floor with a single piece of paper attached to the door. Scribbled on it was the only word that seemed to matter: "Buyer." Diamond smiled.

"We realized our status had been elevated—and that BofA had gone," Diamond says. He reviewed with Paulson and Geithner and their staffs what he and his board had agreed would be the terms. He told them: "Rather than buy Lehman, we're going to extract what we want and ring-fence the private equity and the commercial real estate and leave that in Lehman. We will put in our fee"—a source pegs this at somewhere between $3 billion and $4 billion—"we will put in all the preferred equity, and by our math the gap in valuation is somewhere between $10 to $15 billion to get it funded." In other words, the shortfall was $10 billion to $15 billion.

Paulson was flabbergasted: "What!? I told you there's no government money available for this deal!"

Diamond had more preconditions: "We have to have a guarantee to clear. And I think that has to come from the Fed. We know that the FSA [the British regulator] doesn't have the charter to do it, nor would they do it—we're a UK bank, and this is a U.S. deal. So we will look for third parties. I have very little hope that we can get a third party. . . ."

Michael Klein, one of Diamond's aides, put in a call to Buffett, who once again demurred. "If you fax me something written out about it, when I get back, I'll be glad to read it," Buffett said over speakerphone to the assembled Wall Street luminaries. Then he left with his wife to attend a gala in Edmonton, Alberta.

■ ■ ■

Treasury and Fed officials spent all of Saturday pressuring the heads of Wall Street's top banks and securities houses, including Goldman Sachs,

JPMorgan, Deutsche Bank, Citigroup, and Credit Suisse First Boston, to come together and raise $35 billion to buy Lehman's toxic assets so that the firm could be bought at $3 per share.

Meanwhile, Lehman's representatives—McDade, Kirk, and Shafir, along with the Sullivan & Cromwell lawyer H. Rodgin Cohen—were led to a tiny room on the first floor of the Fed and told to stay put. "It's like we're in a hospital and we're the patient," Kirk joked. But he knew how close to the mark that remark was.

Around 4 P.M. that Saturday, as the Wall Street heads bickered about how much money, if any, they should spend on Lehman, Geithner—according to Paulson—received a call from the Barclays' board in London saying, "We're going to need a shareholder vote. . . .We have a question as to what happens with the trading book."

It was the same red flag that Alastair Darling and Diamond had raised. Even if a merger could be agreed to, Barclays did not have the authority to fund Lehman's trading book on Monday morning. That funding would have to come from elsewhere, presumably the Fed.

Paulson was faced with a Sophie's choice: He could use tax dollars via the Federal Reserve to bail out Lehman or to help it with a merger, or there could be an economic catastrophe.

Geithner hedged on the call with Barclays, according to someone in Treasury. "Tim said, 'We'll certainly keep working to solve it, and don't let that stand in the way. You come up with a deal you can do, and then we'll look at all the options.'"

Diamond recalls that Geithner had told the Barclays board to just "get a deal done, and then we'll deal with the funding issue." Diamond was hopeful he could work with the Fed.

They were looking for a miracle. And to some extent, they got one.

Late Saturday night, the Wall Street CEOs agreed, with some government assistance, to buy the toxic assets, reportedly worth around $35 billion. Paulson now believed he had the deal done, even though the issue of funding the Lehman trading book had not been addressed. Barclays was notified that it should go ahead and bid for a "CleanCo." Everyone was optimistic.

Paulson, meanwhile, was hoping the FSA would come through for him.

In hindsight it appears as though neither party had quite communicated these thoughts to the other—or if they had, that much had been lost in translation.

At around 10 A.M. on Sunday, September 14, McDade phoned Fuld, who was waiting anxiously at Lehman's offices for news, and told him: "We have a deal." Barclays was willing to buy the firm for $5 a share (or roughly $3.5 billion).

But then Sir Callum McCarthy, the outgoing chairman of the FSA and Hector Sants' boss, called up Geithner, "ranting and raving," according to a source, and angrily told him that there was no way the FSA would guarantee the Lehman trading book.

"There was no way forward," recalls Paulson. "The FSA just wouldn't approve the deal."

Sources at the FSA say they were stunned that no one had called them earlier. "Why on earth, if Paulson was serious, didn't he check with us sooner?" someone close to FSA Chief Executive Hector Sants says.

Paulson thought Diamond had spoken to his regulator, and that he'd got them on board.

Diamond appeared to be as dismayed by the FSA's news as Paulson was, and was furious that McCarthy had called Geithner without first coming to Barclays. He believed that he might have been able to make headway with the U.S. Fed and was distressed to learn that an inflammatory phone call from the FSA had seemingly killed the deal. Diamond e-mailed Bob Steel two damning sentences after McCarthy's phone call: "Couldn't have gone more poorly, very frustrating. Little England."

Paulson was devastated. For the second time that weekend he placed a call to Darling, not, he stresses, to ask the UK government for a bailout, but to gauge their mood.

He got his answer. Darling's attitude was the same. It was very bad news for everyone if Lehman failed, but the problem was theirs, not his.

■ ■ ■

According to Treasury sources, Paulson asked his team of financiers, including Steven Shafran and Dan Jester, both retired managing directors of Goldman Sachs, and others from Credit Suisse, to take another look at Lehman's balance sheet.

According to someone present at the Fed meetings, one Treasury staffer estimated that Lehman had overpriced its assets by about $100 billion (Paulson was never told it was this bad); others said the hole was maybe $50 billion to $60 billion.

Paulson lost his cool. He was tired. He was worn out. It was time to tell the Fed and the SEC he could not find a buyer to save Lehman Brothers. He was out of options.

By Sunday afternoon, Lehman was not Paulson's only headache. Sitting in another room in the New York Federal Reserve was a team from American International Group Inc. (AIG). Its stock price was down over 90 percent for the year, the company was being forced to post more and more collateral, and its credit ratings were at risk of a downgrade, which would in turn mean posting more collateral. AIG needed cash quickly, or the company would default and have to file for bankruptcy.

The Lehman situation was bad; this was worse.

Paulson once again put in a call to Buffett, who told the Treasury secretary that he could not afford to let AIG go under. "All bets are off," Treasury sources say Buffett advised Paulson. "You must find a way to save AIG. It's too big and too global."

AIG was the world's largest insurer. It had been widely considered to be a much more dependable counterparty than someone like Lehman or Bear Stearns. It was, after all, an *insurance* company. But the reality was that it had trillions of dollars in bets on the markets, and if its credit rating got downgraded—as most expected would happen within days—it could be hit with collateral calls for billions upon billions it did not have. Millions of Americans had policies with AIG.

Paulson started clearing problems off his desk. First, Lehman needed to file for bankruptcy—a token sign, as Congressman Barney Frank would later say, mockingly, that there was still a free market in America— for one day, at least.

After letting Lehman go, Paulson was pretty sure he would be forced to intervene to save AIG—and God knows who else.

In his mind it wasn't right to equate AIG with Lehman—at the time, AIG looked like it had only a liquidity problem, whereas Lehman had both a liquidity crisis and a capital problem. It was legal for the Fed to make a loan that was secured by valuable insurance subsidiaries; a loan to the firm would, it was hoped, avoid systemic collapse.

"Loaning against stable insurance businesses with independent credit ratings was very different than lending to Lehman Brothers. You can't lend into a bank run and save a company," Paulson later said. "And the run on Lehman had begun before the weekend."

■ ■ ■

The afternoon after Paulson told Geithner and Christopher Cox, the head of the SEC, that Lehman would have to file for bankruptcy, Fuld sent McDade and his team back down to the New York Fed to make sure Geithner fully understood the ramifications of letting Lehman go. When McDade returned, Fuld asked him: "Did they get it?"

"They got it," McDade replied, wearily.

Meanwhile, Scott Freidheim was drafting an assortment of press releases about the possible fate of the firm. George Walker entered his office at one point and took a look. "We've got to take investment management off the table," said the nimble-minded Walker. "Our portfolio managers have to be allowed to continue to manage clients' assets or there will be massive client losses."

Walker was working feverishly to sell Lehman's investment management division. After almost two weeks of round-the-clock negotiations, Bain Capital and Hellman & Friedman agreed to purchase the majority of the investment management division in two equal parts for $2.15 billion on September 29, 2008. The investment management division, which consisted of NeubergerBerman, Lincoln Capital, and Crossroads, among others, was immediately renamed after its largest operating unit: NeubergerBerman. Walker would remain its chief executive.

But the story didn't end there.

U.S. bankruptcy law dictates a subsequent re-auction to ensure that the business had been bought for a fair price.

Against the backdrop of plummeting global equity markets, few companies were willing to top the Bain and Hellman & Friedman bid, which itself was looking less certain as the S&P 500 index dropped beneath the agreed floor of 903. NeubergerBerman could be in limbo and might, like its parent company Lehman, be sold for $1.

To ensure the survival of the business, should the Bain and Hellman & Friedman bid not close, Walker submitted a bid from NeubergerBerman's own management.

On December 3 he won; 51 percent of NeubergerBerman was now owned by the management and 49 percent by the Lehman creditors.

For Walker, who had done a straight stock swap when he joined Lehman from Goldman, it was a remarkable end to a two-year roller-coaster ride.

■ ■ ■

Around 6 P.M. Sunday night, the Lehman board convened at 745 Seventh Avenue. In the middle of the meeting, SEC chairman Christopher Cox phoned Fuld's office. Fuld transferred the call to the board. "The Fed and the SEC are in agreement you should file for bankruptcy," Cox told them. The implication was that if they didn't, they could be personally liable.

Fuld looked stunned. So, too, did Harvey R. Miller, the veteran bankruptcy attorney of Weil, Gotshal & Manges, who had to put together the quickest bankruptcy papers of his career. Too fast, he reportedly said. This is going too fast.

There was also a hitch. Before Weil, Gotshal & Manges could proceed, it needed its payment of around $20 million for the filing. According to Steve Berkenfeld, this was because "they had a claim as a secured creditor against Lehman." As both the firm's attorney and creditor, "they had a conflict."

So, who did Lehman have to ask for the $20 million? The bank apparently in charge of its destiny all along: JPMorgan Chase.

According to Berkenfeld, Steve Cutler, JPMorgan's general counsel, initially balked at handing over $20 million to Lehman, explaining that a "higher authority" had frozen all Lehman's accounts. Berkenfeld says, he was about ready to snap at that point. Many at Lehman groused about Dimon "hovering" around their team at the New York Fed that hellish weekend—wearing black jeans and a black silk shirt and "you know, looking very hip," recalls one of the attendees.

"I don't know if 'higher authority' means Jamie Dimon or if it means somebody outside of your organization," Berkenfeld told Cutler, "but when we take your deposition, *we will find out*. All right?"

The funds were released.

Lehman could now file for bankruptcy—the largest filing in history. It listed $613 billion in liabilities and had $34 billion tied up in open derivatives contracts in 22 currencies in dozens of countries all over the world. Each of those foreign offices were governed by local bankruptcy laws.

Around 9 P.M. that night, Fuld's team—one by one—came by to give him a hug. In they trooped: McDade, Lessing, Russo, Freidheim, Goldfarb . . . all of them. It was like a receiving line at a funeral.

Fuld was stricken, numb. "I think I am going to puke," he said.

Much later, Paulson called. "Dick, you did everything you could," he told him.

Paulson truly believed this; he felt very sorry for Fuld.

"It's a tragedy," Paulson said a year later.

A tragedy that confirmed a view that Paulson had about corporate leadership. "It is not healthy for a CEO to stay too long. When he is in the job for upwards of 10 years, he can become set in his ways and it becomes increasingly difficult for a management team to challenge the boss's decision or to change longstanding policies or practices."

He didn't know that Fuld had tried years earlier to hire Joe Perella for precisely that reason—and had been blocked.

Chapter 20

Damned Flood?

That week was just nuts. Everything happened so fast. None of us got any sleep. Ian [Lowitt] was almost incoherent by the end. I even got asked if I needed a doctor at one point, I was so tired.

—Alex Kirk

While Dick Fuld and his board convened during Lehman's last hours on Sunday, an exhausted Bob Diamond was walking up Madison Avenue with his wife, Jennifer, and daughter, Nell, who had been in constant touch with him as the crisis escalated all weekend. Nell had caught the train up from Princeton to comfort her father, and the three were walking glumly to dinner when his cell phone rang.

"I don't think I can take another call," he said, half-joking.

"Who is it, Dad?" Nell said.

"It's Bart McDade."

"Dad, answer your phone."

The weekend had taken a massive toll on McDade's already low tolerance for fools. He had spent the afternoon at the New York Fed being castigated by various regulators for the manifold sins of Dick Fuld and Joe Gregory.

He feared that no one in the government seemed capable of grasping the carnage that would ensue if Lehman filed for bankruptcy on Monday.

Lehman was on one side or the other of hundreds of billions of dollars in trades. It had hundreds of billions of assets and liabilities strewn all around the world in an unimaginable variety of investments. If everyone who had done business with Lehman, as a client or a trading partner or merely a strategic partner, called their lawyers, there'd be free fall in the markets.

At the very least, McDade needed someone to buy Lehman's New York broker-dealer operations out of receivership—and he knew Diamond would be interested; it was the only part of the firm he had really wanted, anyway.

Diamond's answer, of course, was a resounding "Yes."

The men agreed to meet up early the next morning back at Lehman headquarters, because everyone in London who was needed to sign off on such a deal was asleep.

■ ■ ■

Hank Paulson flew back to D.C. to explain to the press what had happened.

It wasn't all bad news. Lehman may be filing for bankruptcy, but Bank of America announced it had taken over Merrill Lynch the night before.

And for the next 24 hours, Paulson would be lionized in the press for letting Lehman go, for standing up to the Street, for refusing to grease the country's slide to socialism.

"On Merrill and Lehman, Paulson makes the right move," read a typical headline.

But Paulson knew his troubles were just beginning.

He later said he felt that he sounded cavalier the next morning when he said, "I never once considered putting government money into Lehman Brothers." People thought Paulson was saying that he never once tried to save Lehman, which could not have been further from the truth.

"I didn't want to stand up and say, 'Guess what? We're sitting here naked. The United States of America is powerless. And we can do whatever we want for a commercial bank, but for an investment bank we can't. And we've got a problem.' [Even though this] was true. And so what I said was something very narrowly true.

"What I'd meant was, 'If there had been a deal where we could have put government money in, I would have considered it.'"

■ ■ ■

While Paulson talked to the press, Diamond and McDade set up a war room on Lehman's 31st floor, where Fuld could watch them brainstorming through the window of his office—a somewhat uneasy arrangement for all parties.

"It was really horrible to watch him suffer," says one of Fuld's friends.

But Diamond, sorry as we was for Fuld, had to get down to sealing the deal of his career.

To stave off Armageddon while Barclays hammered out a deal, Lehman's clearing bank, JPMorgan, had agreed to keep the New York trading desk in working order by funneling the broker-dealer tens of billions of dollars in loans from the New York Fed. JPMorgan CEO Jamie Dimon would later claim in a letter that JPMorgan did this at the request of not only Lehman and the New York Fed but Barclays itself. Lehman had to survive.

Or, rather, Lehman America did. Lehman's treasurer, Paolo Tonucci, had been instructed not to move any money outside the United States. (Usually Lehman did; it moved $8 billion to Europe.) This meant that on Monday morning, in London, Christian Meissner had no money to pay his 10,000 employees, and no news to deliver.

Meissner was livid. He was surrounded by chaos. His secretary was due to give birth and suddenly she had no health insurance. People stopped coming in to work; no one knew if they'd be paid that week.

"You're on your own," Tom Russo says he told the firm's London general counsel, Andrew Wright, during a phone conversation. After all, if not for the protectionist unresponsiveness of the British at the Financial Services Authority (FSA), many felt that the firm might still be alive. "Please don't ask me to feel sorry for the British," one Lehman senior executive said. "After what they did to us over the

weekend? Please! They got what they deserved." This was payback for
the FSA and for Alastair Darling.

Meissner felt that Fuld had shafted him. Where was "one firm"
now? Why hadn't McDade and Fuld tried to negotiate for Europe and
Asia, too? But Barclays Capital wasn't interested in Europe and Asia.

Meissner implored employees to come to work, since the firm's
value lay in its people. Meanwhile he tried to keep cool and look for a
buyer in markets that were shifting like roiling seas.

■ ■ ■

In New York, Diamond and McDade were hammering out basic
terms. First on the agenda was that the deal could not move forward
unless eight key executives, including Skip McGee, Eric Felder, Jerry
Donini, and Ian Lowitt, stayed. They were apparently offered generous retention packages, which rumors had put at high as $50 million
for McGee (he said this was a "ridiculous" figure).

Significantly, McDade, Kirk, and Gelband were not among the
eight. Gelband would quickly leave for the hedge fund Fortress. McDade
and Kirk knew Diamond already had his own trusted deputies, so they
would be on their own. After ensuring a smooth transition, they left in
November 2008.

On Tuesday, September 16, Diamond felt sufficiently confident
that he'd got a deal that he went down to the trading floor mid-
afternoon and announced that for $1.7 billion (later revised to $1.54
billion) BarCap had bought the U.S. broker-dealer.

He was met with a standing ovation.

Upstairs was Fuld, who sent out a letter saying he felt "horrible"
about what had happened. He wanted to go down to the trading floor,
too—but McDade stopped him.

"We were worried someone might try to hit him," a colleague said.

Fuld had not yet realized how the firm felt about him. A picture of
his face was being defaced by angry bankers on the office wall.

■ ■ ■

As soon as McGee had shaken hands with Diamond to seal their deal,
he flew to London to see if he could help Meissner while Barclays put
together a bid for the European businesses.

But Barclays was not prepared to deal with the costs or headaches involved in laying off most of Meissner's staff, so in a move Chris Pettit would have been proud of, Meissner eventually took an offer for Lehman's international operations from the Japanese bank Nomura, pointedly making sure Lehman's Asian subsidiaries were acquired as well. He saved more than 10,000 jobs.

Meissner felt less like a victor than a hardened survivor. To make matters more depressing, his chief legal officer, Peter Sherratt, told him that one of his legal advisers on the Nomura deal had taken him by the hand and thanked him for "the biggest payday in our firm's history." The lawyers, it seemed, were the real victors in this sorry mess—or rather, the lawyers and Bob Diamond.

Shortly after the Nomura deal closed, Fuld called to congratulate Meissner, who was in no mood to coddle "the Gorilla."

"At the end of the day, we're all defined by our actions," Meissner told Fuld. "I think you and a bunch of your other senior guys really behaved appallingly in all this." He felt Fuld should have negotiated much more tenaciously with Barclays. He should have believed in "one firm." Fuld hung up on him.

Two days later Fuld called him back: "Look, I thought about what you said. I can't really disagree. I just want you to know I'm sorry."

■ ■ ■

Bob Diamond's first big test at the helm of Lehman Brothers came the Tuesday afternoon after the announcement of the merger.

JPMorgan told his team it was turning over the responsibility of facilitating Lehman's line of credit with the Fed to Barclays, a mind-numbingly complex affair involving the transfer of tens of billions of dollars in cash to JPMorgan in exchange for tens of billions of dollars' worth of Lehman's portfolio of securities.

As the markets seesawed in the aftermath of the filing, Diamond's team got increasingly jumpy about some of the securities it was getting back from JPMorgan in exchange for its wire transfers. The result would be a $7 billion legal battle in which both Barclays and JPMorgan would accuse the other of trying to stick them with toxic assets.

Even so, at four o'clock on Friday afternoon, September 19, Judge James Peck of the U.S. Bankruptcy Court in the Southern District of New York approved the deal.

Almost immediately Diamond started to trim Lehman's fat.

A source says he was somewhat sickened by how rarely senior executives had flown commercial. "There is an airport in New York and an airport in London," he noted sarcastically.

Diamond knew that Lehman's rot was at the top.

He had also heard about the friction between London and New York—not just of the past few days, but going back years. Since he had lived in London he knew Jeremy Isaacs well, and he knew both the pluses and minuses of the firm he'd bought.

Diamond decided he needed to lead a cultural change for the new Barclays Capital. He realized Fuld should never have cut himself off from the foot soldiers. So he put his office right on the trading floor. And on his whiteboard wall is a single phrase. It reads:

ONE FIRM

■ ■ ■

Both Hank Paulson and his British counterpart, Alastair Darling, the chancellor of the Exchequer, had known that the repercussions of Lehman going bankrupt would be bad. Just how bad was anyone's guess.

"I always knew that when we had a major bankruptcy, we'd find out how the connectivity of credit default swaps really performed under stress for the first time," Paulson said later. "And I didn't think it'd be good."

Credit default swaps are unregulated financial instruments that act as "insurance" against bond defaults. In the weeks leading up to Lehman's bankruptcy, the price to buy credit default swaps had soared, but even at the 8 or 9 cents on the dollar at which they were trading the week before, they were still a bargain, considering Lehman bonds would trade around 10 cents on the dollar the next month.

Paulson was worried about the lack of transparency of these instruments, which connected Lehman to financial institutions and investors throughout the world. He feared that these instruments, which usually served as risk mitigators, had the potential to become *transmitters* of risk, and exacerbate the crisis.

"I didn't try, initially, to go into the gory details, and neither did Bernanke," he said later. "I didn't want to scare the American public and make the panic worse, and create a bigger economic hole because people were terrified."

By Monday afternoon, rumors were swirling about American International Group (AIG), the market's single biggest seller of credit default swaps.

With AIG's liquidity hole topping $85 billion on Monday afternoon, it had to be bailed out at a very heavy price.

Quickly, the Fed hammered out a take-it-or-leave-it deal: The government would get an 80 percent stake in the firm, its short-term line of credit with the Fed came at a double-digit interest rate, and CEO Bob Willumstad—who had taken the helm only months earlier in an attempt to engineer a last-minute turnaround—was out, to be hastily replaced by Ed Liddy, the former CEO of Allstate Insurance.

■ ■ ■

But the quick nationalization of AIG did not calm the markets, which found Paulson's about-face on bailouts almost as troubling as the magnitude of the taxpayer subsidies needed to plug the gaping holes.

And how big were all those holes? No one knew. The worldwide market for mortgage-backed securities was about $1.4 trillion, and those had been effectively dead for months. But by Tuesday, *all* the markets were dead.

Despite full access to the Fed's discount window, the safest banks and brokerages weren't making overnight loans to one another—and in the rare event that they did, the interest rates they were charging one another were several percentage points higher than they'd ever been before.

News of the Reserve Primary Fund's exposure to Lehman Brothers' debt had flooded the money market industry with redemption demands. And at Washington Mutual, one of the most notorious banks to have gotten in on the boom in subprime mortgages, depositors were lining up around the block to close their accounts. (Some even apologetically brought baked goods to their favorite tellers.)

Paulson now saw there would be a run on the remaining securities houses, Goldman Sachs and Morgan Stanley. On Sunday, September 21, the Fed converted them to bank holding companies—which was what Lehman had asked for just weeks earlier and been denied.

But the mayhem continued, and Paulson had to find another solution. He reasoned that the only way to stem the panic would be for the government to start buying huge chunks of mortgage-backed securities.

On September 20, Paulson submitted to Congress his plan—drafted in bullet points on three sheets of paper—to buy up these toxic assets. Condemned on both sides of the aisle as a tin-eared, dictatorial document, it was rejected nine days later by the House. Another four days after it had been rewritten (and the markets had meanwhile swooned), the bill had grown to 451 pages and it passed—just barely. On October 3, President Bush signed into law the Emergency Economic Stabilization Act, more commonly known as the Troubled Asset Relief Program (TARP), which included Paulson's suggestion—to the tune of $700 billion.

No one was happy. The country was now in a recession and taxpayers appeared to be paying for the lavish lifestyles of the clowns on Wall Street who had dragged them into this mess.

■ ■ ■

It didn't appear that the public's opinion of bankers could get any worse, but it did when Dick Fuld testified before Congress on October 6.

He did not help himself by peering over his half-moon spectacles rather than looking through them (he is very short-sighted), but both the language and the style of his testimony were appalling.

"This is a pain that will stay with me the rest of my life," he said about Lehman's fall. But he was far from ready to admit that the wounds were self-inflicted. Instead he blamed lax oversight, "sensational" media coverage, and the rumor-mongering of short sellers.

Henry Waxman, the committee's pugnacious chairman, gave the broken banker an uncharacteristically measured rebuke. "I accept the fact that you're still haunted at night," he told Fuld. "But you don't seem to acknowledge you did anything wrong."

On October 14, Paulson revised TARP so he could use some of the $700 billion to take direct equity stakes in the major financial institutions—regardless of whether the institutions wanted or needed the government to have such stakes. Buying up toxic assets was too complicated—and as the rapid demise of Fannie, Freddie, Lehman, and Bear had proven, there was too much room for fudging the numbers when it came to valuing them.

In the weeks following the Lehman bankruptcy, even large blue-chip corporations were getting charged near-usurious interest rates simply to fund day-to-day operations, and innumerable small businesses had their lines of credit pulled altogether. TARP was meant to provide banks with a liquidity cushion that would give them the confidence they needed to start lending again. But the financing also gave Congress the right to levy restrictions on Wall Street's notoriously generous bonus pools and summon their executives to Washington for adversarial cross-examinations.

Why, Congress wanted to know, had the AIG bailout alone transferred $13 billion from the Fed into the coffers of Goldman Sachs—to say nothing of the incalculable profits it had reaped borrowing cheaply in its new status as a bank holding company? And where did the Fed get off signing contracts guaranteeing hundreds of millions of dollars in retention bonuses to the employees of the unit at AIG whose prolific sales of credit default swaps had left taxpayers holding the bag for $183 billion? Then there was John Thain at Merrill Lynch, who got his new boss, Ken Lewis, to approve more than $3 billion in Christmas bonuses for his team in November, only to turn around and disclose that Merrill would be reporting $15 billion in additional losses for the quarter—a burden that would naturally be shouldered by taxpayers, who had injected $45 billion into the new merged entity.

And that was just the start. Wall Street CEOs would spend much of the winter and spring getting grilled on Capitol Hill. In the harsh glare of the interrogation room, they would often concede that their pay had been excessive, that the incentives were out of whack, that the system needed to bolster the regulatory systems they had been lobbying for so many years to dismantle. They promised to clean up their acts.

But did they? Within a year Lloyd Blankfein was claiming that Goldman Sachs, the first bank to return its TARP funds, had not needed government aid in the first place and was never in danger of failing, even going so far as to joke to the *London Sunday Times* that he is doing "God's work." Tim Geithner, now the U.S. Treasury secretary, quickly told the media this was flat-out wrong.

After Blankfein came Dimon, then Morgan Stanley and Bank of America, and finally—almost unbelievably—the beleaguered Citigroup. As quickly as they could, they repaid their TARP funds and got back to business—and bonuses. In other words, the devil was back in the casino—and was eager to spin the wheel again.

The Lehman executive committee watched all this and fumed. It wasn't fair; Blankfein had conceded as much back in September when he called Fuld to console him. "There was a flood coming; Bear was on the first floor of the building and you were on the second," he told his vanquished rival. "We were on the fifth. The flood got stopped before it reached the fifth floor."

■ ■ ■

Although he'd gotten out before the "summer of hell," Joe Gregory was just as outraged as his colleagues. After all, he still had $232 million in stock tied up in the company, as well as millions in deferred compensation.

From the Huntington home office where he'd been forced to set up shop—and sell his helicopter—he called former colleagues and raged: "Not only did we get fucked, but people think we are the fucker!" He also told people that if he'd been left in his seat, he could have sorted out the situation; Bart McDade is to blame, he claims, for losing the firm.

Many Lehman people find it impossible to let go. "Sometimes I wake up and I think for a second that Lehman's still alive; it's like it was a person," says Craig Schiffer. "For all the things that went wrong, there was something unique about it, something really strong and magical."

Months later, there was still rage in the eyes of the men and women at Lehman who felt they'd been wrongly singled out and shot in the name, not of merely saving the economy, but, so they believed, saving Goldman Sachs.

"I'm looking at a person who is responsible for this mess," one Lehman senior manager said. "Switch on your TV and you'll see Tim Geithner."

Many ex-Lehmanites believe Treasury and the Fed rushed the math that last weekend, and in Paulson's haste to fix the bigger problems looming he made a massive mistake. Their marks to market, they claim, were not so overvalued—and as proof, they cite the increasing suspicion that the Lehman estate was robbed of a good $5 billion in its last-ditch deal with Barclays.

"I think it's more a story of hubris than a tragedy," a former executive committee member says. "There's a long street of mistakes on Wall Street, and there's a car that's slowly rolling toward a cliff, and there's this guy who gives the last little push, to make it topple down. . . . I mean is he the villain? Yes, on one level he is. But the guys who drove it to the edge are the ones who may deserve most of the blame."

Chapter 21

Closing the Books

Kathy Fuld is a nice person. The trouble is, she thought everyone
else on Wall Street was as nice as she is. They're not.

—*Peter A. Cohen*

Whoever said it's lonely at the top never consulted with
Kathy Fuld, who quickly found that it can be lonely at
the bottom as well. Her fall from grace and the social
ostracism that followed were swift. After Lehman collapsed and
her husband became a pariah (and a poster boy for the naked avarice
of Wall Street), Kathy stopped getting calls from the wives of other
CEOs. At a dinner party with Peter Cohen and his wife, Kathy burst
into tears. "I didn't realize these people weren't actually my friends,"
she said.

By the end of September, she had announced her intention to sell, at
auction, the Fulds' $20 million art collection. A month later, they sold 12
of their 16 Abstract Expressionist paintings for $13.5 million.

Months later, she quietly stepped down as vice-chair of the
Museum of Modern Art's illustrious board. "You need a lot of money

to get to run the MoMA board," explains an insider. And Kathy no longer had enough. The Fulds sold their 16-room Park Avenue apartment for $25.87 million. Like all the other Lehman Brothers wives, Kathy also paid a price for being married to the firm. She once told Karin Jack that her social duties meant she did not spend as much time as she would have liked with her twin daughters. She also confessed that she seldom saw her own family because they did not like Dick.

She was to soon learn that, as one former Lehman wife said, "When your husband leaves Lehman, you become a ghost."

Her husband, Dick, eventually moved his office to the Time-Life Building at 1271 Sixth Avenue, where *Fortune* magazine is located, and where the remaining employees of Lehman Brothers Holding, Inc. helped direct the bankruptcy proceedings.

In early April 2009, he moved to offices at 780 Third Avenue, where he set up his new private equity venture, Matrix Advisors. "You can either look forward or look back," he told friends. After six months of restless sleep, Fuld decided to look forward.

At a party in Greenwich, Connecticut, that summer, Dick Fuld looked deeply tanned and relaxed, far removed from the winter's guilt and sleepless nights. He was charming and funny and wanted to talk about his children. But he held my arm in a vicelike grip when I told him I was trying to piece together the "jigsaw" of events that led to the Lehman bankruptcy. "Believe me," he said, "so am I."

On September 15, 2009, Fuld was reportedly "ambushed" at his Sun Valley home when a reporter rang the bell and said she had an important "family matter" to discuss. Fuld invited her in, and she pounced.

When she asked for a quote, he said, "Nobody wants to hear it. The facts are out there. Nobody wants to hear it, especially not from me."

■ ■ ■

Joe Gregory also stayed out of public view. Reportedly, he sold his seven-acre estate in Manchester, Vermont. Former Lehman employees were appalled to read about his still-lavish spending habits in magazines such as *Vanity Fair*. He may have lost approximately $230 million in stock, but over the years he'd taken out at least that much.

Gregory's healthy portfolio was in stark contrast to the finances of many of Lehman's 26,000 employees, who lost everything. Everyone who worked there—from secretaries to managing directors to the CEO—received half of their pay in bonuses, paid in Lehman stock that could not be sold for at least five years.

■ ■ ■

Erin Callan was briefly saved by Rob Shafir, the former head of fixed income who had mistakenly worn "business casual" to a Lehman off-site and had quit in February 2007 and jumped to Credit Suisse, where he ran the firm's American offices. In July 2008 he recruited Callan to run hedge funds there, because he'd been impressed by her when she had run that department at Lehman.

To the fury of former colleagues, Callan gave an interview to *Fortune* magazine in which she insisted that she hadn't been forced out at Lehman. "It was clear in the 24 hours after we announced second-quarter earnings that the market reaction was just terrible, and there was a rising sense in the organization that a management change was needed. I went back to my office and decided I was willing to step down," adding that she, "was lucky to get out." She was implying, many thought, that she'd been very clever to get out when she had—as if it had been her choice, as if she'd had no responsibility for what had happened. "I couldn't believe it when I read that," seethed one former colleague. But her cocky attitude came to an abrupt end as lawsuits against Lehman, its board, and senior management flooded in. Angry investors wanted to know if they'd been sold a lie. All the institutions that had invested in the firm in 2008 now alleged that the marks had been false. Callan had been the CFO; she'd signed off on the financials and effectively promised that the company was in good health when clearly it wasn't. This was now her potential legal jeopardy.

She quit Credit Suisse, retired to her house in the Hamptons, and dated the fireman she'd once bragged to her colleagues about. Friends said she had a breakdown of sorts. For a woman whose life had been her work, it was a sad outcome.

In an ironic twist, Michael Thompson, her former husband, landed on his feet: He ran his trading business and was happy.

■ ■ ■

Throughout 2009 the lawsuits against Lehman just kept rolling in. One board member told a friend, "I think we'll be in court forever over this."

By November 2009, the cost of retaining the various advisers and examiners necessary to parse the many thousands of claims and counterclaims and go about the laborious work of liquidating the firm had crossed the half-billion-dollar threshold, with no end in sight.

The official liquidators of the estate, the New York turnaround firm Alvarez & Marsal, reaped the biggest chunk of those fees, having billed more than $200 million for about a year's worth of the services of 125 of its employees. In one eyebrow-raising development in June, it was widely reported that Alvarez & Marsal sold the rights to manage the firm's deeply distressed real estate portfolio for $10 million to a group that included Mark Walsh.

As per the requirements of the Securities Investor Protection Corporation, a liquidation trustee, James Giddens, was appointed to investigate the assets and liabilities of the broker-dealer business now owned by Barclays.

In short order, Giddens set his sights on the $5 billion so-called "haircut" that the British bank had been rumored to have slipped through in its emergency takeover of the brokerage—a sum that had grown to $8.2 billion by the time Giddens officially sued Barclays to recover the ill-gotten "windfall" for creditors.

The court has deposed dozens of Barclays and Lehman executives in marathon sessions in its attempt to re-create what took place during the 36 hours between Bart McDade's call to Bob Diamond on the evening before the filing and Barclays' predawn September 16 agreement to buy the broker-dealer, but it is still far from clear how this particularly contentious subplot of the world's biggest bankruptcy will conclude.

Then there is the report of an official bankruptcy examiner, the former federal prosecutor Anton Valukas, who was appointed in January 2009 at the motion of the Walt Disney Company to probe the bankruptcy on behalf of the creditors of other Lehman subsidiaries.

Exactly a year after that fateful Sunday when Lehman Brothers threw in the towel, Valukas appealed to the court for three more months to put together his report. He told the judge he had used the 2001 bankruptcy of Enron as a benchmark for estimating how much time he would need, predicting the task at hand would require reviewing 1.5 million pages. But by September 2009, he reported, he had reviewed

10 million pages and his work was nowhere near done. "If Enron was a mountain," opined the *Wall Street Journal*, "Lehman is a mountain range."

In October the *Journal* revealed what might be the Kilimanjaro of Valukas's quest, a potential lawsuit accusing the Federal Reserve of leapfrogging ahead of other Lehman creditors when it was paid back in full for the cash Lehman borrowed through the discount window in the four days before the Chapter 11 filing.

When it filed for Chapter 11 protection, Lehman reported more than $600 billion in assets on its balance sheet, against $613 billion in liabilities. But as the market worsened, the values of many of those assets shrunk considerably—and the claims of Lehman's creditors (predictably) ballooned.

By November, creditors had filed $824 billion in claims against the holding company, according to an SEC filing. "Some of the claim estimates are just flat-out silly," Alvarez & Marsal chief executive Bryan Marsal told the judge at a hearing.

Amid all the wrangling, attention had turned away from the broader legal (and philosophical) question about Lehman: Had Callan, Gregory, or Fuld lied to investors, or had this simply been a massive case of incompetence?

As of December 2009, federal investigators had yet to bring criminal charges against anyone for the spectacular collapse of the world's fourth-biggest investment bank. But all former Lehman employees were waiting anxiously for Valukas's report, due in early 2010. "There's not a 't' he hasn't crossed and an 'i' he hasn't dotted," says Tom Hill. On February 8, 2010, Valukas filed his report under seal. The report was a mammoth 2,200 pages long. Valukas said in court filings that, if necessary, he would argue before a judge that all of the report should be made public, including many sections that interviewees had asked to be redacted. A date for Valukas to argue for the report's unsealing was set for March 11, 2010.

To the astonishment of many, Joe Gregory brought a $232,999,549 civil suit against the Lehman estate, calculating that the terms of his employment contract said the firm owed him an annual salary of just over $3.1 million for the next 15 years and $700,000 per year for the following decade. Tom Russo sued for the less audacious sum of

$17.3 million. Dick Fuld made no claim, nor did George Walker, Scott Freidheim, Erin Callan, Skip McGee, or Bart McDade. Gregory told people he sued because he had nothing to lose. Fuld disagreed: They'd all gotten rich but they'd lost the firm.

Finally, way past the finish line, the blinkers came off Dick Fuld. Lehman may have gone down, but he was still a Lehman man; and for Lehman men, the kind of men he believed in, it was never too late to do the "right thing." It would not have occurred to him to sue the estate for money. That Gregory would . . . well, finally, Fuld saw the great weakness, the insecurity, and the greed in the man he'd made his number two. He still took Gregory's calls, but he told close friends that he was furious.

When it no longer mattered, Fuld had finally become "the Gorilla."

Epilogue

I kept the photographs of my family in my bathroom, so first thing in the morning and last thing at night I just looked at them. It was the only way to keep going: to remind oneself of what really matters.

— Tom Russo

t its finest, Lehman Brothers was the best of Dick Fuld and Chris Pettit. In the old days, with Fuld battling upstairs, fighting with Peter Cohen, and with Pettit running the troops, the duo was unstoppable. Fuld knew that he'd hear what was going on with the troops from Pettit, who really knew everybody and everything.

Back then, the spoils of money or the trappings of ego hadn't yet begun to rot away Lehman's "one firm" culture. The Ponderosa Boys were all friends with large and generous hearts and jaunty Go-Get-'Em! dispositions. They slept only with their wives. They were honest.

Someone close to Steve Carlson says Lehman became a culture of liars right after the Mexican crisis. "It was then that basically the job became about 'What are we going to spin today to hide our real difficulties?' That's when things started to slide."

Not long after, Carlson left.

In 2006 Lara Pettit was fired from Lehman, she believed, without cause. She was seven months pregnant and had just bought a new house, and she was shocked. Eventually she worked out a severance package with the firm. She asked Joe Gregory if he had known anything about her termination.

"Absolutely not," he had replied. Months later Lara discovered Gregory had known.

Martha Dillman decided to leave Maine and come back to work as a research consultant for the New York–based company Credit Sites. She and Lara were still speaking, but they were not as friendly as they once were.

Mary Anne Pettit moved on with her life; she no longer gets the monthly check she had received as part of Chris Pettit's pension. She is now just another of 64,000 creditors who have filed claims with the Lehman estate, many of whom have, ironically, found the protracted bankruptcy process to be something of a Lehman family reunion.

Because it was easier to file in groups, Craig Schiffer recently found himself reminiscing with Peter Cohen. Peter Solomon spoke to Dick Fuld and found himself in the same group. The ending of Lehman brought them all back together, to memories of the good times—and the bad. They remembered that for a while they'd lived through something they really thought was unique and worth fighting for.

"You had to live it to get it," Schiffer says, "but for a while Lehman just wasn't like anywhere else on the Street."

Only a few of the big names were missing. Lew Glucksman passed away in 2003. At his memorial service in New York, Jim Boshart told how Glucksman had once looked at a dark-haired newcomer whose only role it seemed was to videotape the Monday morning meeting.

"What's your name?" Glucksman had asked the young man.

"Dick Fuld," the man had replied.

"Well, Dick Fuld," said Glucksman, "either you can start working directly for me—or there's the door." That's how it had all begun.

Steve Lessing is thriving at Barclays, where that famous Rolodex is now proving as useful to Bob Diamond as it had been to Dick Fuld.

Skip McGee helped Barclays kick ass in his first year. Barclays made profits of £3 billion in its first quarter of 2009, an 8 percent increase.

George Walker held NeubergerBerman steady. By the end of 2009, assets under management had risen from $158 billion in June to $173 billion. Clients and employees had remained loyal. Walker was holding the ship steady. "We are going to be very boring for a while," he said.

In 2009 Peregrine Moncreiffe was living in Jersey, Channel Islands, with his wife, the artist Miranda Fox Pitt, and their six children. He was running a hedge fund. "I can't believe this would have happened if Chris Pettit had still been at Lehman," he said.

Scott Freidheim moved to Chicago, where he works as an executive vice president for the billionaire hedge fund manager Eddie Lampert, helping with his latest turnaround project, the revamp of Sears Holdings, which owns the retail chains Sears and Kmart. Ironically, just before Lehman's September earnings McDade and Fuld had planned to promote him. They wanted to make a structural change so that the firm was run by subcommittees comprised of executive committee members. There'd be one for risk, capital new initiative investments, advancement, and so forth. Freidheim would have been in charge of each one.

Tom Russo moved to the law firm of Patton Boggs. In 2009 he taught a course, "Background to a Dream," at Columbia Business School on the lessons learned from Lehman. In 2010 it was announced he'd be the new legal counsel for AIG.

David Goldfarb stayed at Lehman Brothers Holdings, working with the estate. He was paid a low six-figure salary but hoped the estate would reward him for all the money he had not taken out.

After staying on to ensure an orderly transition, Bart McDade and Alex Kirk quietly left BarCap in November 2008. (Bob Diamond already had trusted lieutenants in Jerry del Messier and Rich Ricci.) For them, it was time to start fresh and build businesses of their own. The two formed River Birch, a private investment management company, in September 2009. In December, it was announced that McDade was helping to launch a cash equities arm for Evercore Partners, a private equity firm run by the former Lehman partner (and former deputy

Treasury secretary under Bill Clinton) Roger Altman. (Evercore also hired Mark Burton, a former vice chairman at Lehman, in July 2009.)

Mike Gelband went to Fortress Financial Group, a private equity firm. John Cecil founded a consultancy called Eagle Knolls; Jeremy Isaacs started his own business, JRJ Ventures, with Roger Nagioff and Jesse Bhattal.

Ian Lowitt stayed at Barclays.

Mike Odrich joined the liquidators Alvarez & Marsal to build a private equity business there.

Hank Paulson spent a year decompressing and writing his memoirs about the fall of 2008. He also spent some time fishing with his younger brother Richard, who had worked as a fixed income salesman (selling mortgages) at Lehman for over a decade and was "wiped out" by the bankruptcy, according to Hank.

Richard told me that he feels Hank acted heroically under the circumstances. Over time he hopes the story of Hank Paulson will be revised to what he believes it should be, and that the criticism will be left behind. To cheer Hank up, Richard recommended his brother read *Masters and Commanders* by the British historian Andrew Roberts, a book that reconstructs strategic debates and conversations between Roosevelt, Churchill, Marshall, and Lord Alanbrooke during World War II.

Tom Tucker and Steve Lessing talk often, and despite their different careers have remained close. Lessing had bought Finnegan's as a memorial to his friends from the old neighborhood. The picture of Fiver, put there by Chris Pettit, and Rusty Pettit, and Tom Tucker back in the 1970s just before they joined Lehman, still hangs above the bar.

■ ■ ■

As for Chris Pettit—he's never far from the minds of those who know the real Lehman story. When I began my book, Tucker told me that he'd visited a psychic, Jim Fargiano, on Long Island, who had put him in touch with his best friend. In a surreal experiment, I called Fargiano, who is based on a dirt road in Quogue, and found myself unexpectedly conducting an interview with Pettit's spirit.

Fargiano told me he could see Pettit looking down on me and my notebooks and that he "wanted to thank me for the time I was giving Tommy," and to make sure "Tommy knew he was off the hook."

What, I asked, did Pettit's spirit have to say about Joe Gregory? The spirit wrote a word, according to Fargiano:

"Deceived."

Dick Fuld?

"Covers his tracks better."

Fargiano said Pettit talked a lot about wishing he could have traded in his suit for a T-shirt and jeans; he also kept talking about "being in too deep, not able to get out" and "creative accounting."

I asked about love. Fargiano said Pettit had lost his love a while ago.

"What about your girlfriend?" I asked.

The spirit laughed: "Bright kid. Bit self-absorbed, but she was so young—anyone would have been tempted," and returned to the theme of drowning in things going wrong, and not being able to get out. He used the word *targeted* repeatedly.

Fargiano told me he could see Pettit. He was outside, where he'd always wanted to be—never trussed up in a suit.

And then I said good-bye—to Fargiano and, feeling somewhat foolish, to Chris Pettit.

Dwelling again on the whole lurid tale, I picked up an old copy of *Watership Down* and came upon a passage wherein Fiver, who has visionary powers, urges his fellow rabbits to run, knowing that men are coming to kill them:

"Look!" said Fiver suddenly. "That's the place for us, Hazel. High, lonely hills, where the wind and the sound carry and the ground's as dry as straw in a barn. That's where we ought to be. That's where we have to get to."

Maybe, I thought, that is where Chris Pettit finally is.

A Note About the Sources

I lost count of the hours of interviews done for this book when my tape recorder—an old-fashioned AA-battery-charged machine that was the size of a pack of Ultra cigarettes—stopped working. By that point I was on tape 106; each of the tapes had 180 minutes of interviews on them. And I was still only one-quarter of the way through.

To my horror, not only did I have to go back and reinterview those people the machine had simply failed to pick up (it got spotty around tape 80), but I also had to learn how to work a digital recorder—and I bungled that, too, on occasion.

Had the former U.S. Treasury Secretary Hank Paulson not recorded our conversation himself, his insightful and refreshing candor would not have made it into these pages. So I thank him not just for his time and his honesty, but also for handing over the recording.

I must also thank certain members of his team, who wish to remain anonymous and who gave me many hours of their precious time. For one particular senior member of the Federal Reserve, who showed astonishing patience and good humor as we redid one very long conversation, I am most sincerely grateful. The same goes for certain people inside Britain's Financial Services Authority.

Also to the many men and women of the former Lehman Brothers, and also of Barclays Capital (BarCap), who underwent a second and sometimes a third grilling. The only upside of my sorry incompetence was this: I think that by the end, I had got the story down correctly. And I noticed that almost without exception, the stories remained unchanged as they were retold—although the value for me was that they became more detailed, and more emotional.

This gave me faith that the narrators were telling the truth—albeit as they saw it—and that though I had not meant to reinterview people, the reinterviews became the heart of this book.

It was in the reinterviews where people, perhaps relaxed, really opened up. While retelling their stories, they let their feelings rip.

This was the point when I knew that this book would be different, that inside of Lehman there was a soul—many souls, in fact—and that there was a reason people thought of the firm as a person, that they dreamed "she" was alive even after "she" was dead.

It would be my job to explain that soul: to explain the *real* story of what and who Lehman was and why Lehman died. It would be my job to take readers inside the boardrooms and offices of the executive floor and onto the trading floor and show how in the end, as Heraclitus said, character really is destiny.

Because of all the lawsuits facing the Lehman board and executive committee over the bankruptcy, as well as the dispute between Barclays and Lehman, some people were forced to speak off the record.

Others are on the record in places, off in others; but if someone spoke off the record, I always verified what they said by speaking to at least one more source. Thus, if I narrate a conversation that took place in an office, on the trading floor, or on the golf course near Dick Fuld's house in Sun Valley, it may be that I was told about the conversation by someone who was there, listening in. The speakers may have verified this, but don't want attribution.

Where I've taken facts already reported, they are, when possible, endnoted and sourced. But again, I tried to check every reported fact with the players themselves. (I had working with me a team of five outstanding fact-checkers.) Sometimes there was a conflict, and here I did what every journalist does: I went with my gut in the telling of the narrative but noted the conflict on the page, in the text.

When something as momentous as the biggest bankruptcy in U.S. history occurs, people are inevitably not going to agree. And I expect that Joe Gregory will not agree with the general perception of him as characterized in this book: as the Lehman president who did not manage risk, and was preoccupied with things other than running the business. As even his friends admitted, he does not see himself the way others do.

However, the way Gregory is characterized is the way that *every* person—of the *hundreds* who were interviewed about him—saw him. The only exception might be Lehman's general counsel, Tom Russo. But even Russo grew uncomfortable on the subject, saying: "Well, I guess I have heard all the things you are talking about, but I didn't see Joe that way myself."

As a reporter, one's duty is to put all the pieces together—this means as many voices and as many perspectives as possible—until you arrive at a kind of kaleidoscopic picture that gives you a sense of the accurate whole.

There are only two major sources I regret not interviewing for this book. I wish I could have interviewed Chris Pettit. In fact, I wish I had *known* Chris Pettit. His story, his charisma, his noble character, his terrible ending—all of it is a tragedy worthy of a powerful motion picture. But even the best reporter cannot interview the dead—although, as you will have read in the Epilogue, I had a go!

The other is Joe Gregory.

The second half of this book is really Gregory's story, inasmuch as the first half belongs to Pettit.

I talked to Gregory only briefly on the phone—he picked up by mistake when his assistant was out—and in that conversation he insisted he was never fired, and he blamed short sellers for what had happened to Lehman. He told me he wanted to talk for the book but that one of his lawyers was stopping him.

Yet I already had the real, undiluted Joe Gregory. I had his diaries: his own words, not written for a journalist, but for himself. So, I felt this was better than interviewing Gregory himself. I knew from my interviews with all the people who had worked with him that he was seen as a smooth interviewee full of self-justification, and that he would never see himself the way anyone else did. That is the story of his life as told by those who worked with him and arguably his downfall.

His lawyers knew I had his journals. Apparently, albeit astonishingly, he does not have a copy of them and could not remember what he had written. I was asked to send him a copy. Like any good journalist, I did not do so. I did not want to give him any chance to deduce the source from whom I'd obtained them (though I did wonder why he had not kept a copy electronically, since they were written in 2003).

Over the phone I told an associate of his lawyer, Steven Witzel, of Fried Frank Harris Shriver & Jacobson LLP, broadly what he'd written and offered him the opportunity to embroider on any of his own commentary and to answer any of the criticisms about him.

Witzel eventually declined on Gregory's behalf, saying he was sticking with his policy of "not speaking to the press," but to remember that some of his remarks—and others—might be out of context.

Dick Fuld also could not speak to me for this book because of the lawsuits. However, as I point out in the Epilogue, he and I did meet briefly (along with Kathy Fuld), and he was very charming and very apologetic that he could not be more helpful. His lawyer, Patricia Hynes of Allen & Overy, forbade him not just from talking but also from helping with fact-checking.

But behind her back, Fuld was very helpful. Just because Lehman had died, loyalty to Fuld did not. And I thank the people who spoke to me for him—off the record—and checked facts with him for me, in the hope that this would be a truthful and accurate portrayal of the man and what happened to him. Though all the stories about him were run past people very close to him, and who were there with him when events described occurred, I do not know that he personally corroborated every single incident. I just know that the people with him in the room did.

Another person to whom it would have been helpful to talk was Martha Dillman. She told me she did not want to revisit her memories, though she asked Lara Pettit to tell me that the night Chris Pettit died there were three fatal accidents on the lake in Maine. I duly noted this in the text.

In December 2009, just as the John Wiley & Sons team and I were finalizing the manuscript for this book and we were wrapping up the fact-checking, I received 20 e-mails from former senior Lehman executives who knew this ship was finally leaving the docks, readying for the presses. They were excited. They knew that all the dead bodies had been uncovered and quite a yarn was about to be told.

One person wrote to me: "This book could be quite explosive (good for you!) and while I want to be honest, I want to be sure it's done honorably." He was one of those who wanted the truth out there, but to do so he wanted to make sure he was on the record in some places and not in others.

I hope that I have told the "explosive"—but more important, the "true"—story of Lehman. And I hope that, simultaneously, I protected my sources, and that we all kept our honor.

That, after all, is what we as writers are supposed to do.

Notes

Prologue

Page 5 *The stock price rose* Andy Serwer, "Lehman Brothers: A Super-Hot Machine," *Fortune*, April 11, 2006.

Page 6 *I wake up every single night* Richard Fuld, congressional testimony, October 6, 2008.

Page 6 *This was before he learned that Gregory* U.S. Bankruptcy Court, Southern District of New York, nysb.uscourts.gov (Gregory filed on August 5, 2009).

Chapter 1 A Long, Hot Summer

Page 12 *The star-studded, 500-guest event* Richard Johnson, Paula Froelich, Bill Hoffman, and Corynne Steindler, "$3M Party Fit for Buyout King," *New York Post*, February 14, 2007.

Page 12 *Just months earlier* Andrew Ross Sorkin, "JP Morgan Pays $2 a Share for Bear Stearns," *New York Times*, March 17, 2008.

Page 14 *Also gathered were a large number* Heidi N. Moore, "Lehman Brothers: How Neuberger Berman Employees Made Millions," *Wall Street Journal's* Deal Journal Blog, http://blogs.wsj.com/deals/2008/08/28/lehman-the-history-of-neuberger-berman-payouts/, August 28, 2008.

Page 14 *Glucksman was offered $15.6 million* Ken Auletta, *Greed and Glory on Wall Street: The Fall of the House of Lehman* (New York: Random House, 1986), 220.

Page 15 *The firm was founded in 1850* Ibid., 27.

Page 15 *With the post–Civil War expansion* Ibid., 27–30.

Page 15 *He decorated the walls* Ibid., 32.

Page 15 *Bobbie was not much of an investment banker* Ibid., 32.

Page 15 *They were principals* Ibid., 15.

Page 15 *Shearson taking over Lehman* Bryan Burrough and John Helyar, *Barbarians at the Gate: The Fall of RJR Nabisco* (New York: Harper & Row, 1990; HarperBusiness, 2008), 156.

Page 16 *Since Lehman, in their hands* www.boston.com/business/specials/lehman/.

Page 16 *In 2007, Fuld was named* "The Best CEOs," *Institutional Investor,* January 2007.

Chapter 2 The Beginning

Page 18 *During one such inspection* Andrew Ross Sorkin, *Too Big to Fail: The Inside Story of How Wall Street Fought to Save the Financial System—and Themselves* (New York: Viking Penguin, 2009), 18.

Page 19 *An ex–Naval officer* Ken Auletta, *Greed and Glory on Wall Street: The Fall of the House of Lehman* (New York: Random House, 1986), 45.

Page 21 *The team had lost* Ibid., 18.

Chapter 3 The Captain

Page 32 *There was a barber in-house* Ken Auletta, *Greed and Glory on Wall Street: The Fall of the House of Lehman* (New York: Random House, 1986), 123.

Chapter 4 The "Take-Under"

Page 37 *On July 13, 1983* Ken Auletta, *Greed and Glory on Wall Street: The Fall of the House of Lehman* (New York: Random House, 1986), 20.

Page 38 *Unfortunately for Glucksman* Robert J. Cole, "Shearson to Pay $360 Million to Acquire Lehman Brothers," *New York Times,* April 11, 1984.

Page 38 *Peterson made $6 million* Ken Auletta, *Greed and Glory on Wall Street: The Fall of the House of Lehman* (New York: Random House, 1986), 220.

Chapter 5 Slamex

Page 47 *came to be marked* Bryan Burrough and John Helyar, *Barbarians at the Gate: The Fall of RJR Nabisco* (New York: Harper & Row, 1990; HarperBusiness, 2008), 156.

Chapter 6 The Phoenix Rises

Page 58 *Further muddling things* "Shearson Sets Shares at $34," Reuters, May 7, 1987.

Page 58 *The high-yield bond market* Floyd Norris, "Shearson Reversal: Bearishness over Securities Business Led American Express to Alter Plans," *New York Times*, March 5, 1990.

Chapter 7 Independence Day

Page 69 *To fund the spin-off* American Express Annual Report, 36.

Page 70 *By September, Lehman* "Lehman Brothers to Begin Stock Buyback Program," *New York Times*, September 9, 1994.

Page 71 *Less than a year after Lehman went public* "Lehman Debt Is Downgraded by Moody's," *New York Times*, March 22, 1995.

Chapter 9 The Ides of March

Page 90 *Fuld would call him regularly* Kenneth Gilpin, "Perella, a Merger Specialist, Is Hired by Morgan Stanley," *New York Times*, November 16, 1993.

Chapter 11 Russian Winter

Page 107 *Cecil earned more than* "Lehman's Chief Got a 34% Raise," *New York Times*, February 19, 1997.

Page 109 *So complete has Fuld's makeover* Andy Serwer, "The Improbable Power Broker," *Fortune*, April 13, 2006.

Page 111 *In 1997, the* New York Times Devin Leonard, "How Lehman Got Its Real Estate Fix," *New York Times*, May 2, 2009.

Page 112 *Cecil knew that Lehman* Peter Coy and Suzanne Woolley, "Failed Wizards of Wall Street," *BusinessWeek*, September 21, 1998.

Page 112 *Lehman's stock price fell 60 percent* Joseph Kahn, "Lehman Brothers Holdings Posts 23.4% Earnings Drop," *New York Times*, September 24, 1998.

Page 112 *The complex mathematical equation proves* Fischer Black, "The Pricing of Options and Corporate Liabilities," *Journal of Political Economy* 81 (3): 637–654.

Page 116 *'Wounded' Lehman Looks Like* Carl Gewirtz, "Asian Crisis Carries Seeds of New Trauma: Clouds and Silver Linings," *New York Times*, June 15, 1998.

Page 117 *At the end of the year* "Morgan Stanley, Lehman Beat Estimates," *MarketWatch*, January 7, 1999.

Page 119 *Fuld wanted Lehman's stock price* "CEO Richard Fuld on Lehman Brothers' Evolution from Internal Turmoil to Teamwork," January 10, 2007, http://knowledge.wharton.upenn.edu/article.cfm?articleid=1631&specialid=61.

Page 122 *The other overseas member* Jacqueline Simmons, "Former Lehman Bankers Isaacs, Nagioff Start Investment Firm," *Bloomberg News*, December 8, 2008.

Chapter 13   The Young Lions

Page 136 *Fuld asked Odrich to bring* Judith Messina, "40 under 40," *Crain's*, 2001.

Page 139 *Lehman was slowly transforming itself* Taken from Lehman's company literature.

Page 139 *In 2000, to bolster* Ray A. Smith, "Prominent Wall Street Bear Calls It Quits," *Wall Street Journal*, March 9, 2005.

Chapter 14   9/11

Page 142 *When American Airlines Flight 11* www.dronefone.com/wtc/wtc.html.

Page 148 *At Gregory's behest* Andrew Ross Sorkin, *Too Big to Fail: The Inside Story of How Wall Street Fought to Save the Financial System—and Themselves* (New York: Viking Penguin, 2009).

Page 149 *It was more expensive* Lawrence G. McDonald, *A Colossal Failure of Common Sense* (New York: Crown Business, 2009), 214.

Page 151 *Fuld was named one of* www.businessweek.com/magazine/content/02_02/b3765001.htm.

Page 153 *By 2008, the firm had* Suzy Jagger, "No Federal Bailout of Lehman Brothers: The Free Ride Was Over for Financiers," *Times of London*, September 16, 2008.

Page 154 *(Becker left Lehman that year,* Matthew Goldstein, "SEC's Holly Becker Case Slowly Fades Away," TheStreet.com, November 12, 2003.

Chapter 15   No Ordinary Joe

Page 160 *He had left Morgan Stanley* James Moore, "Morgan's European Stars Head for the Exit," *Telegraph*, UK, January 27, 2006.

Page 161 *But Isaacs did not help himself* James Quinn, "From a Runner to a Mover and Shaker Starting Off as a Blue Button on the LSE, Jeremy Isaacs Now Holds One of the Top Jobs with Wall Street's Largest Investment Banks," *Telegraph*, UK, November 20, 2006.

Page 163 *the magazine quoted only one* David Henry, "Cross-Dressing Securities," *BusinessWeek*, March 12, 2006.

Page 163 *A June 2007* Institutional Investor   Pierre Paulden, "Alpha Female," *Institutional Investor,* June 2007.

Page 163 *Callan had the ideal blend*   Much of the information in this section was first reported in two profiles of Callan published in spring 2008: Susanne Craig, "Lehman's Straight Shooter," *Wall Street Journal,* May 17, 2008, and Sheelah Kolhakatar, "Wall Street's Most Powerful Woman," *Portfolio,* March 17, 2008.

Page 164 *(In the Myers-Briggs typology*   A pseudonymously authored memoir written by a former banker at the firm suggests the dearth of "feelers" at the firm might have been due to Gregory's meddling with the Myers-Briggs test results. Joseph Tibman, *The Murder of Lehman Brothers* (New York: Brick Tower Press, 2009).

Page 164 *In 2006 Lehman's subprime*   Bonnie Sinock, "Lehman, Market Trying to Find the Right Size," *National Mortgage News,* September 10, 2007, and Yalman Onaran, "Lehman Brothers to Cut 1,300 Jobs in Mortgage Unit," *Bloomberg,* January 17, 2008.

Page 165 *Lehman Brothers, however,*   The two most detailed chronicles of Mark Walsh's extraordinary career at Lehman are Dana Rubinstein's "Mark Walsh, Lehman's Unluckiest Gambler," *New York Observer,* October 1, 2008, and Devin Leonard, "How Lehman Brothers Got Its Real Estate Fix," *New York Times,* May 2, 2009.

Page 167 *In October 2008, the French utility giant*   Edvard Pettersson, "Lehman to Sell Eagle Energy Unit to EDF for $230.5 Million," *Bloomberg,* October 1, 2008.

Page 169 *We don't have to wait*   "Inflation Is ECB's Biggest Challenge, Says Trichet," *Financial Times,* January 25, 2008.

Page 169 *Russo gave a speech to the G30*   "Credit Crunch: Where Do We Stand?" www.group30.org/pubs_1401.

Page 170 *The timing was so atrocious*   Devin Leonard, "How Lehman Got Its Real Estate Fix," *New York Times,* May 2, 2009.

Chapter 16   The Talking Head

Page 173 *Meanwhile, Bear Stearns CEO*   Kate Kelly, "Bear CEO's Handling of Crisis Raises Issues," *Wall Street Journal,* November 1, 2007.

Page 175 *When the call was over,*   Lehman Conference Call: Lehman Brothers Holdings Inc. (LEH) F1Q08 Earnings Call, March 18, 2008.

Page 176 *On April 1, as Fuld dealt*   "Lehman's Fundraising," www.cnbc.com/15840232?video=99975259&play=1.

Page 177 *That would not be the case*   Einhorn's pubic campaign against Lehman's accounting practices is chronicled in detail by Hugo Lindgren in "The

Confidence Man," *New York*, June 15, 2008. The text of Einhorn's speech at the Ira W. Sohn Investment Research Conference is available on his web site (www.foolingsomepeople.com).

Page 178   *In the Saturday edition*   Susanne Craig, "Lehman's Straight Shooter," *Wall Street Journal*, May 17, 2008.

Page 179   *But on June 4, three days*   Susanne Craig, "Lehman Is Seeking Overseas Capital," *Wall Street Journal*, June 4, 2008.

Page 180   *The next morning, Sunday*   McGee's frustration with Gregory and his weekend visit to Fuld's office were initially reported by Andrew Ross Sorkin in *Too Big to Fail: The Inside Story of How Wall Street Fought to Save the Financial System—and Themselves* (New York: Viking Penguin, 2009), 117–118.

Page 180   *McGee spoke first*   D'Angelin's e-mail was made public as part of the House Oversight Committee's investigation into the collapse of Lehman Brothers. In the Congressional Record it is titled "Lehman Brothers Email Regarding Lack of Accountability."

Chapter 17   The Sacrificial Ram

Page 184   *But that was before Fuld*   Andrew Ross Sorkin, *Too Big to Fail: The Inside Story of How Wall Street Fought to Save the Financial System—and Themselves* (New York: Viking Penguin, 2009), 125–126.

Page 184   *Later Callan would tell* Fortune   Katie Benner, "I Was Lucky to Get Out," *Fortune*, September 26, 2008.

Page 185   *In a typical headline,*   Sean Farrell, "Wall Street's Leading Woman Pays the Price for Lehman's Losses," *London Independent*, June 13, 2008.

Page 186   *The Tuesday following Gregory's ouster*   Lawrence McDonald and Patrick Robinson, *A Colossal Failure of Common Sense* (New York: Crown Business, 2009), 297.

Page 187   *The eight specific tasks*   "The Gameplan," Lehman Brothers, September 2008.

Page 189   *So, with the help of*   "The Impact of Becoming a Bank," Lehman Brothers, July 2008.

Chapter 18   Korea's Rising Sum

Page 191   *There were also the sovereign wealth funds*   "Citi, Merrill May Seek More from Sovereign Wealth Funds," *Dow Jones*, January 14, 2008.

Page 191   *Negotiations in the Middle East*   The China Investment Corporation's history of investing in American hedge funds and private equity firms was detailed by Jenny Strasburg and Rick Carew, "China Ready to Place Bets on Hedge Funds," *Wall Street Journal*, June 19, 2009.

Page 192 *Lehman took this seriously* Lehman's demoralizing efforts to hammer out a deal with KDB were first reported in detail by Andrew Ross Sorkin, *Too Big to Fail: The Inside Story of How Wall Street Fought to Save the Financial System—and Themselves* (New York: Viking Penguin, 2009), 212–216.

Page 192 *There were serious issues* Source: www.koreatimes.co.kr/www/news/nation/2008/10/123_32723.html.

Page 197 *McGee said it had been rejected* But there were articles on September 3 saying that talks had been going on, for example: www.usatoday.com/money/economy/2008-09-02-3485407905_x.htm.

Page 198 *Hours later, a KDB official* Gwen Robinson, "It's Official: Lehman Takeover Story Now Out of Control," *FT Alphaville*, September 10, 2008.

Chapter 19 The Wart on the End of Lehman's Nose

Page 200 *Dimon had two disturbing conclusions:* The role of Jamie Dimon and JPMorgan Chase in Lehman's daily operations and sudden collapse is addressed in greater detail in the Duff McDonald book *Last Man Standing* (New York: Simon & Schuster, 2009), 279–283, as well as Tom Junod, "The Deal of the Century," *Esquire*, September 11, 2009.

Page 200 *what had come to be known as* Andrew Ross Sorkin, *Too Big to Fail: The Inside Story of How Wall Street Fought to Save the Financial System—and Themselves* (New York: Viking Penguin, 2009), 23.

Page 201 *On September 10 at 8 A.M.* Transcript, Lehman Conference Call: Lehman Brothers Holdings Inc. (LEH) F3Q08, September 10, 2008.

Page 203 *As the* Wall Street Journal *later reported* "The Two Faces of Lehman's Fall," *Wall Street Journal*, October 6, 2008.

Page 206 *the FSA would not waive* Katherine Griffiths, "Lehman, Barclays and the Countdown to Financial Crisis," September 12, 2009, http://business.timesonline.co.uk/tol/business/industry_sectors/banking_and_finance/article6831518.ece.

Page 207 *And Bank of America was a particular thorn* Sorkin, *Too Big to Fail*.

Page 207 *Eventually, she said to him* Ibid., 299.

Page 208 *Even so, Paulson had reportedly said* Griffiths, "Lehman, Barclays."

Page 215 *It listed $613 billion* www.numerix.com/uploads/files/InTheNews/SRP_Lehman_Unwind.pdf.

Chapter 20 Damned Flood?

Page 219 *JPMorgan CEO Jamie Dimon* The letter was posted on the Internet on October 17, 2009, by the blog ZeroHedge under the headline "A Rare Glimpse Inside the Fed's Discount Window Courtesy of the Brewing

Lehman-Barclays Scandal": www.zerohedge.com/article/rare-glimpse-feds-discount-window-courtesy-brewing-lehman-barclays-scandal.

Page 221   *He saved more than 10,000 jobs*   "Tension Simmers at Nomura as Lehman Bonuses Loom," *New York Times*, March 27, 2009.

Page 226   *Within a year Lloyd Blankfein*   John Arlidge, "I'm Doing 'God's Work': Meet Mr. Goldman Sachs," *Times of London*, November 8, 2009.

Chapter 21   Closing the Books

Page 230   *In early April 2009*   Susanne Craig, "Lehman Brothers' Dick Fuld has a New Gig," *Wall Street Journal*, April 3, 2009.

Page 230   *Reportedly, he sold his seven-acre estate*   Sushil Cheema, *Wall Street Journal*, November 13, 2009, http://blogs.wsj.com/developments/2009/11/13/friday-diversion-axl-roses-house-sells-again-connie-and-maury-buy/.

Page 231   *"It was clear in the 24 hours*   Katie Benner, "I Was Lucky to Get Out," *Fortune*, September 26, 2008.

Page 232   *By November 2009, the cost*   Linda Sandler, "Lehman Bankruptcy Advisers Get $535.5 Million," *Bloomberg*, December 14, 2009.

Page 232   *But by September 2009, he reported*   "Scaling Mount Lehman," *Wall Street Journal*, September 15, 2009.

Page 233   *In October the* Journal *revealed*   Jeffrey McCracken and Mike Spector, "Fed Draws Court's Eyes in Lehman Bankruptcy," *Wall Street Journal*, October 5, 2009.

Page 233   *By November creditors had filed*   Christopher Scinta and Linda Sandler, "Claims Against Lehman Could Hit $1 Trillion, CEO Says," *Bloomberg*, November 19, 2009.

Page 233   *To the astonishment of many*   In Re: Lehman Brothers Holdings Inc. et al., Southern District of New York, Case 08-135555, Creditor 1000230602.

References

Auletta, Ken. 1986. *Greed and glory on Wall Street: The fall of the house of Lehman.* New York: Random House.

Burrough, Bryan, and John Helyar. 1990, 2008. *Barbarians at the gate: The fall of RJR Nabisco.* New York: Harper & Row, HarperBusiness.

Cohan, William. 2009. *House of cards: A tale of hubris and wretched excess on Wall Street.* New York: Doubleday.

Collins, Jim. 2009. *How the mighty fall and why some companies never give in.* New York: HarperCollins.

Gasparino, Charles. 2009. *The sellout: How three decades of Wall Street greed and government mismanagement destroyed the global financial system.* New York: HarperCollins.

Kelly, Kate. 2009. *Street fighters: The last 72 hours of Bear Stearns, the toughest firm on Wall Street.* New York: Viking Penguin.

McDonald, Duff. 2009. *The last man standing: The ascent of Jamie Dimon and JPMorgan Chase.* New York: Simon & Schuster.

Sorkin, Andrew Ross. 2009. *Too big to fail: The inside story of how Wall Street fought to save the financial system—and themselves.* New York: Viking Penguin.

Tett, Gillian, 2008. *Fool's gold: How the bold dream of a small tribe at J.P. Morgan was corrupted by Wall Street greed and unleashed a catastrophe.* New York: The Free Press.

Wessel, David. 2009. *In Fed We Trust: Ben Bernanke's war on the Great Panic.* New York: Crown.

Acknowledgments

This is my first book. As I wrote in the Prologue, I had no idea when I started it that the material I would find would make this story so extraordinarily compelling and such a delight to research and tell.

I also had no idea of what it takes to write a book. I had no idea of the hours required, not just mine but other people's time; of the vast number of patient interviewees who sometimes were kind enough to put up with a second or even third grilling, and also what a nuisance a book is to the people in your immediate orbit.

Where to begin the thanks?

First, to the men and women of Lehman for sharing your stories, some of them funny, some of them tragic, and in some cases extremely personal and tinged with extraordinary loss. Especial thanks to Tom Tucker and Lara and Mary Anne Pettit for sharing memories that I feel privileged to have been told. I wish I had known Chris Pettit. After writing this book I almost feel that I did.

Many of you—and you know who you are—gave me a great deal of your time but wish to stay anonymous.

Others who are on the record and to whom I am indebted for their time and valuable experience and insights include: Peter Solomon, Robert

ACKNOWLEDGMENTS

Shapiro, Robert Genirs, Peregrine Moncreiffe, Brad Jack, Jeremy Isaacs, Roger Nagioff, Fred Segal, James Vinci, Ronald Gallatin, J. Tomlinson Hill, Peter A. Cohen, Jeffrey Solomon, James Roper, Steve Carlson, Paul Newmark, Craig Schiffer, Cliff Goldman, Doug Ireland, Bob Cagnina, Tom Russo, David Goldfarb, Bob Millard, Alex Kirk, Mel Shaftel, Todd Jorn, Steve Berkenfeld, Andrew Gowers, Marna Ringel, Nancy Hament, Marianne Rasmussen, Brian Riley, Kim Sullivan, Angela Sacco, Madeleine Antoncic, and the inimitable and funny Karin Jack.

Especial thanks go to John Cecil for your never-ending patience. It's one thing when an interview that's one hour long has to be redone; quite another when it's four hours.

Outside of Lehman, too, a huge thank you to Robert "Bob" Steel for your patience, your guidance, and your introductions. You were the person I could always go to if I had a query, and you are a great judge of character.

Thanks also to Bob Diamond, who was one of those who kindly got grilled twice and was most gracious about it. Also I am indebted to the BarCap press team: particularly Michael O'Looney, Kerrie-Ann Cohen, and Peter Truell. Also thank you to Archie Cox for your time.

To a particularly good-humored senior member of the U.S. Federal Reserve: thank you.

Especial thanks have to go to the former U.S. Treasury secretary, Henry Merritt Paulson Jr. for your thoughtful reflections on what became the nightmare of your life.

So, too, thanks to your trusty lieutenant and the dad of dads, Steven Shafran.

I would not have met either Hank or "Shaf" had it not been for the clever, beautiful, and kind Clara Bingham and also the inestimable Michele Davis to whom Clara introduced me.

As for the rest of the former Treasury team, they know who they are—they want to stay in the shadows, but thank you.

Likewise I must thank John Murray and Hector Sants at the Financial Services Authority. Also Catherine Macleod in Alastair Darling's office. And Richard Paulson, Hank's brother.

Also, H. Rodgin Cohen of Sullivan & Cromwell, Warren Buffett, and David Einhorn.

Other people who were essential in giving advice or pointing me in useful directions were: Peter Melhado, Hugh Warrender, Bill Cohan, Jamie Niven, Michael Thomas, Steve Rattner, Peter Rose, Jeffrey Leeds, Cliff Brokaw, William von Mueffling, Richard "follow the money" Plepler, Rob Wiesenthal, Alan Schwartz, Mort Janklow, Donald Trump, John Josephson, Joe Perella, Michael Thompson, Betsy Schaper, Gerald Corrigan, Don Marron, Charlie Ayres, Stephen Rubenstein, Rob Speyer, Jesse Angelo, Lachlan Murdoch, Robert Thomson, Bryan Burrough, Michael Shnayerson, Michael Jackson, Martin Ivens, Nicolas Berggruen, Larry Creel, Bill Detwiler, Jim Burtson, Gerry Pasciuccio, and Ed Frost. And not for any information, because she is immune to my charm and wouldn't give me any, but for continually reminding me that I must, above all, be accurate—my former college roommate and longtime friend, Blythe Masters.

Outside of what was Lehman and Wall Street, there exists, as we know, a different world—one that I haven't been in very much recently, but without some of the people in it, this book could not have happened.

Graydon Carter, my editor in chief at *Vanity Fair*, my counselor, and my friend. Nothing is ever possible without you and your encouragement. Also at *VF*, Doug Stumpf, my patient, clever editor, who has mentored me for years. Then: Chris Bateman, Stan Friedman, Chris Garrett, Evgenia Peretz, Aimee Bell, David Friend, Jon Kelly, Claire Howorth, David Foxley, John Connolly, Jeannie Rhodes, Susan White, Katherine Bang, Jeannie Rhodes, Michael Wolff, David Margolick, Louise Grunwald, Nina Munk, SaraJane Hoare, Francesca Stanfil, Beth Kseniak, Sara Switzer, Lizzie Hurlbut, Robert Walsh, Michelle Ciarrocca, Brian Gallagher, and Michael Hogan, thank you for your support in the past year. Also to the rest of the staff and contributors: So many of you have helped me in different ways over nine years. You are quite simply the best at what you do. Thank you all. John Banta, thank you especially for your good advice. Without it, I would never have found my lifeline for this book: Barry Harbaugh.

Barry, we both know it would take another book to describe the journey we took together. (In all seriousness, a sitcom writer actually would have some good material if they knew the real story. I think we might even be able to push *Gossip Girl* aside!)

Only you and I know how hard you worked, putting in time you didn't have with remarkable good humor and tremendous skill. I look forward to reading your first book. I know it will be awesome, just like you.

Thank you also for leading me to the most diligent and inspiring fact-checking team a writer could have: Ryan Bradley, a wordsmith *sans pareil* who also put himself out greatly during the holidays; Maureen "Moe" Tkacik—whom CNBC should hire right now! Cailey Hall, Stacey Breaks—and two other people who need singling out.

First is Bob Roe, editor extraordinaire. No one moves as fast and well as you!

Second is Emma Givens, my assistant. Emma is one of those assistants to whom the term has no narrow meaning. She is my friend, my organizer—not just my fact-checker, but my life-checker. Thanks to Emma, there was food on my family's table on December 25. This author had a deadline of December 27 and had forgotten all about grocery stores closing.

Then the John Wiley & Sons team: Pamela van Giessen, Emilie Herman, and Mary Daniello, the editors from hell (oh, those deadlines) but also heaven. Emilie: thank you for surviving the crash through the holidays. We made it! Thank you to the others in marketing and publicity: Jocelyn Cordova-Wagner, Sharon Polese, Nancy Rothschild, Deborah Guichelaar, Lucas Wilk, Julie Attrill, Louise Holden, and Emma Knott. As I write this I am only starting to work with some of you and already you are making your presence felt wonderfully.

As for my agent, Andy McNicol at William Morris Endeavor, you rock. And a huge thank you to the very clever Elizabeth Wiatt, for insisting I see her husband Jim when I was in Los Angeles two years ago, and for leading me to WME, Andy, and an incredible team.

Also, thanks to my superb publicists in America: Sandi Mendelson and David Kass; in Toronto: Jennifer Bassett and Candice Best; and in the United Kingdom: Dotti Irving, Mark Hutchinson, and Hannah Blake. Thanks to Julian Niccolini, Alex von Bidder, Rachel Bellon, Bitsy Williams, Nikki Burg, and Tori Howarth for helping me to launch the book.

Ken Auletta: thank you for cheering me on every time we met. You have no idea how much it buoyed me up and how excited I was that you would blurb it. I am honored to follow in your footsteps. You set the bar very high. You always do.

Arianna Huffington, Amanda Foreman, and Simon Sebag Montefiore: thank you for also reading galleys, blurbing the book, encouraging me, and making me feel sure I was writing a book people would want to read; and thank you also for critiquing.

Then there are the thanks to personal friends who were there for me in a variety of ways—on both sides of the Atlantic. Particularly encouraging and helpful for part or all of the way through were: Dan Abrams, Celerie Kemble, Boykin Curry, Len and Emily Blavatnik, Reg Barton, Frances Osborne, Paola Windsor (who lived part of it!), Catherine Ostler, Pamela Gross and Jimmy Finkelstein, Santa Sebag Montefiore, Andrew Roberts and Susan Gilcrhist, Vivi Nevo, Nick Brown, Sarah Murdoch, Dan Peres and Sarah Wynter, Carolina Zapf, Wil Surratt, Fernanda Niven, Catherine Smith, Clemence von Mueffling, Lea Brokaw, Dini von Mueffling and David Richenthal, Stephen and Cathy Graham, Anna Scott Carter, June Black, Bruce and Alex Schnitzer, Peggy Siegal, Jonathan Foreman, Plum Sykes and Toby Rowland, Euan Rellie and Lucy Sykes, Dorrit Morley, Lela Rose, Gretchen Rubin, Molly Jong-Fast, Charles and Dafna Bonas, Anne McElvoy, Aby Rosen and Samantha Boardman, Ariadne and Mario Calvo-Platero, Mungo and Sandy Meehan, Steven Fox, Tina Brown, Jennifer Creel, Susan and Hadley Nagel, Ross and Susie Johnson, Ryan Biracree, Chloe Crespi, Saito Chichi, Kieran McKenna, Sebastian Scolarici, David Frank, Robert Sassoon, Daryl Isaacs, Sarah Crow, Ed Stern, Philip Howard, Greville Ward, Thorold Barker and Jenny Anderson, David Pflumenbaum, Colin Sterling, Anya Strzemien, Rob Fishman, Kenny Lerer, Joe Scarborough and Mika Brzezinski, Willie Geist, Dylan Ratigan, Robin Goldman, Mark Hoffman, Jonathan Wald, Tyler Mathison, Dennis Kneale, Kerima Greene, Bill Griffeth, Michele Cabruso-Cabrera, Larry Kudlow, Maria Bartiromo, Erin Burnett, Nick Dunn, Ellen Egeth, Steve Lewis, Sandy Cannold, Andrea Mantia, Jim Connor, Ryan Ruggiero, and all the team at CNBC.

Thank you to all my family: my parents, Simon and Jill Ward (thank you for being so patient: I know this ruined your trip to New York); to my sisters Lucinda Napier and Antonia Crawshay and your awesome husbands and children, I apologize for being so short on the phone.

An especial thanks to Veronica Wadley, the British editor who discovered me back in 1992. You taught me pretty much everything I know about journalism and have supported me ever since.

Also, the team at home who make my life run seamlessly: Marcia Powell, Victoria Doctora, and the nanny of all nannies, Zezy Barbosa. You know I could do nothing without you.

There is one more person I think about now that this book is coming to a close.

Many years ago when I was a cub reporter on the British paper, the *Independent*, I told the paper's literary editor, John Walsh, a charming, effervescent Irishman, that one day I'd like to write a book. We were on the subway (the so-called London Tube) and I can still recall the uncharacteristic look of derision on his face.

"Are you aware just how difficult that is?" he said. "It's . . . really, really hard."

It was at that moment I decided that by the time I was 40 I would have written a book—a serious book on a significant subject that even John Walsh might want to read. So, thank you, John Walsh, whom I have not seen since, for laying down the gauntlet.

Thanks also have to go to my husband of fifteen years, Matthew Doull—and congratulations to him for his own much-deserved successes accomplished while I was deep in this book.

But this book is dedicated to two young men who know far more about Lehman Brothers than is healthy for two males who turned seven years old this year.

Orlando and Lorcan Doull have put up with "Mummy's annoying book" with humor, wit, and patience way beyond your years.

Without the joy of seeing you each night, of hearing all about your adventures—imaginary and real—and without the mandatory snuggles and chat that you demand every evening, this book would not be worth anything. Nothing I ever write could come close to the greatest accomplishment of my life—which is producing you.

As we say to each other every night at home: "I love you to infinity." This is for you, in the hope that when you read it, you will already be becoming men whose dreams are limitless but who never lose touch with reality.

Mummy

Index

CPSIA information can be obtained
at www.ICGtesting.com
Printed in the USA
BVHW04s1719100818
524084BV00(

31192021532336

9 781118 011492